An Introduction to Ethics

Kevin Gibson
Marquette University

PEARSON

Boston   Columbus   Indianapolis   New York   San Francisco   Upper Saddle River
Amsterdam   Cape Town   Dubai   London   Madrid   Milan   Munich   Paris   Montréal   Toronto
Delhi   Mexico City   São Paulo   Sydney   Hong Kong   Seoul   Singapore   Taipei   Tokyo

Editor in Chief: Ashley Dodge
Acquisitions Editor: Susan Hartman
Program Manager: Reena Dalal
Director of Marketing: Brandy Dawson
Senior Marketing Manager: Kelly May
Marketing Coordinator: Jessica Warren
Managing Editor: Denise Forlow
Operations Specialist: Diane Peirano
Art Director: Jayne Conte
Cover Designer: Bruce Kenselaar
Cover Art: Shutterstock
Digital Media Editor: Brian Hyland
Full-Service Project Management: Sneha Pant/PreMediaGlobal
Printer/Binder: STP Courier
Cover Printer: STP Courier
Text Font: 10/12 Minion

Credits and acknowledgments borrowed from other sources and reproduced, with permission, in this textbook appear on appropriate page within text.

Many of the designations by manufacturers and sellers to distinguish their products are claimed as trademarks. Where those designations appear in this book, and the publisher was aware of a trademark claim, the designations have been printed in initial caps or all caps.

Library of Congress Cataloging-in-Publication Data
Gibson, Kevin, 1955–
    An introduction to ethics / Kevin Gibson, Marquette University. — First edition.
        pages cm
    Includes index.
    ISBN-13: 978-0-205-70854-3
    ISBN-10: 0-205-70854-4
    1. Ethics.   I. Title.
    BJ1012.G535 2014
    170—dc23

                                                                    2013022347

10   9   8   7   6   5   4   3   2   1

ISBN 10: 0-205-70854-4
ISBN 13: 978-0-205-70854-3

With love to Elizabeth who brings out the best in me

CONTENTS

Introduction

Ideas change the world. Every revolution, and every transformation in human history, has been based on an idea about what makes individual lives and communities better. Ideas frame our world, linking us to the past, giving the present relevance and meaning, and allowing us to project ourselves into the future. They provide context for our lives and offer the promise that things can be different. Some ideas are ideals that guide us by articulating a conception of the best possible way of being. Others are practical constructs that help us shape our lives by expressing what our priorities should be and where we should direct our energy and resources. When we analyze or assess our ideas, we evaluate them; we craft value systems. The values we adopt might arise from many sources: our upbringing, education, experiences, or personal reflection. But values are dynamic, and our encounters with the world might render what we once held dear to be less important—or they may completely change the way we think.

Ultimately, our values underpin our deliberations, guide our behavior, and give purpose to our lives. They shape our identity and steer our actions. Values are captured by concepts such as right and wrong, fair and unfair, good and bad, just and unjust, and others that are often hard to label: A student believes the right thing to do is to never cheat on an exam. A child claims that getting a smaller allowance than his older brother is unfair. A diplomat accuses another country of human rights violations. A society views with disgust some unfamiliar practice of another cultural group. Values tend to be the most influential motivators for human action, even more powerful than economic incentives or orders from authority. People work for money and generally comply with laws or regulations, but they rarely risk their lives for those things. Yet time and again people are willing to die for ideals such as freedom, faith, honor, or glory.

Generally we do well enough on our own without looking too deeply into issues, but there are times when we are confronted by new or difficult questions that demand some reasoned framework for analysis. In this text, we will examine the foundational value-based concepts that we use to understand and govern our actions. With the help of philosophy, we can look critically at the assumptions at work behind our judgments to see if they necessarily lead to their purported conclusions. Perhaps we can even propose better ways of thinking about the issues.

Sometimes we find ourselves reflecting on our assumptions after a dramatic event with wide publicity suddenly puts them into sharp relief; at other times we are just unsatisfied with how things are and wonder if they could be improved. The issues we often ponder and deal with are not only the big ones that dominate our actions but also those that may at first glance appear trivial or inconsequential. This is typical because we live our lives in a series of small encounters with one another. Consider the following questions:

- Should we allow people to engage in dangerous activities, or should we encroach on their liberty by regulating them?
- Should we hold companies responsible for injuries their products cause?
- Should we favor some groups over others, or should we treat everyone exactly the same?
- In health care, what determines the best way to allocate limited resources? Do we spread out as much as we can to as many as possible or use some other means such as personal ability to pay?
- Should we educate students in the sciences or emphasize the arts?
- Ought women and men have the same rights worldwide?

All these questions have embedded assumptions, and part of the role of philosophy is to bring these unstated ideas to the surface and examine them in some detail.

Philosophy helps us make thoughtful and reasoned choices that others can defend. Philosophical thinking, whether or not we realize it, helps form the principles that we use to shape our communities, and ultimately the way we deal with other nations and the planet. Many people want to make the world a better place to live—a fine and noble goal. However, in practical terms, our value-based or ethical decisions turn out to manifest themselves in mundane encounters—the way we treat individuals in our daily lives and in the scores of decisions we make all the time about our consumption and disposal of goods in our market economy. Nevertheless, it is important to appreciate that these routine decisions are framed by general principles that have long been the subject of philosophical inquiry.

This book introduces you to the central concerns of classical and contemporary ethics, using examples and cases to highlight particular issues, show how theory can inform our discussions, and reflect on how we ought to treat one another and the world around us.

Chapter 1 situates ethics within the wider discipline of philosophy and examines some of the enduring questions philosophers have examined since the times of Ancient Greece. Chapter 2 looks at the nature of ethical theory and how it differs from legal and religious approaches. The following two chapters deal with the persistent issues of egoism and relativism. An egoist believes a person should promote his or her own interest. The relativist argues that there are no absolute rules and everything needs to be considered in terms of its own circumstances, to the point where we have no right to impose our views on anyone else. Chapter 5 reflects on the nature of the self and our relationship to others. Chapters 6, 7, and 8 present the classical ethical theories of utilitarianism, deontology, and virtue-based ethics, respectively, and examines their various strengths and weaknesses.

Chapter 9 integrates some of the abstract theory to discuss issues of rights and justice. Whatever our personal ethical views might be, in a very real sense, notions of rights and justice connect broad ethical principles to the way we govern ourselves and interact with others. They are fundamental in determining our laws, how we view ownership of property and the imposition of taxes, the care we accord those unable to look after themselves, our handling of end-of-life questions, our attitudes toward military intervention overseas, and the many other ways we create our world.

Chapter 10 looks at some significant feminist insights in ethics: Do men and women have a common nature, or are there essential differences in the way they view the world? If ethical thinking has been framed by a gendered approach that brings in biases, are there responses that can address them? Are there alternative approaches such as care and empathy that provide an adequate philosophical basis for our dealings with one another?

Chapter 11 examines some of the dramatic challenges philosophy has faced in the last fifty years from so-called postmodernist movements. These approaches have questioned not only the assumptions within philosophical traditions but also the way that philosophy has emerged as a unique discipline. Drawing on material from history and psychology, postmodernists point out that ethics relies on certain stories we use to explain how things are, and that we are often unaware of institutions and power relationships that frame these narratives.

Ethical theory can also be informed by non-Western traditions, and so Chapter 12 examines Confucian, Taoist, Buddhist, and Africana approaches to morality. These traditions have stood the test of time and give us perspectives which put community and social harmony at the forefront, or ask us to find moral enlightenment in nature or within ourselves.

The text paves the way for three outcomes. First, readers will become acquainted with the main figures and movements in classical and contemporary ethics, including feminist, postmodern, and non-Western perspectives. Second, it models a critical analysis of the material that encourages readers to take a justified stand on many of the issues and points of view. Third, numerous cases and real-life examples allow the reader to apply general principles to their own particular real-life experience.

This text represents the efforts of many people. I especially want to acknowledge the editorial staff at Pearson Education, my department chair, James South, and my graduate assistant, Jennifer Fenton.

1

Philosophy and Ethics

We all have beliefs and opinions that shape our lives. We often *do* philosophy when we question our assumptions and demand clear meanings, and we can do it without reference to grand theories or technical jargon. However, arguments often grind to a halt and become a contest of wills unless we look more closely at some of the ways people come to their opinions and link them to various conclusions.

WHAT IS PHILOSOPHY?

Philosophy is both an activity and a body of knowledge. Philosophers are rarely content to accept the status quo at face value. We want to know not so much how far we've gone in quantifiable terms, but instead whether we are on the right track. It would be wrong, though, to think that philosophers agonize over every decision and policy constantly—that would make everyday life impossible. However, we sometimes face serious issues, individually and as a society, when it is appropriate to take the time to reflect on what we are doing and why. Thankfully, many great thinkers have contributed to a body of knowledge that will help us sort out questions that vex us at this very fundamental level. Not everyone has to dedicate his or her life to philosophy, but it offers tools to help us confront and resolve some of life's most difficult problems—or to recognize more clearly what makes them so troublesome.

The discipline of philosophy is often associated with the seminal thinker Socrates (ca. 470–399 BCE). At one point, Socrates angered the city fathers of Athens so much that they put him on trial for his life on the charge of subverting the youth. According to the Plato's dialogue *The Apology*, Socrates' response was telling:

> For if you kill me you will not easily find another like me, who, if I may use such a ludicrous figure of speech, am a sort of gadfly, given to the state by God; and the state is like a great and noble steed who is tardy in his motions owing to his very size, and requires to be stirred into life. I am that gadfly which God has given the state and all day long and in all places am always fastening upon you, arousing and persuading and reproaching you.[1]

---

[1]Plato, *The Apology*, 30e

His point is that we can maintain the way things are, but there is value in revisiting our working beliefs. This is true especially when we face novel or difficult issues.

One function of philosophy, then, is to critically examine basic concepts and ideas, and their wider implications for everyday life. By providing us with the analytical framework to examine ideas and competing claims, philosophy allows us to see if they are valid and justified. For example, one theory of justice suggests that we should help those who are unable to benefit from the virtues of the "genetic lottery"—intelligence, health, aptitudes, and even the capacity to do hard work. In other words, the theory suggests we have a responsibility to help others who have, through no fault of their own, a more difficult struggle to survive and prosper. A contrasting theory, however, says that we are entitled to whatever we earn and we don't owe anything to anyone else. By this reasoning, if we are able to use our genetic gifts to generate wealth, we *could* help others, but doing so remains our individual choice.

When we look at these sorts of claims more closely, we realize that there is more going on than a simple matter of arbitrarily choosing this or that theory. If we explore the basic assumptions people make, then we have the possibility of finding areas of agreement and at the same time testing whether our own intuitions lead clearly to the conclusions we draw. For instance, it might seem obvious at first that we are entitled to what we earn and should spend it how we wish, but it turns out that people disagree about notions of property, ownership, and the scope of personal choice. Engaging in open dialogue with others, analyzing their reasoning and evaluating our own, challenges us to explain and justify our views and perhaps revise them if our logic or basic beliefs are somehow faulty.

Philosophy may not give us the means to reach conclusive answers—in fact, it frequently raises more questions than it resolves. On the other hand, it raises the standard of justification from **assertion** to **argument**. An assertion declares something without any support or need for justification. An argument is a connected series of claims leading to a conclusion, and when we proceed to examine every step in the series, we find that each individual claim may be true or false, or the links between them may be invalid. In philosophy all assumptions are up for reexamination. For instance, if we talk about why we should keep our earnings, we have to consider what it means to have the right to property and if that comes about by virtue of the society in which we live. Additionally, we might consider our duties to others and whether our ability to earn has a consequent responsibility to help the less fortunate.

Philosophers contend that it is always worth reflecting on our foundational beliefs and the way they play out in our actions. As Socrates famously observed:

> The life which is unexamined is not worth living.[2]

While this phrase can be read in many ways, it chides us to reflect on our purpose and goals in life. We can go along from day-to-day, but it suggests that perhaps the best life is one where we have taken the time and effort to think deeply about what we do and why. Philosophy as a discipline gives us structure and tools that will enable us to do that well.

These tools include **logic**, which enables us to examine our reasoning to ensure it is consistent and reaches valid conclusions; the **history of philosophy**, which allows us to look at the works of philosophers across ages and cultures so we don't have to constantly reinvent material that has been refined through discussion and criticism over many years, sometimes centuries;

---

[2]Plato, *The Apology*, 38a

metaphysics, which deals with issues not readily addressed by science, such as whether we are minds and souls as well as bodies; **epistemology**, or the study of knowledge, which challenges us to defend that we really know what we claim to know.

WHAT IS ETHICS?

We can initially define **ethics** as the study of the origin and scope of the language of **morality**. **Morals** are the values that may derive from a theory or set of principles that concern good and bad, right and wrong, justice and fairness.

Ethics can be construed as theorizing about the proper regulating mechanisms for our behavior. It tells us what to aspire to and also constrains our actions. It is informed by psychological elements, for example, sympathy, generosity, compassion, kindness, concern for others, or even revenge or outrage. However, these traits can lead to confusing and sometimes conflicting impulses, and thus it is useful to codify them in some way. We can do that by using the power of reasoning to work out priorities, make our actions consistent and predictable, and communicate our ideas of right and wrong, and justice and fairness to others.

There are continuing debates about the origins and mix of our dispositions and reason: Some say that we can see the hand of the divine that allows us to rise above our animal nature, whereas others think that ethical practices are evidence of our evolution as a species. For the present we can put those debates aside and recognize that all human societies exhibit morality, for example, cooperation, child care, and the importance of keeping promises. Moreover, we not only have those traits but also are capable of critiquing and improving our behavior and perhaps that of others as well.

WHAT ARE THE DIFFERENT SENSES OF ETHICS?

In daily language we use the term **ethical** in a variety of ways. Sometimes when we talk about an ethical person or discuss others doing something ethical, the connotation is that a person is doing something unusual and praiseworthy. For example, we may use the term to refer to people who do deeds such as serving at a soup kitchen, as if their actions are somehow distinctly heroic or saintly. We might suspect they are content with either less material wealth or less free time than we are, or perhaps they were born with an exceptional disposition to serve others. The problem with this view is that it makes ethics remote and something which applies only to a select few, with the implication that the rest of us need not aspire to behave or act any better than we already do.

In contrast, we can consider a compelling alternative by treating moral decisions in a broad sense as just as much a part of our lives as any other choices. We are not born with a full-fledged sense of right and wrong, but we learn through trial and error as we mature, and even people who do admirable deeds have inevitably made mistakes along the way. Thus, it is not a matter of such people living in a different reality of personal martyrdom or misguided notions of happiness. Rather, some people simply put more weight on certain values than others. Morality, then, should not be seen as some sort of special state for some individual saints in special situations, but as a common dimension of the regular choices we all face routinely.

When we live day-to-day, we probably don't ordinarily distinguish moral questions from all others, deciding in each such case whether to be good or bad. More typically we judge people on their moral consistency in various situations and fault them if they adapt their values to changing circumstances around them. Thus rather than thinking of moral actions as things like working in a soup kitchen, a more suitable model of morality might be to say that moral elements are mixed in with everything we do. We make choices all the time using a constellation of factors, one of which will be the morality of the issue. The moral aspect isn't always at the forefront and has to compete with other impulses and considerations.

Consider when you buy soap; it probably matters that it is effective, smells good, and is priced reasonably. The question of whether the manufacturer made animals suffer unnecessarily in testing the product may come into the decision, but it has to battle with the other considerations. Perhaps if the concern has been highlighted in the media, or you as the buyer are particularly sensitive to the issue, it will tip your purchasing decision. The point remains that for most of us morality is not a separate and isolated activity, but part and parcel of our regular existence and the various choices we make.

A narrower sense of *ethical* describes a set of rules or conventions within a specialized field. Thus some institutions or professions have "codes of ethics." These codes tend to give specific rules about particular situations in which members might find themselves. For example, a doctor is prohibited by his or her professional organization from having a romantic relationship with a patient, or an accountant doing an audit cannot invest in a company when he or she has discovered insider information not available to the general public. Significantly, although the doctor/patient relationship is a special and privileged one in our society, it is important to realize that medical ethics is *not* a distinct morality with a completely different set of governing principles. Instead it operates as a special case that overlies a general backdrop of principled behavior, such as telling the truth or treating patients fairly. That is, we work from the very widest sense of common ethics first, and then narrow it down to deal with ever more special circumstances. Hence, it is important to begin by understanding the broad picture about the way individuals and communities have reasoned about the proper ways to treat one another.

Seeing ethics only in a narrow sense may lead to two important misunderstandings. The first suggests that we have different sets of behavior for the various compartments of our lives— business, friendship, romance, and so forth. Someone with this approach might claim that we should behave differently in particular situations—"all is fair in love and war" or "business is business," where all morality depends on the situation. While this might be true in some limited spheres, it demands that the individual knows where the boundaries of each compartment are, and that everyone involved has a shared knowledge of the appropriate practices. Thus we expect to be fooled by a magician, perhaps, but in general we operate with background conditions of trust and honesty. In normal interpersonal dealings, we anticipate that we aren't routinely being lied to or constantly duped. As it turns out, moral infractions are dramatic in large part *because* they depart from the shared expectations we have and use in our everyday lives. To illustrate the point, imagine, for instance, what a world would be like where no one could ever be trusted and everything had to be policed constantly.

Second, a narrow view implies that ethics is an external set of rules that we are required to follow, and slavishly doing so discharges our moral responsibility. If this were true, then being ethical would just consist in knowing the rules and obeying them. It would not allow the individual to question values enshrined in the code. In contrast, most of us have significant freedom and discretion in the way we behave, and there is considerable latitude in the interpretation and application of the rules we live by. Even voluntarily joining a rule-oriented organization such as the military or a religious order involves initial assent by recruits, which represents their individual moral choice.

Taking an expansive view at the outset creates a baseline of mutual understandings which can then be refined or made more specific as necessary. Philosophy and ethics provide powerful resources for navigating both the more difficult fundamental questions and problems we face, and subsequently for those decisions we make in our regular activities, interactions, and relationships.

CAN ETHICS GIVE US ANSWERS?

A complaint about philosophy in general and especially ethics is that it does not provide us with answers. This suggests that the goal of ethics is to come up with a computer-style algorithm where we feed in the facts and issues and get a neat answer to our problems in return.

While this has considerable appeal, think about what it would be like if we had this ability. When faced with a value question, we would fill in some sort of questionnaire, feed it into some impersonal machine, and then follow its commands to the letter. Suppose, for example, we are puzzled about whether to use our limited resources to either provide medical care or install traffic lights at an intersection. Both have the potential to save some lives and the cost is roughly the same. We could vaccinate a large population and ensure that, say, five people would not get a deadly disease. Alternatively, we could install traffic signals likely to prevent most accidents in a location that has claimed roughly the same number of fatalities over the last few years. We go to our computerized program, respond to a series of prompts on a screen, and get the response to use the money for vaccinations.

But how does that make you feel? Would you be comfortable delegating your moral decisions to a third party? In effect, that is what we are asking if we demand a definitive answer for each case we encounter.

First, we might legitimately worry that all factors haven't been included in the decision: An automated questionnaire may fail to consider all the relevant factors. Perhaps the vaccine has its own associated risks, for instance, and these need to be brought into the deliberations. Or perhaps some people may feel that there is a morally relevant difference between acting and failing to act, although the results may be the same; these concerns would need to be factored in somehow. Indeed, however we structure the formulaic questions around a moral issue, there is always a nagging feeling that there is more to be asked to pin down the most important aspects of a case at hand.

Moreover, we might be concerned about the way the computer was programmed. What assumptions were made, or what approaches were chosen if there were two or more opposing viewpoints? A program might give more weight to some factors than others, or make logical links between issues that we might dismiss as unimportant. The software could, for example, give great importance to the fact that drivers have responsibility for their driving, whereas it is hard to blame someone for catching a virus. Still, such a link isn't completely self-evident and universally accepted. Even if the machine had flawless logic, we would still likely have some objections to the guiding principles it uses to reach its conclusions.

One recurring theme in ethical thinking is that you are ultimately responsible for your own moral decisions, and there is rarely someone else better suited to make them on your behalf. Consequently ethical theory does not do the work for you—it is a tool that gives an analytical framework to help make appropriate distinctions and discover some of the more subtle areas in a moral argument. Hence it won't, by itself, provide answers, and perhaps it is the process of thinking through a problem that emerges as the most valuable part of reaching a suitable answer.

Theory will help provide the critical questions about which factors ought to be considered in our decisions, what sort of principles ought to direct our behavior, and how we should act.

Summary

Ethical theory is tremendously helpful when we form our arguments and conclusions. Eventually we may adopt a specific theory completely, or we may choose to draw elements from several established theories, or we may combine some of their insights to create something new and unique. Whatever approach we take, studying ethics will enhance our thinking, giving us a theoretical conceptual apparatus with practical implications. Thus clarifying the questions and discovering what an adequate answer will look like are the least we can expect from studying philosophy. At its best, it can provide us with new perspectives and a richer understanding of the world and our place in it.

As we go through life, we will encounter moral issues. We will inevitably need to make choices or take stands one way or another. We are all individually responsible for choices we make and for the consequences of our personal philosophical views and actions. Good argument takes the time to lay out the groundwork and various positions involved, and experience suggests that it is therefore wise to give time to reflection and balanced consideration about what constitutes right and wrong before we make important decisions unreflectively in the heat of the moment.

Moral Foundations

Either consciously or unconsciously we all operate within a moral framework. Occasionally, though, it is helpful to explore the boundaries of our behavior or question how things are always done, especially when we face new or difficult situations. In both ethics and science, we tend to start from our experiences. We encounter the world and recognize phenomena in it—the seasons change; apples drop from trees; only the mast of an approaching ship at sea is seen before the rest comes into view, and so forth. We operate on a few assumptions about the world without necessarily doing the fundamental science to explain what we see; and yet, at the same time we (and, in particular, scientists) find it helpful to generate a theoretical basis for these phenomena to make them more predictable and useful. Similarly most of us have a general sense of good and bad behavior that serves us well in our everyday dealings, but at some point considerable value in developing a theoretical framework allows us to critically examine conduct and make recommendations about how to live better lives.

ETHICS AND THE LAW

A common reaction to moral issues is to say that we can simply look at the law, which will provide the answers we need. Hence if we want to know if it is appropriate to freely share electronic files with others, we consult a lawyer who will tell us what to do. This approach has the virtue of being clear and directive. In general, following the law will be sufficient in most cases and if you are uncertain about what to do, it is the safe option.

The law has moral foundations and the policies that are enacted are deliberated in much the same way as ethical theory has framed them. For example, there is a legal idea called eminent domain where a community can legally override the property rights of an individual. It is generally applied in cases where the community feels that the welfare of the many outweighs that of the few. If a city wants to extend an airport to increase commerce and there is a house in the way of a proposed runway, under the law of eminent domain, the community can demolish the house to make way for the runway. The policy is based on a **results-based theory**—looking at the beneficial consequences overall, not just at the impact on the individual—and could possibly be defeated if opponents could show that the purported benefits were miscalculated through flawed evidence.

In contrast, we cannot legally extract blood from someone with a very rare blood type against his or her will. This is based on the philosophical principle of **personal autonomy**, which sometimes conflicts with theories based on overall benefit. Hence, it appears the law does not come fully formed, but in large part has been drawn from deeper philosophical commitments.

If the law and morality were identical, it would be impossible to have times when an act could be legal but not moral, or conversely, moral but not legal. Perhaps an employer in a developing country legally may not have to provide workers with the latest safety gear available and required in the United States and Europe. Some people may think that failing to do so is morally inappropriate, but the employer isn't breaking the prevailing law. In another example, consider your view of abortion: if the law were changed overnight, would it alter your opinion about its morality? Probably not, and hence we are dealing with two distinct approaches—one that is governed by laws and one that is based on morality. Although they may often overlap, they are not interchangeable. There can also be times when morality may tell us to go against the prevailing legal standards, perhaps by staging a protest, or refusing to be enlisted in a draft for a war perceived as unjust. The fact that the two realms are distinct and do not always overlap tells us that we should not automatically say the legality of an action necessarily implies that it is moral. Thus while following the law is generally a very good threshold for moral behavior, it should not be an absolute yardstick for morality. This is especially true in cases where technology develops more rapidly than the law, for example, in cases of sharing electronic data or using social media.

Another key difference of law and morality is in the focus of moral responsibility. If we make our own decisions about right and wrong, they can certainly be informed by our sense of ethics, legality, and convention, but ultimately we have to take the responsibility for our own choices and acts. Imagine a hypothetical world where we constantly defaulted to the law as our guide. It would be full of legislators making the law, police enforcing it, and judges assessing punishments for those who transgress. We would all have to become encyclopedic about the current regulations. However, in reality the law is not static and uniform. Lawyers are hired to interpret the law in a way that best favors their clients. Various readings of the facts, issues, precedents, and appropriate regulations show us that the view of morality *as* the law leaves us with a state of affairs that ultimately resolves into the same kind of debates that we currently find within philosophy itself.

ETHICS AND RELIGION

Philosophy and religion also overlap in many areas, but they are distinct fields and deal with ethical issues from different perspectives. They may reach the same conclusions—for instance, both would probably agree that taking the life of an innocent is wrong, or that charity is good. However, the starting point and methodology will be different and the two should not be confused.

Religious commitment involves alignment of one's life with a divine being. Ideally, every action is an attempt to be more harmonious with a supernatural force that informs and guides the life of a believer. The divine may be known by a revelatory experience, perhaps through encounters with a text such as the Bible, a religious organization like a church, or a spiritual being. Typically a canonical text is considered to be divinely inspired. Further, the mystery of the religion invokes faith, and the believer will accept some basic tenets on that basis. Certain teachings are held to be authoritative and intertwined with the faith, insofar as questioning them would be regarded as heretical. A further hallmark of religion is its various rituals, including worship and prayer.

In contrast, philosophical inquiry does not require an act of faith. In the Western tradition at least, it favors rational argument to demonstrate its conclusions, and it fosters analysis and debate. Texts are not held to be immune from criticism, and indeed, much of the discipline involves close critical reading and responses to classic works. No single text is held to be authoritative, and the history of philosophy often reads like an unfolding dialogue that emerges from earlier works.

These differences are significant when we consider the study of ethics. A religious approach will demand some connection with the supernatural and certain dogmatic assumptions that fuel moral action. For instance, the Ten Commandments that Moses brought down from Mount Sinai give many people an ethical anchor, but at the same time they may feel that these religious laws are immune to interpretation or criticism. That is, people feel the Commandments should be obeyed simply because they come from God, and therefore they do not need any further justification. Even though a philosopher might agree with the Decalogue as a set of moral principles, he or she need not start from the same place. We could imagine that they could be considered a reasonable set of conventional rules to govern a society, but it is not essential to philosophical inquiry to make reference to a spiritual author.

Although ethics does not depend on a religious backdrop, it need not be antagonistic to those with religious commitments. For a believer, religion typically governs one's whole life, and not just morality, and many philosophers have deep spiritual lives that are based in faith. At the same time, they feel it is worthwhile to engage in inquiry about the nature and scope of moral behavior. Saint Thomas Aquinas, for example, argued that a life of faith can be congruent with philosophical investigation based on logic and experience.

The religious believer might maintain that a full and rich life requires knowledge of the supernatural, a view contested by the atheist. However, as an empirical matter, an ethical life need not depend on being religious, or having any particular faith or worldview. We can see this because someone could create a moral system and live a good life without any reference to a supreme being. We can have both theistic and atheistic ethics where we scrutinize the consistency of the recommended behaviors and their outcomes. For instance, whatever the origin of a moral intuition, it would be appropriate to question theories that lead to suffering or oppression. Certain ethical attitudes will spring from religious beliefs, to be sure, but the philosopher can examine them on their own merits without having to question the underlying faith commitment. Conversely, someone of faith should not see ethical theory as a challenge or threat, but rather as a useful analytic tool, which is capable of refining and clarifying how we should treat one another.

THE NATURE OF CONSCIENCE

Another approach to morality is to say that we have an inner feeling or voice that tells us right from wrong, in other words a *conscience*. For example, in the Disney movie *Pinocchio* the character Jiminy Cricket cheerfully sings about letting conscience be a guide for your actions, leading us to believe that we can judge each moral question by reflecting on whether it makes us feel good or uneasy. Thus, for example, when faced with a choice of whether to peek at an answer sheet accidentally left on a teacher's desk or not, we might reflect on whether (and to what extent) we would feel guilty for being dishonest. Most of us have had this type of experience at one time or another.

There is an issue of timing, because having a conscience is often thought of as carrying a burden after the fact for having done something wrong. This dynamic is often portrayed in TV crime dramas where the confronted suspect voluntarily confesses all because the crime is weighing on his or her mind. This is not new: In Shakespeare's story of Hamlet, the title character arranges a play to mimic the apparent murder of his father by his uncle. The idea is that this will flush out the culprit because someone with a guilty conscience is troubled and will not be able to keep the secret indefinitely. Hamlet's uncle sees the play and storms out, which Hamlet takes as proof of his guilt.

Despite widespread acceptance of the notion, many philosophers have questioned the very concept of *having a conscience*, believing that it may just be shorthand for some other psychological dynamic at work such as conforming to societal norms. Let us look at it more closely.

First, do all of us react similarly? If we all had the same moral sense, then perhaps we would all react similarly when faced with moral choices or at least those who choose the wrong path would regret their actions and seek to redress them.

Laura Bohannan, an anthropologist, lived among the Tiv people in Nigeria. She was confident that the story of Hamlet would have universal meaning, and told them of a chieftain killed by his brother, and the desire for vengeance by the dead chieftain's son. To her surprise, the Tiv interpreted the story quite differently. They thought that the brother was the proper heir and instead of being shocked that the queen cut short her mourning and married the new king, they thought it entirely appropriate. Their cultural framework shaped their moral judgments which were at odds with Bohannan's.

It appears that moral judgments based on conscience have to be taken in the context of the society and its conventions. Perhaps what we mean by conscience is an immediate response based on our sense of conformist judgments where we assess our actions in terms of how others in our cultural group would respond. Additionally, various opinions about the moral acceptability of practices such as the treatment of animals suggest that conscience may be a function of upbringing just as much as nature.

As children, our behavior is largely influenced by others, mainly our parents. We are encouraged to behave in specific ways and rewarded or punished accordingly. If we are taught to protect, love, and care for animals, for instance, our response to killing animals for sport may be condemnation. However, if we are encouraged to believe that killing animals for sport is actually a means to practice a survival technique, we may be more open to the idea. Similarly, some feel guilty when engaging in activities, such as jet skiing or disposing of plastic in landfills, which may harm the environment. Others have no problems doing so. If conscience is really a function of our human nature, then we should all react to issues similarly, which is clearly not the case. Hence it is difficult to establish what is actually an *innate, raw, or unbiased* response because of the influences of others beginning at very early stages of life.

Furthermore, conscience can be fluid in nature. We can imagine someone who is reluctant to steal office supplies from work, but is told by her coworkers that "it's no big deal" and that "everyone does it." The reluctant employee may take a ream of paper, but agonizes over her action all night long even though she realizes there is very little likelihood of being found out and, even if she were, the consequences would be minimal. A few days later, when she runs out of toner for her home printer, she decides to take some home, this time justifying her actions by telling herself "it would never be missed" and that "she is worth more than she is paid." Sleep comes more easily this time and after a while, she is completely undisturbed by her actions and wouldn't even describe them as morally wrong.

The issue here is that even if we hear that inner voice of conscience, we are adept at ignoring it or interpreting it in various ways. The remedy might be to assess potentially moral actions quietly and reflectively, but there is no guarantee that our findings will be any different from the justifications we've already made. In other words, this may be a case where we choose to explore multiple kinds of justification without any real governing principle to arbitrate between them, and whether decisions are made hastily or at leisure would not affect their validity.

Conscience is used in another sense when we talk about people who have stood up for their beliefs and face punishment as a result, as in the phrase "a prisoner of conscience" describing someone who will not recant political views in the face of a repressive regime. In a slightly different sense, the term has recently been applied to cases where, say, a pharmacist refuses to dispense birth control pills to a customer because of his personal religious beliefs. However, conscience in this context need not be referring to the mysterious inner voice. These cases describe a mode of behavior that is based on an individual moral stance. The fact that some people are willing to make sacrifices based on their strongly held personal beliefs does not by itself verify that they are responding to an unprejudiced moral sense or that their views are any more correct or justified than others.

One of the continuing issues in ethics is the difficulty of putting our concerns about behavior into words and then persuading others (or being convinced by their arguments). If we leave conscience as a lurking, subjective voice, then we will preclude that possibility. But if we think of it as a useful starting place reflecting primitive ethical intuitions, it opens up the opportunity for moral discourse and arguments.

ETHICAL PROJECTS

Other approaches place ethics in the context of a wider project. For example, some theorists will argue that our current ethical views are shaped by evolutionary biology, asserting that we have successfully survived as a species because we have developed psychological mechanisms that promote cooperation and nurturing. This is known as **sociobiology** and draws on work in zoology and anthropology. In this case, it is plausible that ethics could be reduced to a natural science of observation and prediction. Others believe that mankind is unique among the animals, set apart because of our ability to reason. **Natural law** theorists believe that human nature reveals fundamental truths reflected in the way we behave (e.g., that we form family units). Oftentimes natural law is used in conjunction with a **theistic** world view, which suggests that we have been created with certain natural dispositions to the good and the right by God and our mission is to discern those truths through reason.

Some take the ethics project to trace the implications of deeply rooted convictions about the nature of people and existence. For example:

- **Foundationalists** believe there are certain core moral anchors, and there are both sacred and secular versions of this thesis. For instance, many believe that the key moral precepts are the Ten Commandments found in the Old Testament of the Bible and any ethical question can be answered by reference to these few central ideas. However, the set of core tenets need not be religious in nature; we could create a system of similar moral claims without reference to a divine origin. Their project typically involves a marriage between these central tenets and prescriptions about the way people *should* behave.
- **Coherentists** are not concerned as much with immutable truths but try to understand the justification of moral language in terms of its internal consistency. For example, if someone says human life is invaluable, coherentists ask if the same line of argument

be used for both the debates about abortion and capital punishment. Dealing with these kinds of knotty problem, coherentists believe, will help establish sound analyses that can be applied to difficult or novel cases.

- **Ethical egoists** believe the fundamental moral unit is the individual and he or she ought to always promote his or her own good. This means the person does not accept external values, whether they are from conventions, laws, or divine commands unless he or she sees them in his or her interests to do so. The egoist may cooperate with others, but ultimately the arbitrating factor in making any ethical decision is whether there is any personal payoff involved. An egoist viewpoint is often seen at work in the literature of strategy and business.

- **Relativists** focus on the idea that there are no fixed points in ethics and all claims must be expressions of preference. Just as some people prefer coffee and others soda, decisions about lying, cheating, or stealing are considered individual expressions of personal choice. What goes for one person or group applies only to them, but has no privileged status that means it should be imposed on anyone else. However, as a practical matter we don't live in societies where anything goes, and standards are rarely arbitrary. Thus the relativist is challenged to explain why some behaviors should be encouraged and others sanctioned.

- **Cultural relativists** accept the claim that there are certain acceptable conventions within a community and look at the differences between different societies. This leads to a view that ethics is a societal construct, but should not be regarded as reflecting any objective or universal truths. For example, bullfighting is popular in Spain, but would be considered barbaric in some other countries; or the government has a say in family size in China, which many in the West would consider an infringement of a basic human right. Yet at the same time, some countries have gone to war with others to prevent genocide or liberate a repressed people, and the cultural relativist faces the challenge of justifying such acts.

Thus there are clear differences in diverse approaches to the study of ethics and the objectives involved. Whatever someone's starting point, though, all these perspectives are open to critical scrutiny, and philosophers have created strong arguments on all sides. The benefit from these clashing views is that every objection demands that the proponent respond with ever greater clarity and sophistication. In the next section we will look at the various strategies that philosophers used to tackle ethical issues, and some of the key distinctions they use to present their arguments.

VARIETIES OF PHILOSOPHICAL ETHICS

The study of ethics is often broken down into a number of subfields. As the discussion becomes more specific, technical terms are used to clarify the distinctions. Although not everyone would agree with the distinctions or accept the classifications, it is nevertheless worthwhile to grasp an overview of the various schools of thought.

Descriptive Ethics

Descriptive ethics focuses on actual behavior. Thus if we say we care about buying dolphin-safe tuna or recycling, but if the research shows people are unwilling to pay more or alter the way they act, then our talk may be less significant than our actions. In studying ethics, we can gain useful self-awareness from empirical research in descriptive ethics. Even if the particular manifestations of morality differ across time and culture, all societies have had a sense of what constitutes justice and goodness, and descriptions of practice are useful in working out the emergence and application of value-based attitudes.

To understand descriptive ethics in a broader context, let us begin with a simple statement:

All human societies kill animals for sport.

This is a descriptive sentence. It is important to notice several features of the sentence: First, it is a statement. That means it asserts a fact which can be either true or false. Philosophers sometimes use the term *proposition* or *propositional content* when discussing the truth or falsity of a fact-asserting or declarative sentence. Statements, however, need not be true; their function is to make a claim along with conditions which would either affirm or deny it. In this case, if a society venerates its animals and never kills them for sport, then the claim is still a statement, but, as it turns out in this case, a false one.

Second, by itself the statement conveys no values: It only says that the activity takes place. We may react with alarm, disgust, or a complacent shrug, but the sentence doesn't demand any specific response. The same would be true if research indicated that one-third of all job seekers lied on their applications. But these empirical findings do not tell us whether such actions are good or bad, only that they happen.

Professionals in certain disciplines (e.g., zoology, anthropology, and psychology) specialize in examining human and animal behavior and report their findings. For example, zoologists tell us that dolphins support sick companions and will push them to the surface to breathe, anthropologists report that poor people give proportionally more of their incomes to charity than the rich, and psychologists indicate that bystanders tend to avoid helping others in an emergency. These researchers do not present their conclusions with an "ought to"; instead they leave it to us to draw our own moral implications.

A note of caution is appropriate as it is not unusual for a merely descriptive sentence to have an embedded persuasive element. For example, in the following:

No decent society kills animals for sport

the word *decent* imports an implicit value element into what initially appears to be a neutral statement, and so we always need to be wary, in so far as some words and phrases introduce a personal bias that frame statements likely to alter the perceptions of its audience.

Metaethics

Metaethics looks at the nature of moral language, how we use it, and asks questions about the meaning of moral utterances. Additionally, it touches on a range of other issues in philosophy, since it questions the knowledge claims involved, which is the province of the branch of philosophy called epistemology. Since metaethics is largely concerned with examining moral language, the key elements are conceptual analysis and examination of the reasoning involved. If we have good reasons to accept some ideas and reject others, and we can concur on ways to ascertain the validity of certain claims, then we are more likely to identify flawed ways of thinking such as vague terminology and sweeping conclusions, and move toward moral consensus.

The work of writers in this area often discerns the set of beliefs that people have and the reasons behind what they say when describing their own values and trying to influence those of others. For example, here is a sentence with an explicit value component:

It is wrong to torture kittens for fun.

In exploring the nature and meaning of the sentence we could ask whether it is a statement of fact or an expression of personal feeling. If it is a fact, then is it fixed in a certain context, for instance, here and now, or is it true for all people everywhere and always? If it is an expression of a personal view, could someone's view ever change, and should other people hold the same belief?

These sorts of questions are important in discovering how ethical discourse functions: If you dislike the idea of torturing kittens, but feel that other people are entitled to their own opinions about how to treat their animals, your view won't have much leverage in persuading others to alter their behavior. Alternatively, you may take the position that torture of any animal is, and always will be, wrong in any circumstances, and that your claim is on par with scientific facts.

Metaethics is usually divided into two camps: **cognitivism** and **noncognitivism**, each with its own subfields. Cognitivism (from the Latin word *cognoscere*, meaning "to know," or "to recognize") is the philosophical view that moral statements make knowledge claims. Thus cognitivists believe that moral statements reflect facts, and they should be treated in the same way as other factual claims. Importantly, they don't say that all statements are true, only that they are capable of being shown to be true or false someday. In some cases, we may not yet conclusively know the truth, but a hypothesis is susceptible to proof that future technology or research will provide. For instance, consider the claim that pregnant women who drink over 300 mg per day of caffeine, or eight cups of coffee, may cause birth defects in their children. While we may not have a definitive answer at the moment, in the end the claim itself will turn out to be either true or false. In the same way cognitivists talk about moral claims such as "x is bad" or "y is unjust" very much as if they were irrefutable statements about the world, just like sentences about gravity or electromagnetism.

Similarly, the cognitivist may say that the mission of ethics is to determine how best to obtain the truth or falsity of moral statements, and deny that there is any room for personal interpretation. Hence it may indeed be true that it is wrong to torture kittens, and the cognitivist maintains that such a statement has the force and irrefutability of a scientific claim. It is important to note that moral disagreement does not necessarily undermine the cognitivist view. Just as people historically have had the false perception that the world is flat and the idea has been subject to scientific discovery, individuals may get their facts wrong about morality. Nonetheless, the cognitivist holds out the promise that one day we will have the appropriate means to establish the truth one way or another.

Cognitivism is typically broken down further into **naturalism** and **intuitionism**. Naturalism asserts that moral talk turns out to be shorthand for natural facts, that is, the kind that can be established through demonstration or scientific proof. Thus the naturalist believes that we can translate moral terms into physical, sociological, or psychological hypotheses that can subsequently be tested. For example, it could be that:

Torturing kittens for fun is wrong.

means

Most people disapprove of torturing kittens.

or

All sane people release certain brain chemicals when they witness the unnecessary suffering of kittens.

The preceding statements are simple and crude, and most naturalists would say that once we parsed out what we mean by "good" or "wrong" or other value components, their meanings will end up being far more complex and subtle. At the same time, naturalists believe with research and sufficient data the study of various cultures and human physiology will yield scientific findings corresponding to the value components of our sentences. That is, they believe there is no mysterious quality of "good" or "right" that could not be reduced into descriptive sentences of observable data. One view along these lines is that given sufficiently advanced imaging of the brain, for example, every value statement could be translated into a fact about brain states, with the corresponding belief that value differences may be explained as chemical imbalances in the body.

Some philosophers, notably G. E. Moore (1873–1958), feel that naturalism rests on a fallacy. They say that any purported translation from a value statement to a factual one will fail to fully capture its meaning. The evidence for this is that we can always ask "But is it good?" to any factual claim. For example, if the naturalist maintained that "Ending malnutrition is good" translates into "All sane people approve of ending malnutrition" or even "All humans react with the release of certain brain chemicals when confronting malnutrition," Moore would say that the factual statements are still subject to the value question of whether all people approving something makes it good, or whether our bodily responses tell us how to judge something morally.

Moore himself represented another cognitivist school known as **intuitionism**. It accepts that moral statements can be determined as true or false, but contends they arise from a human sensibility that we all share, which enables us to determine right from wrong. It explains apparent variations by saying our moral senses are often clouded and we need to refine them to make accurate judgments. If we had appropriate clarity about a moral question, they argue, we would achieve universal agreement. Someone who relies on conscience alone would be an intuitionist, and as we have seen he or she faces the task of explaining a sense which is elusive and unclear to many.

In its defense, we cannot deny that often people have similar experiences and reactions to some moral issues, such as intuitions that promises ought to be kept or that babies should be cared for. As an analogy, think about the nature of *love*—many people experience it and are more certain about it than many other facts. They could be persuaded that they are subject to perceptual mistakes, but will maintain that their experience of love is raw and immediate. When asked to explain what it means to be in love or how they could demonstrate it to others, they find themselves hard-pressed to do so. However, we don't necessarily give up on the concept of love just because it is hard to explicate, and the intuitionist would say much the same about our moral sensibilities.

Noncognitivism, in stark contrast, focuses on the belief that moral language expresses or exhorts only our personal attitudes and is incapable of expressing objective facts about the world. One noncognitivist view, **emotivism**, suggests that a moral statement translates into a sincere representation of our reactions such as the idea of "Torturing kittens-Ugh!" They would deny that there are universal moral facts, and believe that morality is a question of personal reactions, which may vary significantly. Another version, **prescriptivism**, gives additional force to our reactions by suggesting that our responses and utterances not only express a personal view, but they serve to encourage others to think the same way as well—for example, "Torturing kittens is wrong and you should think so too!"

The cognitivist/noncognitivist split is not the only way of slicing the metaethical pie. An alternate version uses the terms **realism** and **antirealism**. In ethics, a realist is someone who believes there is an objective truth to moral claims. That is, the realist would say that there is a reality to moral matters that does not depend on individual perception or interpretation. A realist would assert that there is something we perceive about the act as we understand it and we recognize this reality in our moral assessment of the act. Therefore, all realists are cognitivists insofar as they posit that moral statements have a factual basis. In the 1930s, W. D. Ross, an English intuitionist, claimed some duties such as *doing good* and *preventing harm* are self-evident and obvious, and are therefore real because the moral assessment by anyone with normal sensibilities would always be the same.

Conversely, the antirealist position asserts that there is no objective moral reality, implying that all antirealists are also noncognitivists. But, that does not necessarily mean that there are no standards or that all moral decisions are a function of individual preferences. The antirealist denies that there is any ultimate moral reality, but at the same time is likely to agree that we live by a set of practical conventions.

To explain, let us try another analogy. People build dwellings, which take various forms with functional elements such as sleeping areas, and dedicated spaces for cooking and bathing. We would expect to find some basic concepts such as sound structure and weatherproofing as part of any design. However, these do not show there is some objective or ideal form that a home should manifest, but rather that humans tend to react to their surroundings in similar ways. Some aspects of a dwelling will depend, to a large degree, on the environmental conditions. Architectural and aesthetic values will also vary depending on the particular time and society in which we live—for example, the Soviet regime favored brutal concrete buildings, whereas other cultures look to spectacular ornamentation. The point is that in a human endeavor it should not surprise us that basic common features come about from functionality, and others vary by emergent conventions.

The same could be said of a wide range of activities, such as sports, the college curriculum, or the discipline of philosophy. From within the convention there are certain ideas of better or worse, but when we look at each activity as a whole, it is clear they have been crafted by our own design. Thus we prize strength and agility in many sports, but these often represent ancient martial qualities, and are traditional rather than natural—we could just as easily value elegance, balance, or endurance. Similarly, the subjects we study at college and the way they are approached has developed from a set of accepted conventions, but we can imagine a radically different approach—perhaps one that involves service learning or requiring life skills training.

The antirealist view in ethics does not deny that morality exists. Instead it claims that human societies have developed a set of functional and mutually beneficial standards for behavior that are social constructs, and do not represent an objective or eternal moral reality. The common features of the convention simply mirror what works best in any human community. Hence while these codes and principles are internally consistent and we often find similar behaviors praised and sanctioned, antirealism maintains that they reflect the most practical or efficient functional underpinnings inevitably emerging as part of humans living together.

Normative Ethics

Normative ethics deals with setting norms or standards. In other words, it asks *what we ought to do*. Normative ethics is divided into two subfields: ethical theory and applied ethics.

Ethical theory deals with the theory and justification of moral principles. It tries to explain what is good and why that is so, and what makes an act right. If we return to the kitten case, we might say that torture is wrong because it causes unnecessary suffering or that it degrades us as human beings. We are now able to move beyond mere assertion toward providing principles to support our claims about what we ought to do and how we ought to act. However, these principles need to be justified, not just asserted, which involves developing arguments showing their internal consistency and coherence. There are several levels of justification in which we often move from looking at individual judgments to developing a universal rule and establishing a general principle.

Applied ethics, also called practical ethics, applies the principles of ethical theory to particular focused areas and cases. Philosophers in these areas make explicit arguments about how we should behave in specific cases. For example, there is considerable literature that applies ethical analysis to human rights, the environment, or the treatment of animals. Other areas deal with concerns where special standards might apply. For instance, in medicine issues such as confidentiality and informed consent are examined, in the law there are questions about attorneys as zealous advocates, and in business what the appropriate levels of social responsibility to the surrounding community should be.

Many philosophers have had little difficulty in bridging the gap between ethical theory and its application. Their works are peppered with examples to illustrate the points they make, and so it is difficult to maintain that theory is divorced from application. Nevertheless other philosophers believe it is most useful to deal with the theoretical backdrop in isolation before we can apply theory in particular cases involving practical decisions.

Traditional ethical theories fall into three main groups: consequentialist, deontological, and virtue-based. **Consequentialist** theories, as the name suggests, look to the potential results of our actions to determine whether they are right or wrong. **Deontological** theories arise from the Greek term *deon*, meaning "duty," which focus on motives or intentions. For example, there are cases where the greater good might be served by breaking a promise. Perhaps a recently deceased relative had extracted a deathbed promise that you spend a huge amount of his money on a monument to his memory, but you want to donate the money to a worthy cause instead. The tension arises when we have to discern where the moral focus should be—on the potential benefits, as a consequentialist would, or on the motivating obligations and duties, as a deontologist would. **Virtue-based theory** does not present direct principles or rules that would indicate what the best course of action is in particular cases, but instead tells us what matters most is developing a worthy character, suggesting that *who we are* is more significant than *what we do*. This theory looks at someone's actions over the entire sweep of his or her lifetime, and judges him or her by the way he or she engages virtues guided by a core set of values.

Some ethical theories are described as **teleological** (from the Greek word, *telos*, meaning "end" or "destiny"). The general idea of teleological theories is that life should be purposeful. Thus a consequentialist might say that we should work to increase overall welfare by doing the maximum good for the maximum number, whereas others could argue that we should try to do our moral duty, or live in harmony with nature or glorify God. A virtue theorist might say that all human life should be aimed to encourage human flourishing, using all our gifts to fulfill our best potential.

Recent Challenges to Ethical Theory

The accepted teachings in ethical theory have been radically questioned in contemporary times. **Feminist** philosophers have suggested that classical views may have ignored some of the special concerns of women and insights they offer. These philosophers confront many of the assumptions that have been presented in the ethical canon. For example, the role of reason has often been held to be dominant in contrast to that of emotion, which has typically been described as a feminine trait and downplayed in moral discourse.

Postmodernist philosophers have a wide range of perspectives on ethics. In general, they react against the **modernist** assumption that academic theoretical discourse has a privileged truth-telling function, and they look to the experience or phenomena of what goes on when we use ethical language. Postmodernists may claim that the concepts of ethics allow us to organize our experience in certain ways or construct notions of what it would be like to have an ideal life. Their focus shifts from looking at morality as a distinct practice to trying to make sense of the world through experience informed by ethical language. In other words, each of us constructs our own narrative based on our lives, and the function of ethical language is not so much to argue as it is to present a story that makes sense to others.

Summary

A frequent reaction to any ethical inquiry is often for people to rely on an immediate intuitive response, and then try to persuade others through various rhetorical techniques. Parents, for example, will often engage in moral instruction by simply telling a child that something is wrong and threatening punishment if questioned. Nevertheless, at the end of the day this kind of approach is unsatisfactory: It leaves no room for questioning, argument, or progress in the ways we determine basic and everyday notions of right and wrong, good and bad, or what is fair and just.

The nature and scope of ethics can initially be intimidating, especially in its use of technical language and fine distinctions. Yet there is real value in looking at ethics by systematically distinguishing the various starting points and assumptions at work. Further, once we have established some common foundations, it will allow us to develop principled arguments to defend our views and persuade others through rational argument rather than assertion or bigotry. It is worth examining ethical claims in such a rigorous and methodical way since they may govern some of the most important features of human life, including ordinary interpersonal behavior, social policy, human rights, the environment, and ultimately issues of life and death.

3

Egoism and Hedonism

Moral philosophy relies in great part on basic assumptions about human nature: whether we ultimately care only about ourselves, those we love, or mankind and the earth more generally. Some see the spark of the divine in human action. In this chapter, we will examine arguments for and against putting the self first and their implications for moral action.

Egoism refers to putting the self—the ego—as the paramount focus of moral concern. Egoists only act from self-interest.

SELF-INTEREST OR COOPERATION?

In William Golding's book *The Lord of the Flies*, a plane crashes, killing all the adults and stranding the surviving group of boys on a remote uninhabited island. Initially the boys agree to work together for the common good. They cooperate in finding food, building shelter, and maintaining a signal fire, but as time goes on, they become more savage and individualistic, to the point where they start murdering one another. The book poses the question whether civilization is, in fact, only a thin veneer that hides a much darker side of human nature, and if there were no such external constraints, would communities rapidly spiral into anarchy and violence? There are similar stories of people stranded in lifeboats who initially get on well, but as resources begin to fail and hope of rescue fades, they turn on one another. In stark contrast, many other books such as the *Wizard of Oz* highlight cooperation and heroic self-sacrifice in the face of adversity.

Psychological egoism interprets actions in terms of what benefits we will derive from them, and predicts that we will do whatever is best for us. Thus it holds that we are looking for some payoff, and even a charitable act would be interpreted as seeking self-satisfaction. Take cases of apparent **altruism**, where people do good for others or for their own sake (e.g., Mother Teresa who worked for the poor of India). The psychological egoist would argue that whether she realized it or not, Mother Teresa was ultimately working to fulfill her own needs, perhaps a psychological desire to feel good about herself, or an attempt to earn salvation, and although these motives may be hidden from the individual doing the act, they nevertheless drive all we do.

Ethical egoism is the normative claim that says we *ought to do whatever is in our self-interest*. It often accepts psychological egoism as verifiable and makes the further claim that not only *do* we act in our self-interest, but also the moral claim, that we *ought* to.

Self-interest may take many forms, of course. Thus someone might deny himself a high-fat treat on the grounds that he is looking for long-term health; another might give to charity because it makes her feel good about herself; others might go for self-indulgence because they don't worry about the future. The point is that they are all putting themselves at the center of the moral universe and, moreover, think it is right that they do so.

It is worth emphasizing that rational egoists may be motivated by what is best for themselves, but that doesn't mean that they will always take a short-term perspective or ignore others. For example, it would be completely rational to donate blood on the self-interested grounds to support an institution that may someday save your own life.

There is a long tradition of egoism, and it has taken many forms. Here we will look at three central figures, Niccolo Machiavelli, Thomas Hobbes, and more recently Ayn Rand.

MACHIAVELLI

Niccolo Machievelli (1469–1527) worked as an administrator and diplomat for the Florentine republic during a time of great political turmoil. He is most famous for his book *The Prince*, which was published posthumously. It is a reflection on how best to rule a principality, and in the book he recommends that a ruler should be bold and ruthless, acquiring and using power to his own advantage at every opportunity. The ethical notions of right and wrong become less important than maintaining power and order in any particular case, and thus a prince should do whatever is expedient or necessary to maintain his position: Generosity and compassion might help in some cases, but brutality and intimidation in others. What unifies Machiavelli's use of cruelty and kindness though is that the primary focus of all action he prescribes for the prince is survival and dominance in a culture of mutual animosity. Thus if we believe that our personal interests matter most, and also think everyone believes the same thing, the result is that we have to be constantly wary that others will be out to get us if it helps their cause in some way. It will also make us suspicious of their motives, because we might interpret even an apparent act of benevolence as designed to create an obligation to return the favor in the future or put us off our guard.

It isn't clear whether Machiavelli was sincere in everything he wrote, but his work has been widely cited as the source of the motto "Might Makes Right." He is also famous for saying that it is desirable to be loved and feared by one's subjects, but given the choice, it is ultimately better to be feared.[1] Essentially his philosophy is to promote the self through dominating others by any means necessary. However, as we find throughout the book this requires constant vigilance, strength, and strategic alliances: Imagine a world where mutual betrayal is more normal than mutual trust. It portrays the world as being divided into those who create their own destiny by imposing their values on others and those who merely adopt conventional morality, and hence *The Prince* resonates with the true egoist.

The notions of right and wrong are seen through the lens of what is good for the prince: Whatever he does to promote his own interests are necessarily good, and those which are likely to hurt him are wrong. Torturing a peasant, for instance, might be something the prince thinks he needs to do to prevent a rebellion, and because it helps his cause, it is automatically the right thing to do. Thus there is no independent or universal moral system involved. Machiavelli says that it is going to be useful for the prince to appear just and benevolent, but only insofar as the perceptions help him keep in power. Hence if he creates a system of laws that allow people property

---

[1]Niccolo Machiavelli, *The Prince*, ch. 15.

rights, it is likely to benefit commerce and keep the peace, and similarly appearing to be honest in diplomatic dealings may be to his benefit. Yet these are merely means to the end of keeping the prince's fortune and sovereignty, rather than good in themselves, and the litmus test for any act will be whether it helps the prince's own interests or not. In other words, honesty or justice become a mere tool that can be used or abandoned at any point rather than external measures of ethical action.

HOBBES

Thomas Hobbes (1588–1679) lived during the time of the English Civil War, when the idea that kings were appointed by God was overturned and members of the same family may have taken different sides in a bloody conflict. Like Machiavelli, Hobbes believed that mankind was naturally self-interested and competitive, but in contrast he had a different perspective on power. While Machiavelli advocates domination as the appropriate response to our natural state, Hobbes believes in enforced cooperation.

Hobbes's mechanistic philosophy suggests that we are fundamentally animals motivated by various appetites. He denied the notion of absolute moral standards, but instead asserted that moral terms are just manifestations of our own preferences: We label what we approve of as good and what repels us as bad. He combines this with a view that we are more individualistic than communal, so that without a governing authority the natural human state would constantly compete for scarce resources effectively, a perpetual state of interpersonal strife. He asserted that the human natural state is a state of war in which we see everyone else as a potential adversary. Unchecked, he thinks we would live in "continual fear, and danger of violent death; and the life of man, solitary, poor, nasty, brutish, and short."

Like Machiavelli's, Hobbes's view begins with self-interest. His solution to this natural state of enmity is rationality, in the sense that we make a reasoned agreement to cooperate and restrain our ambitions for the sake of the common good. His book, *The Leviathan*, draws its name from a Biblical sea monster in the book of Job that can be conjured up at any time, to remind us of our human frailty. Under the system that Hobbes devises, we agree to subject ourselves to a supreme authority, and in return we are rewarded with peace and prosperity. So in the natural state, as he suggests, no one would bother to plant seeds and work the land if it was certain that the resulting crops would be stolen by others. However, if we put a system of laws and punishments into place, then it sets up the framework for mutual prosperity.

This kind of arrangement arises from **benign self-interest** in which, though the prime motivation is still self-interest, the egoist realizes that he or she will benefit by contracting with others, leading to a system that increases welfare generally. However, the egoist is indifferent to the welfare of others except insofar as it affects his or her own interest. Paying taxes to maintain a community firefighting service, for example, would be acceptable as long as there were no preferable alternative arrangements that would benefit the egoist more. The central focus is on the advantage of the individual, and so if there were a more effective and cheaper private service available to the egoist, with the downside that it would not serve the indigent, then it would be consistent for him or her to opt for it rather than aid the community as a whole.

On the other hand, if he or she is also personally emotionally affected by the plight of people whose houses are destroyed, then he or she might choose to pay to avoid having that happen. Thus self-interest need not preclude helping others, but helping others is often seen as a means to one's own self-interest, or an inadvertent effect of it. This also means that a sophisticated egoist will uphold the law, even though it may be inconvenient and damaging in the short run. For instance, egoists may ideally wish to exempt themselves from rules about speeding, but come to realize that they are better off in a society where such rules are maintained.

Therefore, although Hobbes's view of human nature seems cynical to many, he takes it to mean that we should approach morality from a rational point of view that takes into account our long-term best interest. The keys to such a system will be creating means that allow people to work out what is best for them and giving them the ways to achieve it. Thus if we consider health care, for example, people are notorious for their ability to irrationally discount the future health risks that they know will lead to harm by smoking, eating fatty foods, or not exercising. However, the truly wise egoist would reason about what would be in his or her best interests in the long term, and supporting a system that looks after the elderly when they are no longer able to take care of themselves might then be a good strategy. Similarly, such wide perspective and long-term thinking might result in a system of mutual cooperation and benefit, but it would depend on people having ready access to information and fighting the psychological tendency to focus on immediate and expedient outcomes.

RAND

A contemporary version of egoism is found in the works of Ayn (usually pronounced Ann) Rand (1905–1982). Rand was brought up in Russia where her family's business was seized by the Soviets after the revolution in 1917. Subsequently she moved to America and earned her living as a screenwriter in Hollywood. She is best known for her philosophical novels, *The Fountainhead* and *Atlas Shrugged*. Rand used the term *objectivism* to describe her views, where an individual governed by reason measures achievement by productivity and the individual's paramount goal is his or her own happiness.

On Rand's view, we strive to achieve happiness by exercising our uncoerced personal choices. When this is manifested in free market capitalism, we all get what we earn through our own effort, without anyone depending on us, or vice versa. Central to her writing is the primacy of the individual who has no obligations other than the ones he or she voluntarily undertakes. The objective element comes about because there are external facts about reality that we have to acknowledge—for instance, human nature and our needs. If we can adjust our lives to fit the objective reality, she believes we will achieve happiness. Rand's heroes are self-made types who then can trade their goods and services; if they tap into an unfulfilled human need, say, personal computing, then they will merit rich rewards.

A natural objection is that some people may not be able to compete in the marketplace, and yet we still consider them as morally considerable. Rand's response is that the minority of adults who are unable to work have to rely on voluntary charity, but there would be no reciprocal sense of entitlement. From Rand's perspective, people may voluntarily give to others, but misfortune is no reason that the better-off have to provide for others without reward or, in her terms, engage in *slave labor* on their behalf. A person's economic value is determined by the willingness of others to trade with him or her as a result of free market choices. If we choose to give some of our money away to charitable causes, that is fine, but it should be a voluntary act, not one forced on us by a government that may often serve interests other than our own. She regards her view as contrary to what she calls "tribalism" (the notion that we are responsible for others in our community) and "altruism" (doing good without regard for reward).

Rand believes that everyone operating out of self-interest as manifested in his or her actions in the free market will bring about the maximum human happiness. She thinks that a central government would be very bad at determining what would make us happiest—that is, discovering the objective reality—and would prefer to let us choose for ourselves. At the heart of her theory, then, is the basic assumption that we do indeed know our own preferences, and fulfilling them will make us happy. Often the counterclaim is that we think we know what we want, but those desires are malleable and subject to outside influences. For example, the advertizing industry is built on the premise that people can be influenced to buy goods and services. Further, happiness may be elusive: The Russian author Tolstoy noted that everyone feels he or she would be content if he or she had just ten percent more wealth than they do, but that becomes a shifting goal that may never be achieved.

STRATEGIC ETHICS—GAME THEORY

The logical extension of assuming that we are all egoists is to behave in a way that primarily maximizes benefits to ourselves. We may cooperate with others, but only so far as it maximizes the eventual personal payoff. Thus one way ethics can be thought of is as a game—a very serious game—of strategy among self-interested players. A strategic action is one that you take without knowing what the other party will do, and in the absence of full predictability we need to make our best assessment. This will involve rationally working out how people are likely to react in any given circumstance, based on our knowledge of human nature and psychology.

Strategic self-interest can be modeled mathematically. The term **game theory** describes scenarios where individuals have to make decisions that will affect their outcomes. If we start with the assumption that people are self-interested and rational, then we can develop models that will help us work out the potential results of various actions. Although we use the terminology of *games* and *players*, these names are somewhat misleading as they originated in work done in the cold war to assess options under the threat of nuclear annihilation, and thus we should not discount it as trivial.

At the simplest level, though, we can think of two children sharing a pizza, where one divides it and the other chooses one part. Given that both sides want as much as they can get, it would be rational to assume that the chooser would take the largest piece. Therefore, it would be a rational strategy for the cutter to divide it as evenly as possible to minimize any potential loss.

It appears that maximum gains are found in cooperation, but in the absence of full trust and information we recognize that someone is likely to defect on the group, a dynamic known as the **prisoner's dilemma**. It gets this name from a story of two suspects who are separated by the police, and then independently offered a deal that if one confesses while the other does not, he will get off lightly whereas his partner will get a longer sentence. If both confess, then they both get the worst outcome, with the clear implication to each that they should confess before the other gets a chance to. The best outcome for the prisoners, though, is the one not advertised by the police: If both keep quiet, then both will be released without charge. If they trust each other fully, then the best option is for them to say nothing, but if there is any lingering doubt, the light sentence is preferable to the long one, and hence the dilemma each faces.

The same forces operate when we think about many mutual endeavors. Take the way we regard environmental resources: We know that it is probably in everyone's mutual best interests if we individually cut back on the amount of pollution and waste that we cause. However, doing so may go against our personal ideas of what is best for ourselves, but if everyone thinks the same way and we don't make any binding agreements with one another, then it is likely that someone will break the deal and look for instant payoffs. However, if we know that the deal will be broken, then it makes sense for everyone to default to what is best for them without regard to anyone else. For instance, if fish are scarce, then all the trawler operators might agree to lower their quotas to give the stocks a chance to build up. However, that forces up the price of fish and the incentives to cheat on the agreement, and, of course, everyone involved faces the same temptations. Recall that Hobbes's view is that the only way we can stop rampant self-interest is to create strong enforcement and punishment mechanisms that force us to actually do what we know to be best.

The game gets much more interesting if there are multiple encounters (termed *iterations*). Thus if the prisoners are mere acquaintances and are unlikely to see each other again, they may make different choices than if they are lifelong pals who anticipate working together in the future. Scientists wondered what would be the most successful strategy where two parties played repeated games and arranged tournaments where computers went through hundreds of thousands of iterations. The winning strategy was also one of the simplest. It is known as **Tit for Tat** and works by initially cooperating and then reciprocating every move the other side makes. The reciprocation element means it doesn't hold grudges or punish the other party with a greater penalty than it suffered, qualities the programmer describes as "nice."[2] If we extend the findings to moral behavior, it makes sense for us to be mutually cooperative rather than always seeking our personal immediate gain, because other options are likely to result in inefficient distrust where everyone is just looking out for himself or herself.

In another realm, researchers have found that animals often exhibit cooperative behavior, and sociobiologists have identified forms of the prisoner's dilemma in animal behavior. Parasites, for instance, thrive on a host, but if there are too many, they will kill it and themselves as well. It seems that they achieve equilibrium where they are restrained from reproducing to a greater extent than the host can tolerate. Some bats, it seems, will share their food with those who have none, and research shows those who have benefited are more likely to help those who have previously helped them, and monkeys routinely pick parasites off another expecting the favor to be returned.[3]

One remarkable implication of marrying ethics to strategic models is that it means morality need not have to be an exclusively human activity since we could program a computer to prompt the best result. Consider that humans are fallible in our reasoning: For example, we become invested in our earlier decisions, tend to be selective in the evidence we use to confirm our decisions, and tend to discount contrary evidence.[4] If we set up a program that equates maximizing self-interest as the goal, it would give us transparent, predictable, and accurate responses, and we might be able to rely on it more than our personal judgments. At the same time, the reservations we might have about delegating not only mathematical calculations but also moral judgments to computers might well give us some insights into why morality may be more than rational self-interest.

The prisoner's dilemma is a rational exercise, without any necessary ethical connotations. However, we can see that the moral qualities of trust and cooperation are desirable characteristics for extended relationships, and it can go some way to showing why even from an egoist perspective cultivating certain moral traits may be desirable.

---

[2] Robert Axelrod, 1984. *The Evolution of Cooperation.* New York: Basic Books.

[3] H. Goscilo and P. Petrov, "The Vampire Bat," available at http://www.pitt.edu/~slavic/courses/vampires/images/bats/vambat.html, accessed July 9, 2013.

[4] M. Neale and M. Bazerman, 1991. *Cognition and Rationality in Negotiation.* New York: Free Press.

CHALLENGES

There are several arguments against egoism. First, egoists have to face the challenge of whether the theory applies to themselves or should be a general rule. Additionally, egoism requires a robust notion of personal identity that relies on certain commitments about the self. Egoists maintain that we care most about ourselves individually, but other philosophers believe that there is evidence this assumption is incorrect and human nature is, in fact, as much concerned about the welfare of others as our own self-interest. Let us examine these claims in turn.

Egoists who believe that *everyone* should maximize his or her own personal welfare face a logical problem, because what applies to them individually cannot be made into a general rule: What is best for one egoist will diminish the welfare of others, and they would be acting in the same way. There will inevitably be times when the liberty and interest of one person will clash with those of others, and there are not enough resources to give everyone what they want. Thus if the egoist recommends personal advancement as a general rule that applies to everyone, he or she will effectively be advocating actions which will sometimes thwart his or her personal ambitions. This leaves the egoist with two options: Either accept the inconsistency or narrow the ethical theory so it applies to the egoist alone; that is, I should always do whatever I think best, and ignore the interests of others unless they give me some advantage.

Egoism also relies on a sense of personal identity called **atomistic**. This reflects our common-sense intuition that we are all separate beings with individual personalities, wants, and needs. Hence it follows easily that we should look after ourselves and may have to compete with others. We should note at the outset, though, that not all cultures put the individual at the center of moral concern—for instance, some stress the value of family, clan, or community more. And so it is possible that atomism may seem self-evident only due to our own cultural and historical location. Additionally, it prompts questions about how connected we are with one another, and whether we are responsible for anyone else and their actions. We might think of parents of young children: They typically put the welfare of the child ahead of their own, and if the child behaves badly or breaks an object, they are held responsible. Some feminist philosophers propose that the primal human experience is one of being cared for, and so the starting point for ethics ought properly to be not as isolated individuals but rather as part of a dynamic relationship of caring. A bond like that of the parent suggests that individuality may not be as straightforward as we typically think of it, and the egoist may inevitably not just be concerned with a single individual but those he or she cares deeply about.

The second test for the egoist is the associated view that humans naturally feel connected with one another. This need not be grounded in evolution, of course, and is a question of empirical psychology. That is, are humans naturally competitive and aggressive, or perhaps sympathetic and nurturing? David Hume (1711–1776), a Scottish philosopher, thought that morality arose from our sentiments, and decried those who felt that humans were basically selfish. Note that here again the argument does not say that we are always altruistic or that we ought to be, since it is sufficient for his purposes to show that we aren't exclusively competitive or aggressive. He points to the fact that animals and humans care for their offspring and are grateful when they are looked after. Moreover, we all have friends, and their well-being matters to us and we often put ourselves out in order to help them.

A further challenge to egoism is a family of views known as **natural law**. Theorists of this view argue that at the core of human nature and activity is a set of general moral principles. Thus we find that humans naturally form couples, or develop friendships. From these observations they conclude that there are inherent human values that go beyond self-interestedness.

The philosopher and theologian St. Thomas Aquinas (c. 1224–1274) posited that the fundamental value all human beings share is, "Good is to be done, and evil avoided."[5] Aquinas explains that given the fallibility of human reasoning, the more particular we attempt to make this principle, the more subject to error it becomes. Nevertheless he provides a list of universal goods derived from natural human inclinations: Knowledge, rationality, and, he derives the universal values of life, community, and society from the natural human inclination for sex and procreation.

Although Aquinas sees the divine at work in natural moral principles, natural law could be derived from purely secular values, in that we find traits in all human societies that encourage community, and thus it may be that part of human nature is indeed other-regarding. Although it may be true anthropologically that people can be selfish and competitive, there is considerable evidence that they are also compassionate and cooperative by nature.

Altruism means people benefit others without an obvious payback. For example, a man might donate anonymously to charity, and never expect any recognition or personal benefit in return. Or seeing a child who has wandered into the path of an oncoming vehicle a woman tries to save her at considerable risk to herself. If altruism is truly part of the human makeup, then it poses a direct counterargument to egoism. Contrary to psychological egoism, altruism contends that people are not always motivated by benefits for the self. If we observe common instances of altruism, it might seem to be just as much a feature of human nature as self-interest.

Take the case of Raoul Wallenberg, a Swedish diplomat stationed in Budapest, Hungary, during the Second World War. He issued Jews with passports that said they were Swedish citizens awaiting repatriation, and housed them in buildings where he flew Swedish flags. The German officials accepted the documents and allowed the bearers diplomatic immunity. Some stories recount him going to deportation trains handing out passports to anyone he could, despite the presence of armed guards. It is estimated that he saved over 100,000 people who would otherwise have been sent to concentration camps. Wallenberg was eventually taken into Soviet custody and reportedly died a few years later in prison, but he is remembered and praised for his moral courage. In fact, one of those he saved was a future U.S. Congressman, Tom Lantos, who said of him, "He had no official authorization. His only authority was his own courage. Any officer could have shot him to death. But he feared nothing for himself and committed himself totally. It was as if his courage was enough to protect himself from everything."[6]

It is hard to account for Wallenberg's actions without invoking the idea of altruism: Although we might concede that he acted from selfish psychological desires, the fact remains that he did significant good for others at a tremendous personal risk. Why would he act that way when he didn't need to? Beyond the self-verifying claim that we all do whatever is best for us (and we can determine what was best for someone by looking at what they did), there are two linked explanations for altruism. The first is drawn from the emerging field of *sociobiology*, and suggests that humans are not primarily individualistic, but communal beings. The second suggests we make rational decisions that favor the family or community.

At this point, consider Plato's story of the *Ring of Gyges*. A poor shepherd finds a ring that gives him invisibility, and he uses it to eventually become the king by using his powers to deceive and ultimately murder those who stood in the way of his newly found ambitions. The point of the story is to illustrate that in the absence of external restraints we will inevitably maximize our

---

[5]St. Thomas Aquinas, *Summa Theologica*, Part II, Q. 94, Article 2.

[6]"Unesco pays tribute to Raoul Wallenberg" available at http://www.unesco.org/bpi/eng/unescopress/1999/99-101e.shtml, accessed June 6, 2013.

own welfare, something that undergirds the ethics of Machiavelli, Hobbes, and Rand. However although the shepherd might have acted that way, it is entirely plausible that he could have used his new powers to help others or prevent harm.

A common observation is that parents will often sacrifice for their children, for example, working two jobs so their children can go to college or making sure the child has decent clothing before buying anything for themselves. Animals also show evidence that they will sacrifice themselves for the sake of the herd, which contradicts our understanding of Darwinian evolution. That is, if the individual truly matters most, we should expect that no animal would put itself at unnecessary risk. For example, Vervet monkeys and ground squirrels have been observed sounding an alarm that incidentally attracts the attention of a nearby predator, an act that would obviously minimize its own chances of reproductive success.[7] A number of studies have shown that animals have very strong kin bonds, and will sacrifice themselves to save their offspring. How then can we account for sacrificial behavior that seems paradoxical?—the altruist is likely to die with fewer successors, and hence it is a trait that should die out. Interestingly, Darwin's own response is that man, like some animals, is a communal creature and therefore what matters most is not the survival of the individual but the survival of the group, and thus any behavior that promotes group welfare will be fostered. He explains that primitive humans would have acquired instinctive social feelings, such as discomfort, at being separated from their companions, and that their giving mutual aid for their livelihood entailed social feelings of sympathy, courage, and even love.

The salient point for issues of egoism is that it turns out that we are not naturally separate individuals, but joined by ties of love, friendship, and sympathy that go beyond the convenience of cooperation to explain action in the absence of reward. Thus one way of challenging the egoist is to question the assumption that humans are individualistic. All human societies are communal, after all, and we might question why so much moral weight is assigned to the view that we exist as isolated atoms.

HEDONISM

A common theme in egoism is that individuals have their own personal preferences in much the same way that people prefer one flavor of ice cream to another. That is, people have different views, but they aren't right or wrong in any absolute sense. Next we consider another area of our lives to see if an egoistic approach is realistic, and examine some of the variations of personal happiness for any common features or constraints that should apply. **Hedonism** is a theory that contends we are motivated by seeking pleasure and avoidance of pain, sometimes thought of as maximizing personal happiness. Here we will look at some cases to test our intuitions about whether personal values may have a common core, or all are a matter of individual choice.

The first hypothetical is a young man, Eric, who lives a life of indulgence. He has a trust fund and spends it on recreation, food, and alcohol. He is willing to try anything that promises pleasure, and is not too concerned about the legality of his actions. He drives cars fast and enjoys taking risks, thinking that life is short and he might as well enjoy everything he can.

The second is a young woman, Jennifer, who enjoys marijuana to the point where she no longer interacts much with anyone else. Her acquaintances describe her as a "pothead," and

---

[7]D. Chaney and R. Seyfarth, 1992. *How Monkeys See the World: Inside the Mind of Another Species*. Chicago: University of Chicago Press. p. 219; P. W. Sherman, 1977. "Nepotism and the Evolution of Alarm Calls." *Science* 197: 1246–1253, at 1252.

while they enjoy hanging out with her on the occasional Friday night, they tend to avoid spending frequent amounts of time with her, especially during the workweek, because she mostly seems to be having an internal conversation that she finds mildly amusing.

Let us now introduce some science fiction elements: Josh, the third, loves playing video games. He lives by himself, and he spends all his waking hours trying to achieve high levels within the games. He has no real friends, only gaming partners. His ambitions are confined to beating the machine, and he claims he is content with that. He is then chosen to try out a total immersion video game, called *As Good As You Think* played with highly advanced virtual reality equipment. Once attached to the machine, the player has highly enjoyable adventures, cannot feel pain, and possesses super powers. Optional extras allow the player to be fed intravenously and never have to exit the program.[8]

The fourth is a religious recluse, Larry, who spends his days in quiet contemplation and routine work sheltered away from the busy world outside. He does not feel the need to mix with others, and finds fulfillment in simple tasks and minimal distractions. Having lived in a world of materialism and competition, he now has found inner peace and contentment through his spiritual journey.

If the hedonist is correct, then we all should calculate the maximum pleasure we can experience, and then act that way. Yet there seems something amiss with the preceding characters that appear, initially at least, to represent various forms of hedonic action. It might be that it is a simple miscalculation about what will bring about the most pleasure—perhaps romantic entanglements will result in regret and bitterness, or living like Eric and Jennifer will damage our mental and physical health. An initial problem, then, is working out how to value and compare our individual experiences. Eric may enjoy bungee jumping, for example, an activity that would fill others with dread; in contrast, some people may like nothing more than curling up with a good book, which Eric would consider boring and pointless.

Many people would find some of the lifestyles in these stories offensive or misguided. The point is that the disquiet we may feel with any of these suggests they fail to tell the whole moral story, and we should assess them in comparison to other approaches that recommend, say, that we do have duties to others or to make contributions to the world.

The question remains whether there is anything *morally* wrong with the behavior in these examples. We might have intuitions to the effect that some of the characters are living a truly "wasted" life—they are unproductive and contribute little to society or others. This kind of reaction would imply that we are not always willing to "live and let live" but feel that members of a community probably have obligations to the society. A similar line of criticism might be that by avoiding engagement with the world we might also fail to live up to our full potential—if we have the capacity to do so much more and be a positive force in the world, then perhaps we should.

Larry the recluse's avoidance is more physical than mental, but perhaps the same sorts of criticism might still apply. However, the case is unusual because people are not naturally reclusive—we live in communities and are social beings. While this form of life is good for Larry, it would be impossible to universalize it. That is, we may say that we should strive for our own self-interest, but it wouldn't work if everyone manifested his or her self-interest in the same way as Larry. So perhaps another hallmark of a plausible ethical theory is that it takes account of the facts of our normal existence; for the most part we are social beings and form close relationships with others. If that is true, then a life of pure egoism would not work either as an ideal or as an ethical theory.

---

[8]This example echoes Robert Nozick's Experience Machine in his *Anarchy, State and Utopia* (1974). New York: Basic Books.

Summary

We have seen that psychological egoism makes a strong case that we are all motivated by personal outcomes, and even when we think we are looking out for others, we may be doing so because it gives us personal satisfaction. Let us summarize the arguments on both sides.

First, we should return to the distinction between psychological and ethical egoism. The psychologist believes that we are, by nature, self-interested and thus our actions can be explained and predicted in those terms. At some point, though, the explanation becomes self-verifying because it relies on an unknowable motivation, one that may be opaque to the individual. Imagine someone gives money to charity, and believes her actions are to benefit others. The donation not only takes away from her disposable income but also causes her some hardship. She thinks that sharing with others who are less fortunate is a necessary function of being a decent person. The psychological egoist may retort that while she thinks she is acting for others, her acts of charity are actually giving her satisfaction and buying her psychological peace. She may deny this, but the psychological egoist responds that he knows her motivation better than she does herself. However, the conversation goes on in the absence of any real information. Both explanations will fit the facts—the donation—equally well, and there is no easy critical test to choose between them.

Consequently, we may admit that psychological egoism is plausible and could be correct, although we should recognize it as a working assumption, not proof. By itself, this is a fairly harmless concession, in that it gives us one way to explain much of what we do.

The distinction becomes critical, though, when we move from the harmless concession that it is one model for our behavior to an assumption that it is a universal truth, which is less persuasive. Still more pernicious, though, is the move from an explanation of *how we are* to *how we should be* that ethical egoism makes. We can still concede that people are basically self-interested but then say that we should not be. We have all sorts of psychological impulses to act in ways that we resist because we impose a reasoned filter. Even if we accept the egoist's account of human nature, it is one thing to recognize that we have certain dispositions, and quite another to say that they should be followed as ethical guidelines.

Thus it is worth reading beyond the descriptions of self-interest to see what sorts of solutions philosophers have offered to deal with them. For instance, Hobbes proposes an overriding authority—a benign sovereign—who would punish people who acted against the common good, whereas other theorists believe that rational people would necessarily realize the mutual benefits of cooperation outweigh any immediate personal advantages and act accordingly.

The strict egoist presents us with two questionable assumptions. The first is that people always act according to their own best interests, and the second is that self-interest does not embrace the well-being of others, unless it is self-beneficial. While undoubtedly the claim is true of many people, it may not be a universal truth. It isn't obvious, for instance, that we would all use great power for self-aggrandizement, and quite plausibly it might turn into a story of a noble heroine who helps people in distress, along the lines of many comic-book superheroes. Hence, although the premise of the egoist is that we will always promote ourselves above others, this isn't always borne out by our experience. This is especially true in small groups like families or communities, where very often people do look out for one another without any clear demands for rewards.

Another consideration is that it may be the case that the debate itself rests on the faulty assumption of a strict dichotomy, that we are either purely altruistic or purely self-interested. But in fact, if humans are not atomistic, but rather innately social beings who are tied to those we are in relationships with, our feelings of beneficence and of self-interest may not be as easily pulled apart as the egoist suggests.

In a similar vein, some economists have recently challenged the prevailing view that we always act out of self-interest. Amartya Sen (1933–), for instance, recognizes that we sometimes act in ways that are confusing to classical economics. For instance, we might spend money to preserve penguins as a personal commitment, even if they had no perceptible effect on our living standards. He goes so far as to describe people who neglect commitments and concentrate only on personal welfare as rational fools.[9]

In short, the egoist starts with the assumption that we are all independent and looking out for ourselves in a competitive environment. For this to be fully persuasive, we need to ask whether their claims are universal truths, or perhaps are sometimes true but sometimes not. Commentators sometimes use the metaphor of the jungle, saying that human society is "red in tooth and claw" and it is a "dog-eat-dog" world—just like Hobbes imagined. Still, the people in Hobbes's world have not got to that point, but instead realize that without some constraints things could go to the extreme; that is, they are able to pull back from complete egoism because they see where it would lead. Moreover, wholesale adoption of the egoist program seems to imply that we agree with their view of human nature and discount altruistic or generous motives.

Egoism suggests that we all strive for our own self-interest, and some argue that egoism says that amounts to experiencing pleasure and avoiding pain. However, we find that the concepts are not as clear-cut as we might initially believe. For example, if we give to charity, we can derive some satisfaction from the act. That need not imply, though, that the giving is caused by our self-interest, only that it is correlated with it. We see that working out the best outcome in any particular case will involve comparisons of various dimensions of pleasurable activity, and these may vary from person to person. Additionally, egoism of this sort relies on a sense of individual personhood, which clouds the fact that we naturally live in social groups that necessarily involve relationships and mutual obligations. To be a consistent egoist, one needs to be disinterested in the welfare of others, except insofar as it will affect our own interests. While this is a plausible stance, it does not seem to reflect how we actually live our lives.

Finally, although the jungle metaphor is appealing, it may not reflect how things really are. To illustrate the point we might look to one of its first uses in Rudyard Kipling's *Jungle Book*, where the animals learn the laws of survival. In the case of the wolves, the verse actually speaks to our interdependence:

> Now this is the Law of the Jungle—
> as old and as true as the sky; And the
> Wolf that shall keep it may prosper, but
> the Wolf that shall break it must die...
> As the creeper that girdles the tree-trunk
> the Law runneth forward and back—
> For the strength of the Pack is the Wolf,
> and the strength of the Wolf is the Pack.[10]

---

[9]A. Sen, 1977. "Rational Fools: A Critique of the Behavioral Foundations of Economic Theory." *Philosophy and Public Affairs* 6: 317–344.

[10]Rudyard Kipling, 1903. *The Second Jungle Book*. London: Macmillan.

Relativism

Ethical relativism is the view that no universal or absolute rules would apply to everyone regardless of context. All moral judgments, according to ethical relativists, must be considered in light of the particular situation, and so we can't condemn any action ahead of time. For instance, the moral claims that genocide, killing, and torture are always wrong, whatever the facts, could be challenged by saying there are always exceptions and mitigating circumstances that might justify a specific case. Ethical relativism contrasts with classical ethical theories that assert some underlying universal moral principles will apply to everyone and in every case, whatever the circumstances. The dispute between these two ways of looking at morality centers on the way we describe the moral choices: An **absolutist** will say that some moral acts are always right or wrong. The **relativist**, on the other hand, might not agree with someone else's beliefs, and may consider them to be misguided and harmful, but ascribes those differences to personal opinion and preference rather than deviating from a moral principle that applies to everyone in all times and places.

Another way to understand relativism is to think about what we each desire. Because our answers differ, we could argue that there is no universally agreed-on goal and we must decide for ourselves what is right or wrong behavior to lead the life we want. Hedonists believe that pleasure is the highest good. The challenge for the ethicist is whether our varying views can be captured in a way that avoids the relativist position.

CASE—EDWARD DOWNES

In 2009, a well-known British composer and conductor, Sir Edward Downes, committed suicide. He and his terminally ill wife, Joan, had traveled to Switzerland to end their lives with the help of a Swiss group called Dignitas. At eighty-five, Downes was blind and almost completely deaf, and was dependent on his wife for his daily care. Joan, a former ballet dancer and Downes's companion for fifty-four years, had been diagnosed with pancreatic cancer and given weeks to live. In addition to having been devastated by his inability to enjoy music any more, Downes had told people that he didn't want to live on without his wife.[1] Friends of the conductor said the act did not surprise them, and felt

---

[1] "Conductor Dies in Aided Suicide," available at http://news.bbc.co.uk/2/hi/entertainment/arts_and_culture/8149166.stm, accessed June 4, 2013.

he was entirely rational in realizing that his quality of life had diminished to the point that he preferred to end it.

The case received wide publicity, and reactions varied from condemnation by groups that believe it is wrong to assist people who are not terminally ill to kill themselves, to praise from others who feel it vindicates a person's right to determine his or her own fate. In the UK, suicide is not illegal, but helping others to do so is an offense punishable by up to fourteen years in prison. The British authorities chose not to prosecute Downes's son, who had made travel arrangements to Switzerland and accompanied his parents on the journey, although it appeared he knew his parents' intentions and stood to gain financially from their demise. They concluded that he had acted solely out of compassion, and they dropped the case. Nevertheless, shortly afterward the government decided to not revise the existing guidelines that make assisted suicide a criminal act, and the British Medical Association reiterated its opposition to assisted suicide.

Putting the legal issues aside, the question in the Downes case is whether taking one's own life is morally wrong, and whether it is ever appropriate to prevent suicide when the individual involved appears rational and uncoerced. Some philosophers, such as Immanuel Kant, who fall into the absolutist camp, taught that it is always morally unacceptable in every circumstance. Relativists believe it depends on personal choice in the specific circumstances.

The fact that some people condoned Downes's suicide whereas others thought it tantamount to murder seems to strike a blow to the ethical enterprise—after all, if a single act can provoke a wide range of moral responses, then it seems there is no single truth and everyone has to find his or her own values. It also implies that we can be responsible only for our own acts, as other people will make their own decisions regardless of what we think is right or wrong. Accordingly, we may criticize or try to persuade others that our standards are correct, but in the end we have no right to force our values on anyone. One consequence of taking a relativist position is acceptance of the fact that there may be cases where we find practices morally repugnant but we are forced to deny that our reactions can be universalized to all situations.

For example, this view can be seen in the case of students' perspectives on academic honesty. Many American colleges have an honor code along the lines of "I will not lie, cheat or steal, or tolerate those who do." Nevertheless, there is a general reluctance for students to turn in their classmates. This may be because of a social stigma against being a "snitch," but if we look more closely, we see that the discomfort at turning others in may also be motivated by students' acceptance of moral relativism. Students often say that they believe they are responsible for their own conduct, and while they may feel disturbed by improper behavior of others, they are uncomfortable censuring them, which they believe is not their business. So while a student may consider it is his or her personal responsibility not to cheat, whether other students comply with academic honesty is considered a matter of the individual's own beliefs and opinions.

This view emerges from the common observation that people and communities have differing moral standards. Because we observe a range of differing moral perspectives across peoples, cultures, and times, it seems that moral judgments can perhaps apply only to individual cases and be specific to particular situations. In the United States in the twenty-first century, for example, slavery is regarded as morally wrong. But the practice has been accepted in parts of the world at different periods in history, and we might not be able to condemn the practices during the times and places it was not considered immoral. Relativists take the fact that there are counterexamples from different periods in history and across cultures in which a particular action has not been condemned to say that there are no principles that everyone agrees on. Subsequently they may claim that slavery is not wrong absolutely and universally (slaveowners in ancient Greece did not think it was), but it is wrong depending on the historical period or culture in which it is practiced.

The relativist challenge is strong one: For almost every case where we think that people would agree on an act being universally condemned or praised, it appears we can be shown a counterexample. For instance, we might think that incest has been continuously condemned in every society, but then it turns out that it was routinely practiced among the pharaohs of ancient Egypt. Killing babies might seem to be viewed with distaste in all cultures and throughout history. But in the philosopher Plato's famous treatise *The Republic*, it is suggested that it was in fact acceptable to kill "defective" infants during the time of the city-states.[2] Similarly, we might think that stealing is always wrong and that this principle can be agreed upon universally, but then we are presented with tales of Robin Hood who is praised for stealing from the rich to help the poor. Moreover, lying may be bad, but there could be situations where terrorists demand to know the whereabouts of an intended victim, and lying could actually save a life.

One way relativists defend their view that morality is merely a matter of opinion is to point out those moral differences we tend to tolerate, or at least, don't condemn. For instance, we tend to tolerate differences in opinion about whether people should give to charity, and if so, how best to go about doing it. Some people believe that the use of their taxes to support public services suffices as adequate means of charity, while others believe they should tithe through church, and still others may believe they should give to local, or even global, foundations. Similarly, we tend to tolerate differences in opinion about whether people should send their children to public or private school, or whether it is alright to homeschool them. We see that different moral opinions exist, we accept them, and moreover, we generally don't condemn people for differing on the matter.

The relativist seizes on these differences in people's views about less controversial subjects such as charity and schooling, and then makes two associated claims: First, that the wide variety of values show that morality depends on the time, place, and context of the action. And second, because everything is, literally, relative, then there are no moral absolutes.

CHALLENGES

The relativist position may not be as robust as it initially appears. While these examples of exceptions to what seem to be universally valid moral prescriptions are telling, there are going to be some claims where it is hard to find counterexamples. It is difficult to imagine a plausible case where it is acceptable to violate someone's bodily integrity through rape, for instance. And harming the innocent, like children, for fun would find few defenders. Yet rape has been used as a weapon of warfare as recently as the Rwandan Genocide and the Bosnian War. Applying the moral relativists' reasoning, we have no means to condemn such practices. Given these dangerous implications of relativism, we have good reason to critically examine the theory.

Remember that moral relativists point to the problems associated with absolutism as reason for accepting relativism. Because it seems that there are cases where exceptions to universal principles need to be made, and that there are a range of moral perceptions on many issues, they propose relativism as an alternative view. But perhaps in doing so, they have succeeded in setting up a false dichotomy of sorts—between a theory that prescribes absolute and rigorous values and a theory that prescribes none. As it turns out, however, in order to stem the relativist

---

[2] Plato, *The Republic*, 460c.

argument, we need not claim that all morality is absolute, only that we have to make moral judgments taking into account the whole situation in which it occurs. This means that we need to understand the complex context in which actions and practices take place, and we can indeed make general moral evaluations upon having such an understanding.

Another response to the relativist is to consider the different/wrong distinction further. The fact that values differ across cultures and through time does not logically imply that they are all right. It may be true that the Egyptians practiced incest or that landowners in the Southern American states thought slavery was proper three hundred years ago, but it could be the case that they were wrong, and there has been moral progress since then. Some philosophers have referred to an expanding circle of moral concern—centuries ago, the ruler had sole authority over all his subjects, but since then the moral sphere has widened to include property owners, commoners, both men and women of all ages and races. This suggests that some variations are not just a case of preferences in context, but that the people involved were misguided or wrong and now we are more morally enlightened than we were in the past.

Several other lines of attack further diminish the relativist position. One problem with a view that there are no underlying principles and that people are free to follow their own inclinations is that it gives no traction to criticize anyone else. Think of an instructor grading students. One gets an "A," whereas another gets a "D." When they approach the teacher, he says that the evaluation process is a matter of personal opinion, and that he gives grades based on his mood at the time. His response would be inadequate to most students because they feel there ought to be some rational principle at work behind the assessment. Similarly, if a bully capriciously hits weaker children, we condemn his actions, and his explanation that he just felt like causing them distress seems arbitrary and cruel.

Furthermore, if relativism is a *moral* stance, as opposed to, say, a sociological report, then relativists have to accept that their own theory applies relatively, and this leads to a paradox. That is, the relativist would have to acknowledge that others are free to adopt their own moral positions, which need not be relativist. The relativist cannot then consistently say that relativism ought to apply generally—otherwise it wouldn't be relativism, which denies anything but the value of the individual's own choice. Yet if the theory of relativism amounts to no more than a personal view, it lacks the leverage to move it to a universally applicable theory.

The relativist position suggests that because there are widely varying moral choices, there cannot be a single correct one, and they all have equal merit. The reality of variance does not, by itself, mean that there is no common factor. To make an analogy, in issues of religion, for instance, we might say that the plurality of religious beliefs and denominations is a sign that believers are mistaken and we should abandon spiritual endeavors. Yet we often arrive at the very opposite conclusion: We could take the fact that there are many religions to show that there is a strong spiritual thirst shared by many people, and the fact that there are many diverse types may demonstrate that there are varied routes to a similar goal, or, put differently, there are varied manifestations of the same phenomenon. The point is that we cannot deny the validity of an activity—whether ethics or religion—based on variations within the practice.

The ability to make moral judgments depends on such elements as overarching principles, presenting assessable and defendable reasons, the consequences of one's actions in terms of the benefits and harms involved, the interests of others, the common good, and the environment, among others. The relativist will have to ignore all these factors unless they have direct bearing on his or her own welfare. It is simply true that there are diverse standards around the world. Yet this does not mean that they have equal moral standing. One aim of ethical theory is to make moral judgments subject to rational analysis and not just individual preferences.

RELATIVISM V. ABSOLUTISM

Sometimes the relativism debate is framed in terms of being between two isolated camps, the relativists and the absolutists, with no bridge between the two. One reason may be that the philosophers involved are engaged in different projects. Those who look for absolute, unchanging moral truths are concerned with finding moral anchors from which they can build a solid set of moral deductions. Hence they believe that a set of moral rules persist throughout time and place. Thus if it is wrong to kill the innocent, then it will be wrong whatever time and place, without exception. These rules might be religious or secular—perhaps the Ten Commandments, or a code like the American Constitution. The benefit is that with a secure base we can then be most concerned with working out how those general rules apply in more particular cases. Some legal scholars, for example, take the American Constitution as framing some basic rules from which we can extrapolate when working out more specific cases.

Additionally, it might be a mistake to equate relativism with the idea that anything goes: Not all relativists necessarily believe all moral claims have equal standing. Instead, they suggest that morality is not about finding enduring truths, but about making sure that our moral judgments are consistent and cohere with one another. Take a nonmoral example: If we think of a dog show, there are no absolute standards involved—purity of breed, the way the dog responds, or its bodily proportions are all somewhat arbitrary. However, they all make sense within the context of a competition, and the canine association works to make sure the standards are consistent and don't call for conflicting ideals. Similarly, the coherentist argues, moral rules may not have some external or fixed foundation, but in order to have a functioning society we need to agree to conventions and work on justifying standards within the system.

Thus at the very basic level we have some shared understanding on what it takes to get along with each other. These agreements may be few, but they are sufficient to deny that there are no moral governing moral principles—there are at least *some* that all humans need to have in order to have any sense of community at all. Importantly, in this debate we don't have to show universal agreement to defeat the strongest version of relativism. All we need to show is that there is some unanimity despite the appearance of variance. If we can counter the claims that *anything goes* and *any and all ethical assertions are equally valid* by showing that there are at least a few settled moral issues, then the relativist's line of argument will fail.

An absolutist (sometimes called a foundationalist) would see the relativist as free-floating without any fixed point to make moral judgments, whereas the relativist would see the absolutist as inflexible and uncompromising to circumstances. As is often the case, the truth probably lies in a mixed view. Instead of two distinct camps, imagine a ball with a surface covering like a crust. The hard core of the ball represents the absolutes, and the covering the discretionary action. Some would argue that there is almost universal agreement on many things and the differences are quite minor, and others would say that there is a very small core and a very thick crust above it. This model gives us a sense of there being some broad universal moral agreements at the core of human endeavors, together with an area of discretionary judgments open to debate. We may find that we agree on very broad overarching values, but engage in various practices to protect those values. Importantly, though, it gives us a way to combine both the foundationalist anchor and the relativist reliance on context and choice.

Evidence for this model is found in the social sciences: Anthropologists tell us that some elements are common to all human societies. For instance, we think it is right to keep contracts. Although this might initially sound trivial, on reflection we can see it is essential to communal living. In trade, each party needs to believe that the other will fulfill its promises, and someone who gains a reputation for not keeping his or her word would be ostracized. Communities need this sense of mutual trust to survive over time. Furthermore, researchers tell us that all communities have means to care for children and the elderly.

Some might counter by saying there are, for example, habitual or opportunistic liars, which is certainly true. However, the very fact that we distinguish lies as being abnormal shows us that they are regarded as outside normal discourse. They also become self-defeating in small communities, where there it is imperative that people rely on each other. We could say the same about other counterexamples—there may be some people who abandon their children, but they aren't the norm.

The issue here is that we naturally look for principles that undergird our behavior, and these form the basis of moral claims about justification and validity. The relativist has to deny any common principles, and therefore truncates moral discussions that we might have over how to better integrate these values at the outset. While relativism is a plausible philosophical stance, the logical consequence is that the relativist has to be prepared to live in a world without mutual principles that undergird justice and fairness, something that many of us would prefer to avoid.

Once we engage in discussions about *principles*, the perceived differences in behavior may become less pronounced. For example, initially it looks like a significant divide exists between countries that allow or ban capital punishment, say, or wide variation in the way they deal with end-of-life issues such as voluntary euthanasia. It is undeniable that these differences exist, and so we can concede that behavior varies. However, when we subject the apparent dissimilarity to greater scrutiny, we should go beyond the actions people take to look at what makes them act that way.

Consider the case of dealing with the homeless. Some might say that it is best to encourage them to work and not give any handouts, while others believe that we should provide charitable assistance. Even though the two approaches seem at odds, when we look at the motivations, it turns out there is considerable agreement. Neither side believes homelessness is a good thing, and both want to assist people in that predicament. The difference is only in how they put their beliefs into action. If we not only look at the manifested behavior but also take into account the reasoning involved, we find there is much more agreement than we might initially think.

Likewise, in judgments about end-of-life decisions such as the Downes case, it would be wrong to characterize the various camps as promoting suffering or death. It is much more likely that they would describe their actions as allowing the individual maximum respect. Both parties may agree to the principle, although the concept may be put into practice in one society through heroic measures to prolong life in one case and allow the person to end his or her suffering in another. Though the views are almost completely opposite, they may, in fact, be drawing on the same motivation, and when we move the debate to a more abstract level, we may discover much more agreement than the relativist believes there is.

MORAL IMPERIALISM

While the relativist maintains that all moral judgments are dependent on the context and may not apply when the circumstances are different, **imperialism** comes about when one party is so sure of its moral position that it feels it is appropriate to impose its standards on others. Imperialism has two elements: first, the belief that there is a single set of moral truths, and second that these truths can be expressed in only one way. The first claim is plausible—as we have seen, it could be that there is a set of moral truths (e.g., respect) expressed in abstract principles that lead to different behaviors due to variations in interpretation and context. It is the second element that is more worrisome.

The problem can be illustrated historically in cases where colonizing powers felt they were civilizing native peoples when they demanded compliance with their domestic norms, believing that their values were superior. This would not be such an issue for us, perhaps, if we felt that their values were in some sense more enlightened or advanced; we can imagine it wouldn't be objectionable from our vantage point, for example, if the dominant power prevented cannibalism or banned slavery or torture. However, the practice gets more troubling if the imposition applies to a tribal tradition of polygamy or dressing to cover genitalia, especially if the people involved see no problem and the practices seem to do no harm. This picture gives a much more graduated view, where some actions are always going to be wrong (or always right), whereas others depend much more on the circumstances. If this is correct, then it would be appropriate to intervene if one of the fixed moral issues is being compromised, but much less so when the act is more dependent on the specific situation. The difficulty, as usual, is working out the motives, the justifications presented, and the effects of the act.

Recall that the image of the two incompatible views, one where everything is dependent and the other where there must be fixity, tends to unnecessarily polarize the discussion. Instead, a better image is probably of a core of agreement in principle and a surface of differences in practice. Then debate is not so much about whether relativism or absolutism is correct, but becomes how much is common and how much should be discretionary.

One way of thinking about this is in terms of human rights, where proponents argue that some inviolate rights apply to everyone regardless of circumstances. Hence it may be always wrong to enslave or enact cruel punishments, and therefore is appropriate to educate others about what makes them wrong. However, once we move away from the core of settled issues, there is less of a mandate to interfere with others. This is especially true if we do so without some kind of cultural sensitivity. For instance, it might always be appropriate to stop the practice of sati, where a widow is burned on the funeral pyre of her husband, but less proper to interfere in a case where animals are killed for sport, such as in bullfighting.

Part of the analysis has to be working out at what level the disagreement occurs: Take the case of lying as one instance. All societies agree that routine lying is wrong. However, many Westerners are perplexed in Asia when they find that a refusal—seen as a personal slight that may hinder the relationship—is rarely stated directly, and what appears to be an agreement remains unfulfilled.[3] Thus a European visitor might think his Japanese host has not told the truth, whereas she was attempting to save face and preserve the relationship. This is not to say that lying is acceptable in Japan, but the visitor may not be aware of such subtleties in communication in that culture. Within the culture, though, intentional lying is still condemned as wrong. Thus it turns out there is considerable moral consistency across cultures, although it gets manifested in different ways.

MORAL IMAGINATION

Philosophers have recently taken a greater interest in the area of discretionary action. They believe that moral principles may not always directly map on to our moral experiences, and as such, we should spend less time dwelling on absolute moral principles and more on teaching

---

[3] "Japanese Refusals," available at http://www.carla.umn.edu/speechacts/refusals/japanese.html, accessed May 15, 2013.

people how to apply broad universal principles to various situations. *Moral imagination* is the creative exploration of options present in any situation. Individuals necessarily think in moral terms when presented with a value-based situation, but rather than defaulting to a simple formula, moral imagination frees them up to see if there are solutions that are both reasoned and culturally sensitive. It incorporates many insights from social psychology that tell us about ways of thinking that trap us in standard routines and perspectives. These conceptual schemas can help us deal with the mass of information that we encounter everyday by blocking out unnecessary stimuli and getting us to focus on important data quickly.

This zone of moral deliberation is sometimes referred to as **moral free space**—not in the sense that there are no rules, but more to indicate that we are able to make free decisions within its constraints. For example, Uluru, a large rock in Australia, is a favored tourist destination, but the Aboriginals regard it as sacred and any intrusion as desecration. Eventually a compromise was reached where climbing was not prohibited, but strongly discouraged through an educational center at the base of the monolith. The solution did not impose a moral principle in an unsophisticated way, but instead required extensive discussions and mutual respect between all the stakeholders. Thus the language of moral imagination tells us that any application of moral theory ought to involve the creative ability to conceive of various possibilities within a situation, and then a principled evaluation of them.[4]

In one sense, moral imagination is a way of reframing the debate of moral absolutism and relativism that capitalizes on their strengths. In the Edward Downes case, for example, it may be too simple to cast the issue as suicide being either morally always right or always wrong. Rather, an imaginative approach will inform us about the various moral principles at work, and then let us evaluate proposed options in light of them.

Summary

At first, it looks like the fact that some people endorse some behaviors while others think them repugnant defeats any attempt to make morality more than individual preferences. It seems plain that morality varies over time and from culture to culture. For example, Edward Downes went from England, where assisted suicide is illegal, to Switzerland, where it is allowed. Additionally, the legality need not govern the morality of the case: When he committed suicide, it caused significant public debate, showing that people disagreed even within the same culture. It is not surprising, therefore, that it is often said that there are no rights or wrongs, just personal choices.

Yet as we have seen, mere variation by itself does not mean there are no underlying standards, or that some people might be mistaken in their moral beliefs. Perhaps, akin to the spiritual quest, there are many ways of approaching the same goal.

There are significant risks in adopting a thoroughgoing relativist position. It would mean that we could not criticize others, yet alone intervene on moral grounds—for example, we could not justify military intervention to prevent genocide. Additionally, we find there is probably considerable agreement over many issues, starting with basic anthropological findings that all societies look after children or care for the sick or the elderly.

The picture that emerges is that there are likely some core beliefs that we all share at an abstract level. For example, few would deny

---

[4]The term was popularized by Mark Johnson, 1993. *The Moral Imagination*, Chicago: University of Chicago Press.

that the elderly should be afforded dignity and respect. However, the manifestation of those accepted beliefs can vary dramatically from person to person, time to time, and culture to culture. One response might be to abandon a search for ethical theory altogether. Another choice, though, is to discuss the nature and application of ethical principles in a reasoned way. In science, theories are taken as practical working hypotheses built on basic assumptions, but always with the thought that they could be overturned if a superior theory emerged. Perhaps we should approach ethics in the same way, as a means to work out the best kind of behavior and a full and rich life. Not everyone will agree, of course, but the search itself will nevertheless be instructive, as it will provide grounding principles and rational discussion of the most important issues we face.

5

The Authentic Self

Ethical theory draws in large part on fundamental ideas about the self. Typically we believe we make our own decisions and should be responsible for the consequences. However, philosophers have often taken more nuanced views about the link between the self and ethical behavior. In this chapter we will focus on four philosophers who have addressed the issue of human nature and ethics.

SUMMERHILL

Summerhill, a private school founded in 1921 by the educational pioneer A. S. Neill in England, aims to follow the interests of the students, and classes are optional. If students wish to play or spend time by themselves during the day, they are allowed to. Children are encouraged to express their feelings without judgment by adults. Rules are created democratically, with children and teachers having equal say in communal meetings. The overriding principle—resting on the belief that freedom leads to happiness—is that children should be happy. Instead of being coerced or guided by adults, the students read books and create experiments or art at their own pace and as they wish. The staff acknowledges that students do not always attend lessons, but when they do, they are motivated to learn what interests them, rather than being drilled with facts that they find useless. Thus students can cruise the Web for information, negotiate with teachers about what period of history to examine, or try their hands at craft projects. Contrary to what many people imagine, the students do not run wild or constantly laze around, but actively engage in play and study. When they leave school, students report that they are more self-confident, self-disciplined, and emotionally balanced than their peers.

Summerhill's curriculum model—letting children take emotional, intellectual, and even physical risks and trusting them to make their own decisions—challenges almost everything we commonly think about child development and education. Neill contrasts the Summerhill curriculum model with traditional models that establish expectations for children at an early age, designating a certain path and particular learning goals, which will lead to their happiness. Interestingly, he points out, many of us know that this notion of there being one path to happiness is not true, yet we sustain the model, perhaps because we don't believe there are any other alternatives. The Summerhill approach is focused on fostering happiness first, and Neill believes that most of the work young people do at regular school is a waste of time—appropriated for a test, and then never used and forgotten. Neill also points out that while we routinely accept that children need to learn mathematics, history, geography, science, art, and literature, we often ignore the importance of emotional and interpersonal development. He believes that all outside interference, whether by anxious parents who think they know what is best for the child, or educators with preset goals, actually diminishes us, by replacing creativity with learning—largely in the form of accumulating facts and formulas. In contrast, the founder's paramount goal was to produce a school where children had the freedom to be themselves, and to do that he created an environment where children need not have discipline, direction, suggestion, moral instruction, or religious training.

Although it has never had more than a hundred pupils at one time, for almost a century Summerhill has been highly controversial, and something of a thorn in the side of the educational establishment in the UK. It typically fails the standard benchmarks for academic achievement, but it turns out that when its pupils do choose to sit for national exams, they tend to do well. The school attributes this to the fact that its students opt to study subjects they are attracted to instead of those they dislike. Looking at the Summerhill example, we might ask whether teaching as we regularly think of it, either in the home or at school, restricts children's creativity, regiments them unnecessarily, and makes them feel inferior and overly dependent on adults. However, we might also ask whether certain guidelines are necessary for their development. Would we be better off with an educational system like Summerhill's, where the emphasis is on fostering the individual rather than maximizing the data learned?

We can expand the question that Summerhill poses about how educational conventions shape or stifle our distinctive interests and apply it more generally too. The work of Jean Jacques Rousseau, Friedrich Nietzsche, and Jean-Paul Sartre tends to emphasize the formation of an authentic self, free from social influences. In contrast, the work of Martin Buber tends to emphasize that the individual should not be the focus of ethical theory, and that we become fully alive only when we are in relationship with others.

ROUSSEAU

Jean Jacques Rousseau (1712–1778) spent his life moving from place to place. However, he was highly influential and became famous for his autobiographical, political, and educational works that often caught the popular imagination while antagonizing the authorities. For instance, he is the author of the paradoxical phrase "Man is born free, but everywhere he is in chains." One of Rousseau's main concerns in his writings is how to preserve the individual's liberty and authenticity in a world where people are shaped and dependent on society. In order to do this, he first looks to the past, imagining how human nature was in ancient times and then conjecturing about the development of human society.

Rousseau was an *essentialist*, meaning that he believed that humans have an intrinsic core or *essence* that distinguishes them from other animals. He acknowledged the special power of humans to reason, but posited two other intrinsic human qualities that are evident before reason becomes apparent in human development. The first is *amour de soi*, meaning "love of self" or "self-respect" (i.e., our deep concern with our own welfare and preservation). However, it should be contrasted with the kind of self-love encouraged by egoism, which leads to *amour-propre* (self-love, or pride), where individuals are trying to outdo everyone else. Rousseau maintains that it is appropriate to look out for one's own preservation as this would lead to virtuous behavior. Amour-propre, on the other hand, is the source of all the damage humans inflict on one another.

It gives us a false perspective, because it encourages hypocrisy and illusion in the attempt to compete.

The second intrinsic human quality Rousseau posits is our natural disgust at seeing other sensible beings, particularly of our own species, suffer pain or death. In this way Rousseau responds to Thomas Hobbes's notion that, left unchecked, people would be merely self-interested and competitive. However, he is also aware that the human story is one of violence and oppression. He suggests that the reason for this state of affairs, despite the fact that humans are essentially good, is the development of society. In a natural state, humans are self-sufficient and happy, without undue ambitions or desires, but as we build communities, we become corrupted. And so, Rousseau's evaluation of Hobbes's view of human nature is that Hobbes conflated the ills of current society into his account of human nature, and so wrongly considered the constructs of society to be intrinsic human characteristics.

According to Rousseau, in ancient times humans had no need for communities and thus were not compelled to compare themselves to one another. Only when people started to form communities—which foster internal competition and external aggression, leading to systematic domination and oppression—they began to see themselves as others defined them, thus accounting for the emergence of vanity, deference, esteem, or contempt. He blames the emergence of society for creating wants that are not needs, and pitting individuals against one another. Furthermore, contrary to many of his contemporaries, he believed that the notion of private property serves us badly, as it is a further source of a societally formed sense of self-worth and a distorted understanding of *amour de soi*. However, if we have few needs, then we have no real reason to compare our wealth to others, and we wouldn't rely on the opinion of others to establish our self-worth. Rather than developing into competitive, vain, and aggressive people, free from the constraints of society, Rousseau believes that we could develop into our naturally peaceful and self-sufficient selves.

Rousseau extols the self-sufficient man over the social man, with the latter only being conscious of his or her existence through the judgments of others. Thus the independent person is self-creating in that he or she will be self-aware, and have a sense of self that does not rely on outside judgments. In modern terms, the individual should be authentic to their inner self, and not rely on others to impose their views. For example, a child who is told that he or she is ugly or dumb will often accept those opinions and act accordingly. Similarly, we may be led to understand that success in life correlates to acquiring certain goods or adopting a particular lifestyle. Authenticity, on the other hand, will require self-knowledge and confidence in our own beliefs, rather than meek acceptance of what others may tell us as true or right.

Consequently, Rousseau believes that education should concentrate not on conforming the child to social expectations but on actualizing the child's inner potential. He explains in his philosophy that the first impulses of man's nature are always right, and that notions of sin, obedience, duty and obligation are foreign to man in this natural state. That is, in his natural state, man does not need morality, obligation, and duty because he is not filled with the vices of the aggressiveness brought to him through society. An ideal upbringing, outlined in his book *Emile*, would allow the child to make his or her own discoveries by trial and error, and the role of the educator becomes one of creating the right sort of environment that will enable students to become aware of what makes them happy and how the world works. This entails removing the child from societal influences during his or her upbringing and education. Such an environment is designed to shield the child from unnecessary distractions and comparisons.

Rousseau is sometimes described as an *ethical naturalist*, in that his morality is based on natural inclinations. The natural inclinations he focuses on are self-preservation and compassion. He contrasts the *good*, which is a natural trait, with *virtue*, which is a social skill. He acknowledges that humans inevitably do form communities, and that we cultivate skills, including the use of reason, that help us get along. Nevertheless, he feels that communities distance us from our natural selves and introduce an element of politics into our lives, in effect enslaving us to artificial norms. Thus he stresses the innate freedom of humankind in its natural state, while at the same time pointing out the paradoxical yoke that society imposes on us. That is, on Rousseau's view, the human is naturally free, and in this state, naturally good. However, he or she exists at the same time, and quite paradoxically, in the bondage of social conventions which will eventually compel him or her toward aggression and avarice.

It is instructive to revisit the Summerhill experience and contrast it to a more regular classroom: Summerhill is not completely anarchic, with individuals all doing whatever they want. There is a very deliberate community, but it aims to ward off what Rousseau sees as the evils of society—striving after conformity to social norms and rules, and from this, arriving at the devastations of vanity, pride, envy, self-love, competition, and aggressive interaction. The students at Summerhill are encouraged to follow their interests and not compare themselves in terms of academic or athletic achievement. Rather like Rousseau's presocietal man, who is uncorrupted and naturally good, they are free, and whether they are happy is the fundamental gauge of their success. On the contrary in most educational environments, there are set rules and levels of achievement, and the measure of a student's success is his or her obedience to those rules and performance on various exams. Therefore, in a regular school, those who do all these are encouraged, and those who don't are sanctioned.

This all has a moral correlate, of course. In our current society, certain behaviors are promoted, and there is a premium on following convention, being polite, and having good manners. While this leads to a level of peace, Rousseau's thought challenges us to consider whether it actually does so at the cost of squelching personal aspirations or through the oppression of children by adults? Imagine the things around us and the activities we are told to engage in, and even the goals that we have set for ourselves—do they really make us happy, and are they really authentic? Part of the Summerhill philosophy is that quiet time, in which nothing is done or produced, is perfectly acceptable and healthy, a philosophy which contrasts markedly with the way we often live our lives.

A related question is whether there can even be an authentic self. Rousseau did not use this term, but he did believe that humans are alienated from their true selves because of the way society is structured. The natural man is instinctual, and morality is needed only when people form communities and become aware of obligations to one another. While Rousseau acknowledges that the development of society is inevitable, and therefore we cannot escape from the ways in which it suppresses our natural state, we can do our best to educate children to realize their own interests and what makes them happy.

The obvious objection to the view of human nature and development articulated by Rousseau and exemplified through the education philosophy of Summerhill is that some people might find that they are natural bullies, or enjoy destroying property. Although doing so might be uninhibited and genuine, is there any way we can describe such behavior as good if it harms others? Rousseau would probably respond that he is perfectly aware that children do small harms as part of their exploration of the world—for example, boys using a magnifying glass to burn ants—but as they mature, they realize that it is their nature to be peaceful and kind. He believes that we have an innate conscience, and that children misbehave only because of the aggressive and competitive vices associated with the expectation to conform to social norms and meet societal expectations. Educating the child absent such conditions, Rousseau maintains, will result in people who are strong and good, that is, true to uncorrupted human nature.

We might take issue with Rousseau's naïve psychology in that it sometimes seems to have an unrealistically rosy view of what people would be like if they weren't corrupted by societal influences. However, perhaps the point we should take from Rousseau is not so much that his fundamental beliefs about human nature are empirically correct, but that his writings encourage us to distinguish between the norms we formulate for ourselves and those that emerge from social constructions. For example, in current society, we may believe it is correct to eat some animals but treat others as pets. Rousseau forces us to confront whether many of the ideas we hold are, in fact, anything more than what is conventionally acceptable. Consequently, perhaps when making judgments about our behavior, we should abandon such morally loaded words as *good*, *right*, and *just* and instead use to such terms as *justified*, *proper*, and *correct*, words that suggest we are being judged merely in a context of external societal rules and not on the basis of some higher principle. Importantly he reminds us that we typically and unconsciously adopt external conventions as if they were eternal verities, and he encourages reflection about what is artificial rather than authentic in what we do.

Much of Rousseau's views may strike contemporary readers as dated and quaint, and some of his work can be criticized for its sexism—for example, Rousseau believed that women deserved little education beyond homemaking. However, it is important to separate the strands of his thought and to not dismiss his work completely because of some of his positions. He remains relevant for our study of ethics in that he offers us two important insights. The first is that moral terms such as *good* and *bad* may be used to represent artificial constructs that society sanctions, rather than some absolute value. Humans often follow rules unconsciously and rarely question set conventions. Moreover, even the fact that communities adopt similar codes, such as prohibitions against stealing or obligations to tell the truth, would not convince Rousseau that morality is based on universal traits such as reason. Instead he would argue that these codes simply point to the fact that humans generally agree on what makes a society function reasonably well and thus they adopt similar standards as a practical matter.

The second insight Rousseau offers is about our own human nature. Is there some inner self that has been suppressed or shaped by societal conventions that we should try to recover? This view is not egoism in the sense that a person should regard himself or herself as more morally significant than others, but rather a call for the individual to search for an authentic set of inner truths. Ironically, these truths might accord perfectly with what society dictates—the difference is that they come from within and are not imposed. Thus someone might, as Rousseau suggests, be naturally compassionate, gentle, or generous. It would be important, though, to realize that acting in such a way is motivated from within, and not because someone is simply following duties or external expectations.

NIETZSCHE

While Rousseau has been seen to challenge the prevailing conception of human nature, we now turn to the work of a philosopher who became notable for challenging the entire historical context of the notion of human nature. Friedrich Nietzsche claims that many of the traditional moral systems are created and sustained by the powerful and dominant by perpetuating false pictures of human nature and human moral purpose to keep the masses in order. That is, most of us take up societal and institutional values like sheep, goaded not by the nature of society but rather by the interests of the special few. The truly self-mastered man that Nietzsche advocates, however, is one who rejects and rises above such coercion and control.

Friedrich Nietzsche (1844–1900) is perhaps most famous for his pronouncement that "God Is Dead," and for the purported link between his philosophy and the rise of fascism. Unlike that of most professional philosophers, his work relies heavily on irony and uses devices such as cryptic aphorisms. Because of Nietzsche's unusual style, it isn't always clear what his true meaning is, or whether he is entirely serious. Nevertheless, his writing and thought has been highly influential. Moreover, his work draws on classical literature and philology—the study of the nature of languages—and his writings frequently refer to figures from Greek and Asian literature that demand a certain level of knowledge on the part of the reader. Therefore, viewing it from a different angle by way of an example will be helpful to gain an overview of his philosophy and to understand his ethical ideas more clearly.

Imagine that you are visiting a distant culture—or, maybe even a science-fiction world where you land on a planet inhabited by humans—and are observing this new, unfamiliar community. Apparently the people of this culture share many of our features: They are mortal, have roughly the same lifespan, have males and females of the species, and have a highly developed language. Yet they have organized their society differently from those we are acquainted with. There is rampant sexism and other forms of discrimination: Women and children are treated as property of the men. They have a strict code of conduct, and even the most minor of infractions leads to capital punishment. They are generally not discontent in their lot, because they believe that compliance in this life will lead to greater happiness in their next reincarnation, and there is no social mobility in their highly stratified social structure. There is no scientific or intellectual progress. They subscribe to a religious faith with many gods, who they believe control their destiny and monitor every action they take. There is no medical care, since they do not want to anger the gods by altering their destiny. They believe their moral goodness is secured through obedience to the social conventions, which they think reflect the will of the gods. Against this background, everyone is reasonably satisfied, and even those in subservient roles accept their arduous lives with optimistic resignation.

From your standpoint, people face unnecessary hardship, and are stifling their potential. If you could intervene, what sort of appeal could you make that would allow them to see what you see? A first step might be to have them imagine that things could be different. For example, if their gods were loving and merciful instead of arbitrary, then they might be less fatalistic and be motivated to work to improve their welfare. If they reflected on their nature, they might wonder if the divisions of social classes and the discrimination were more products of social conditioning than inevitable aspects of their existence. But what would happen if they took notice of what you said? The news might, in fact, be unwelcome. It is one thing to be a drudge, but another to have a heightened consciousness about your position and not be able to do anything about it. As the saying goes, "Ignorance is bliss." If enough of the oppressed population rebelled, then things might change, but there is no guarantee that things would change for the better. Would it be preferable to leave them ignorant of your insights?

In this example, you have just played the role that Nietzsche takes on as the narrator in his ethical works. He assumes the role of the lone prophet telling us how things really are, and encourages us to chart our own path. However, what he says tends to make people uncomfortable. His message places a huge burden on the individual to confront the realities of his or her existence and subsequently challenges him or her to work for change. Because of the enormity of the undertaking and the social and personal difficulties that will be encountered in trying to dismantle the oppressive social and moral framework that is now in place, only the honest and courageous will be able to rise to the task.

In Nietzsche's view, many of the things we believe we know or take for granted are wrong. We have created myths to avoid the ugly truth: that humans are not at the crown of creation, that we have no eternal soul, and that there is no God who cares for us. If we recognized that we are on our own, then we would have to accept that it is we who create values, and that there are no eternal truths to console us. Seeing this also means accepting the fact there is no objective good or evil; these are labels we have created. Moreover, we construct social arrangements and values that we cast as permanent and purposeful to find relief from the psychological anxiety about our real situation. The language we use also beguiles us; for example, the idea of fate or nature makes an entity where there may be none, and yet we often invoke these ideas as part of our everyday talk without noticing that they are just human inventions.

Although not everyone will want to escape the romantic illusions we create to cope with our existence, according to Nietzsche the few who do will find it liberating: They will no longer have to be confined by stifling conventions masquerading as eternal truths. When they look back, however, they will see those left behind as timid, dishonest, and weak.

Nietzsche's particular target in his writings was the Christian Church, with its commitment to certain social and moral systems that it believed to be commanded by God. He believed the Church preached quietism—acceptance of its teaching and abandonment of personal ambition. He claims that the implications of accepting the Christian teachings of sinfulness, a vengeful God, and damnation are that everyone must work solely toward his or her own salvation, and consequently would be incapable of seeking after any sorts of temporal comforts. This picture, he believed, was a miserable one, where people live in fear and trembling before a God that punishes them arbitrarily. Such teaching consequently makes people weak, as they deny their natural inclinations to create morality, and rather demean themselves to accept fixed values as sheep that follow a shepherd.

One common objection that some have raised is that if we abandon all notions of human nature and fixed values, as Nietzsche at first glance seems to do, wouldn't this lead to a philosophy of nihilism, where there are no ethical principles at all? In response to this concern though, Nietzsche thought that nihilists, like Christians, were weak and afraid of life. His philosophy promotes no such view. He argues rather that in the absence of God or conventional morality, the individual ought to embrace life completely, as it is he or she alone who is responsible for creating values to live by. Nietzsche's response is to develop a philosophy based on strength, not weakness. He named this powerful person, the superior one who is capable of being fulfilled by his or her sense of purpose, the *Übermensch*—the "Superman."

Although Nietzsche calls into question conventional morality, he does not dismiss morality altogether. Rather, he believes that the way society endorses certain behaviors acts to suppress the individual spirit. In an investigation he calls his *genealogy*, he looks to cultural history to see why in the past such conduct has been sanctioned or endorsed. He argues—in his investigation into the ancestry of morals with ancient Greece, where character was paramount—that virtue amounted to what virtuous people did. Certain leaders, particularly dominant members of society, were able to justify their own actions through fabricating a list of virtues that the rest of society accepted at face value. On Nietzsche's analysis, these dominant members of society—aristocrats, masters, or knights—defined "nobility" simply by those actions that *they* performed, and the rest of society—a crowd of the powerless—didn't possess the courage or will to exhibit these dominating traits. This mass of lesser people then classified behavior into two categories: good and evil. They created these categories to persuade one another that conventional actions were the better ones, glorifying meekness, obedience, patience, caution, and prudence as virtues. Meanwhile, the *Übermensch* disdains this petty system. As indicated by the title of Nietzche's treatise *Beyond Good and Evil,* the *Übermensch* literally dismisses the idea that human morality can be captured by these two classifications of behavior. Nietzsche, taking on the persona of the *Übermensch*, calls himself an *immoralist*, not in the sense that he does bad things, but in the sense that he is free of the shackles of conventional values. However, we should be careful here: Nietzsche is not advocating anarchy or pandemonium. On the other hand, he believes the superior person is the creator and arbiter of his or her own values, and is not fettered by typical notions of good conduct for its own sake.

In *Thus Spoke Zarathustra*, perhaps one of Nietzsche's most famous writings, Nietzsche introduces the *Übermensch* through the development of the character of Zarathustra. In his portrayal of Zarathustra's spiritual journey of self-mastery, he makes use of the literary device of prophetic writing, often in the form of inverted Biblical parables and symbols, and moreover, asserts rather than argues for his philosophy. At one point the protagonist announces that man is something that must be overcome, and this can be done only when we realize that good and evil are illusory constructs. He asserts that our inclination to take control and exert command over others is suppressed by the Church's teaching, but in fact it is a natural and appropriate human tendency. Zarathustra warns us that those who cannot become masters of their own fate will inevitably become commanded by others. But this radical moral freedom is also balanced by increased personal responsibility. We must constantly find out what is right by ourselves instead of accepting prevalent codes or rules, and then we are compelled to live by the standards we make and apply them to our own acts just as much as to the behavior of others. To make one's own laws is surely most difficult, and entails a risk of oneself, for one becomes judge, avenger, and victim to his or her own law.

The Superman that Nietzsche is speaking of is the supreme individualist. Thus it is particularly ironic that the notion is associated with the conformist and collectivist political system of fascism. While some of his writings and slogans were co-opted by the Nazi party, for example, their followers often adopted propaganda uncritically from party authorities, this was exactly the dynamic that Nietzsche disparaged. He feels that the individual is the one who has to decide, and he would reject any system either secular or religious that inspires blind obedience and servitude.

Nietzsche's writing frames concepts in his favor somewhat in that he appeals to many readers who want to come away feeling they are uniquely honest and courageous, and distinct from the everyday crowd. In fact, this may explain the enduring popularity of Nietszche's work, particularly among those who wish to be labeled as "nonconformists." However, a deeper understanding of his work leads us to realize that his world is one of black and white, and that he leaves little room for compromise between positions. This is because his resolution to the problems he associates with various moral theories is a sheer rejection of those theories, rather than some sort of critical navigation through them. For example, he seems to rely on an *ad hominem* fallacy in rejecting any and every practice associated with or stemming from Christianity.

At this point, let us return to the remote culture described earlier. We can see there is some importance in taking the perspective of an outsider who can radically reassess that the patterns of behavior and morality that the community has come to assume are natural and inevitable. Given how things are, change is unlikely to come from within unless someone can step back and look at some of the fundamental conceptual underpinnings of the society. In our own case, it took intellectual mavericks to champion the cause of emancipating slaves and promoting women's rights, for example. Thus there is real value in Nietzsche's call to examine not just the modes of behavior we have, but presumptions we may have about human nature and the proper way to organize society. If values are human constructions instead of eternal verities, then it would be appropriate to consider how things came to be as they are, and whether what we do is for the best.

Nietzsche's reliance on Greek myths throughout his writing to make his point is open to question, though. Is he correct in saying that there has always been a dominant class who has discerned that they are the value-creators and should impose those values on the unthinking masses? Certainly, anthropologists tell us that human communities tend to have leaders who shape the values of the group. Nevertheless, leadership may not imply dominance, or that there shouldn't be overriding principles such as justice or respect for persons. China, for instance, used a Confucian model of social order for many centuries. Nietzsche's response to such an objection might be that these are simply sugarcoated instances that belie the underlying truth—say, that China had a ruling elite, or that a system of justice actually represents the value system of a dominant few.

Another criticism that might be leveled against Nietzsche is that his distinction of society into leaders or followers is neither as strict or necessary as he makes it out to be: We could imagine that there are times when we are masters of our own fate, and make our own value-driven decisions, but at other times it is useful to be part of a societal convention that happens to suit our needs or aims for mutual benefit. It could be that the will to get along is just as strong as the will to exercise power and dominate.

Despite these criticisms, Nietzsche changed philosophical ethics by making it self-conscious. That is, before his critical work, moral philosophers often started from certain fixed assumptions, such as what human nature was like or that there were some eternal truths to be discovered. While we can still stipulate those as starting points for discussion, after Nietzsche we are aware that even those foundational claims cannot be taken for granted and are subject to scrutiny. His work signals a sea change in the discipline, and anticipated the challenges posed later by existentialist and postmodernist writers. We will examine one of these philosophers more closely next.

SARTRE

In addition to being one of the leading philosophers of the twentieth century, Jean-Paul Sartre (1905–1980) was a fiction writer, playwright, and leading figure of the *Existentialist* movement. Many traditional moral theories are grounded in assumptions about what is essential or unchanging about human nature. The term *existentialist* emerged from the slogan that *existence precedes essence*, meaning that when we remove all preconceptions about what it is to be human, we are left with the stark fact that we find ourselves alone in the world. This realization means that we can't think of ourselves as conditioned by other people or societal expectations, but are creators of our own values. This is both liberating and frightening: We must recognize that we are free to choose the way we live our lives, but at the same time we have to take responsibility for our choices—we cannot abdicate them to mysterious external forces. If, for instance, we believe in fate, then we are relieved of the burden of responsibility for the decisions we make, as they can be attributed to some other source. But according to Sartre, if we recognize our freedom, or that we are the source of all values, we must also recognize our responsibility.

This is not to deny that there are limiting factors for our choices: There are, for instance, genetic realities that we are born with, or social and economic realities we inevitably find ourselves in. Sartre describes these elements as "facticity." Nevertheless he believes it is wrong to blame those circumstances—our facticity—for the subsequent choices we make. That is, whatever situation in life, humans always have complete freedom within those limits to define themselves, and those choices imply personal responsibility. Thus even though someone is imprisoned and has no physical liberty, Sartre argues that he or she makes decisions about personal conduct and can be held accountable for those choices. Importantly, while some have criticized existentialists such as Sartre as lacking the resources from which to get any notion of morality given that he believed in a world without God, fate, or human nature, the very absence of something external to blame is precisely what, on his view, makes us responsible.

Making our own choices does not mean that we must constantly rebel against rules and conventions, however. We may conform to the rules all around us, and in effect, look like we are merely obeying the rules and blindly conforming to the norms. However, in Sartre's view, if we have consciously chosen to follow them instead of unreflectively conforming, we are acting ethically. What matters for Sartre in determining the rightness and wrongness of acts is *why* we choose to do as we do, that is, our motive. The fact that humans are individuals with total moral freedom is an overwhelming prospect for most people, causing us great psychological anxiety. For Sartre, to confront this anxiety and make conscious choices while acknowledging responsibility is to be ethical.

According to Sartre, working out the right thing to do and then being responsible for the choice creates a burden, and most people would rather shift responsibility to someone else, or to fate or an institution like the Church. Once we are told what to do, we no longer have to confront a range of options, and we can also shift the blame if the outcome isn't what we thought it would be. Similarly, when we hold one conscious choice, as one might do when one privileges one moral principle for all cases—such as pursing personal happiness or looking after the less advantaged—we close ourselves off from other possible choices and we become, in effect, less capable of authentic moral decision making.

Thus we all face a constant struggle against the temptation to avoid the harsh problems that a personal morality involves. Perhaps someone is offered an opportunity that would involve breaking a prior promise. Sartre believes that defaulting to an external authority or set of commandments to make a decision about how to behave in this instance is likely to make our lives easier in one sense. For instance, in such a case it is far easier to simply rely on the principle, "Never break promises," to avoid the burden of reasoning through the choice before us. But, in Sartre's terms, failing to deal with the dilemma internally will lead to an *inauthentic* decision.

Being moral for Sartre includes knowing oneself, and then being true to that self. Existential authenticity means that an individual is acting in accordance with his or her own values. At one point, Sartre gives us the image of a waiter who smiles and shows deference in front of the clients, but he seems too enthusiastic as he balances his tray on one hand above his head. It is as if the man is putting on a mask—in ancient Greek drama, a *persona*—when playing the role of the waiter, but his behavior belies his real self. Of course, there may be waiters who are genuinely unctuous and happy in their work. However, the waiter may not be aware of his freedom and the decisions that keep him in that role, or, alternatively, he may know that he is, in effect, acting. The important point is that the waiter's enthusiasm is motivated by his unquestioning, or in Sartre's words, inauthentic, acceptance of the role of "waiter," not because he has consciously chosen to be friendly and polite to customers. Ultimately, Sartre challenges us to consider why so much of what we do, especially at work, seems to be role defined. His answer is that it is what society demands, and we easily conform to these expectations. However, these roles are not merely imposed on us: He argues that the actor also has to be a willing participant in the drama. If the players all know their roles, each knowing how he or she is supposed to act, it gives a comfortable predictability to the employer, customers, and the staff. It relieves each individual of the anxiety of having to work out things for themselves—we are then all able to "switch off" while in our roles, and simply do what is expected of us.

In contrast to this inauthentic role-playing, Sartre believes we should be constantly reflective about our acts, and we should be *authentic*. If we deceive ourselves or dissociate from the choices we make, they no longer represent our freely chosen values, and he contends this amounts to living in a state of *bad faith*—what he terms *mauvaise foi*.

Consider as an example the fact that in America, many students go to college: From an early age they are told that college is the means to a successful life and sometimes told that it is the only means. Moreover, the school system is geared to funneling them into higher education. It is probably beneficial for students to graduate from college, and few regret the experience. Yet Sartre would have us look at the nature of the decisions along the way: Were the students aware of the choices they made, or did they defer to external pressures and expertise? When they got to college, did they then adopt what others told them were the characteristics of good college students, as if they were taking on a role in a play? It is important to remember that Sartre has no problem with someone confronting a decision and eventually deciding that it is best to follow a conventional path. He is more concerned with unreflective thinking or the belief that there is no choice to be made in the first place.

In some of his essays Sartre portrays man as "condemned to be free"; that is, he is condemned to his facticity, but free in that he is responsible for every choice he makes in the world he finds himself in. We must then, in Sartre's thought, *invent ourselves* despite whatever world we find ourselves thrown into.

Sartre goes on to give an example to illustrate both the freedom and weight of personal responsibility. Sartre tells of a student who came to see him in the early years of the Second World War. Seeking counsel and advice on what to do, the young man explained that his brother had been killed in the German offensive in 1940, and his father, a suspected collaborator, was separated from his mother. The student wanted to leave France to join the Free French Forces, but he lived alone with his mother and realized that his departure, or potential death, might be devastating to her. At the same time, it wasn't clear that he could reach England, as he might be interred in Spain on the way. The young man's internal conflict was that he felt a direct and personal commitment to his mother and yet a far more general and uncertain duty to his country. Through this example, Sartre points out that in many cases, ethical theory appears to come up short. That is, we find ourselves in messy conflicts that following one simple moral principle would not seem to resolve.

Interestingly, Sartre tells us that although the student had sought guidance from him, he would not give it: The student had the freedom to act, and only in making the choice himself could he exercise that freedom. Sartre felt that it would be wrong for the student to delegate the decision to a mentor, because in choosing the mentor the student would already have an inclination of the answer he would get—going to a collaborationist priest, for example, would pretty much determine advice to stay with the mother. The dilemma would be resolved only by the student making a choice, and then acting on it, and subsequently taking full responsibility for it as a free personal decision.

Sartre notes that not making a choice is not an option: Even vacillating is a choice the person makes. Moreover, he denies that decisions are ever arbitrary. We cannot, for example, toss a coin and then blame our subsequent actions on some kind of fate. We frame the options, and then set up our own decision procedures. In the case of the coin toss, we have already outlined the various possible choices, and we have decided the appropriate decision procedure for making that choice. Thus there is no getting away from the fact that we are the ones shaping our own destiny.

The picture that Sartre paints could be considered nihilistic: Why should we bother to embrace life's decisions actively instead of just passively accepting whatever comes along without agonizing over it or trying to aspire to more virtuous action? However, this is very much contrary to Sartre's view. He believes that our acts affect the world in some way, and our choices as actions define who we are: People are not born heroes or cowards but create themselves as such by the choices they make. Because the future is uncertain and we are not subject to some particular fate, we constantly have the opportunity to shape it. Sartre's fundamental notion of existential choice thus becomes advocacy of social engagement. We become who we are only by making decisions in a social context, and conversely, the social reality is a function of individuals working together. Just as there is no essential human nature for Sartre, there are no predetermined social laws, contracts, or hierarchies, for we are constantly engaging our facticity, sustaining such practices, revising them, or creating them new. In this way, Sartre views his account of existentialism as a doctrine that is more optimistic than any other, since it grounds our destiny in ourselves and tells us our only hope is found in acting toward the creation of it. Despite this optimism, if every decision relies on reflective individual commitment, the task can be overwhelming, and it is not surprising that the figures in Sartre's novels and plays are often paralyzed by the tasks they are faced with.

One potential objection is that Sartre could still be charged with ethical relativism: If someone authentically wants to be a Nazi, and commits to it, could he or she be criticized from an existentialist standpoint? That is, if the decision is the focus of moral activity, and the person makes a reflective and considered choice to commit genocide, does Sartre have any way of condemning him or her? One answer Sartre gives is that the freedom also carries its own responsibility: We cannot later make excuses that we were swept up in enthusiasm for a cause, or persuaded by circumstances or other people. In other words, we are accountable for every choice we make, and there are no excuses. Moreover, in *Anti-Semite and Jew*, Sartre points to oppression, violence, and racism as a perversion of our natural recognition of the other. That is, Sartre holds that we live in a world of interpersonal relationships, and this fact of our existence calls us to oppose oppression, violence, and racism.

To some, human choice may seem arbitrary in the absence of a divine or secular absolute authority. Sartre admits this, but asks what alternative we have. Humans are the authors of values and so must create meaning for themselves. Beyond the freedom to choose, he believes, there are no preordained constraints or fixed points to guide us. If God did exist, he says, it would change nothing, and he sees the reliance on divine commands as just another way to avoid taking responsibility for ourselves and thus avoiding the anxiety personal choices provoke.

Another defense against the charge that his view implies ethical relativism is found in Sartre's play *No Exit*, in which three damned souls are forced to confront one another in a locked room in the afterlife. All have performed evil deeds: Garcin, the soldier, deserted the army and cheated on his wife; Estelle married for material advancement and later killed a child she had as a result of an affair; Ines had led a life of cruel manipulation of those around her. However, only Ines is honest about her actions and, moreover, refuses to allow the others to sugarcoat what they did. The play illustrates two relevant points: that we are free to make choices, but that we also must face the judgment of others who may not permit us to hide behind the stories we make up about our own lives. This means, as one of the characters declares, that "Hell is other people"—not because they punish us, but because they reveal to us our shortcomings and our inauthenticity. Thus Sartre feels that it is not the case that ethics is unprincipled: The common aspiration should be to live authentically.

Although he completely denies the idea that humans have some type of essential nature, Sartre maintains that it is part of the human condition to choose to be concerned about other people. In his view, information about others—the child, the foreigner, even the idiot—enables us to understand them. He goes on to argue that we can also pass judgment on others, since they could falsely believe they are forced to make certain decisions, which he condemns as cowardice. Thus the key factor is whether individuals have somehow abused their freedom. Because freedom is the central concern of all people, it should be evident in every choice. And because our own freedom and that of others is interdependent, any personal act will have an effect on others, however small. Thus he contends that our responsibility is very great, because it pertains to all of mankind. Nevertheless, he contends that the sort of freedom he is talking about is highly abstract, and could be manifested in many different ways.

If we return to the student's question once again, Sartre has already stacked the deck by framing the issues in a certain way and using connotative language—for example, that by staying he would be helping his mother. Although entirely plausible, the situation could be described using other terms that might incline him to another decision, perhaps, that his mother would be better off establishing her independence from others. The point is that although Sartre claims we have free choice, we may in fact be trapped in ways of seeing the world and linguistic expressions that already confine those choices. In order to escape them, we would need to have some remote perspective independent of culture and language. Since that is impossible to achieve, perhaps Sartre's notion of radical freedom is much more bounded by social constructs than he believes it to be.

Sartre's work is most powerful when showing that we often live mindlessly—we constantly follow one path and then delude ourselves about what we did. In response to this thought, he says that we have control over our actions, and need to take responsibility for what we do, whatever our personal circumstances. His advice to the student may not have been consoling, but there again, Sartre doesn't offer comfortable words: He wants us to face the blunt reality of the world without relying on the crutches of ethical systems or external guidance.

Yet at the same time, Sartre perhaps overplays the idea of the individual mind—the ego—and our ability to live authentically. The dominant idea is that of the anxious human trying to deal with his or her infinite freedom alone. This view seems to downplay, if not deny outright, the value of relationships in our lives. It may also understate the power and influence of outside institutions, such as the government or education, in shaping the way we think and act—both for good and for ill. In the next section we will examine a philosopher who held a radically different approach that suggests, against Sartre, that mutuality, not individuality, is the prime mode of our existence.

BUBER

Martin Buber's (1878–1965) moral philosophy is perhaps best explained as a dramatic presentation of the philosophical idea of *intersubjectivity*. His most famous work, *I and Thou* (1923), does not read as traditional philosophy, and because his sometimes poetic essays tend to challenge basic assumptions about how we see the world, they bear repeated readings. Nevertheless, his work is important for contemporary ethics in that it disputes the classic notion of the autonomous individual making discrete decisions and focuses instead on the ways we encounter the world as social beings.

Buber believes that the traditional description of personhood is incomplete. To understand why, imagine a picture, perhaps of a landscape. The picture will typically have a foreground and a background, and we distinguish the two in contrast to one another—that is, we can't think of the foreground without its background, and vice versa. In that sense, the elements of the picture are not separate, but exist in relationship to each other. It is fundamental to the elements that they are put in relief to one another: Even though we may talk about, say, the figures in the foreground, and may not consciously think about the background, the two aspects exist only in relation to each other. Similarly, Buber suggests that it is wrong to think of people as independent and discrete beings. In effect, we only come to understand our existence in relation to the external world—we know that we are separate only because we have something to say we are *separate from*.

Buber uses two compound words to explain his view that isolated existence is impossible. The first is *I-It*, where we encounter the world as objects. These objects may be inanimate, such as rocks or tables. Here the person relates to them from self-interest, and, as he puts it, *monologically*. That is, the encounter essentially reflects the person's own attitudes, and we tend to look to how we can benefit from the object—can I use it, or what good is it to me?

The second kind of encounter is much more rare. In an *I-Thou* relationship, we recognize the other not as an object, but as a being that resonates with us. Importantly, although the language to describe the encounter suggests two independent entities, what Buber finds important is the moment of connection where the separateness of our existence falls away. This is not simply two people having mutual respect, in the sense of Kant saying that we should treat others as ends-in-themselves. Instead, Buber is saying that we can define ourselves only when we interact with the world. Most of the time we treat the world as a collection of objects, and indeed we often treat people in much the same way. However, there are those times where we surrender our guard, and open ourselves to a special rapport or communion with others in what theologians call a *numinous* experience. The word *numinous* literally means an experience of the divine, and Buber believes such a communion is possible not only with people but also with nature. He recounts instances when he was enthralled with nature in the case of being epitomized by a tree, and at another time when he gazed into the eyes of an animal. Thus the relationship is paramount, and he strives for the exchange of values. We come alive for Buber when there is a meaningful relationship at work, and conversely if we didn't engage in the world, we would not be truly alive.

The I-Thou relation for Buber is one of life and value, but it is fragile and may collapse into an I-It. Yet with love and art, it is possible, he believes, for the I-It to transform into an I-Thou. Elsewhere, Buber introduces the notion of Other (with a capital "O") to signify the connection with a being in this kind of shared experience, sometimes known as *mutuality*.

When we experience the world, we often do so in the form of I-It. That is, we relate to the world as an individual perceiving an object. In this experience, we perceive beings and events as things, or as objects, and we analyze their various parts. We relate to them as owners, and consequently as strangers detached from them. However, it is the I-Thou that establishes the world of relation in which I face a human being not as an object of my perception or as a thing individuated from other things in space and time, but as a unified Thou with whom I am in a living relation.

Buber's thought is elusive to many. However, perhaps that is just the point: The classical ethical systems start with a concrete idea of the subjective self, and then consider ways that we should interact with one another. Buber challenges that notion of identity, and suggests that every time we try to pin down what it is to be a person, we will inevitably fail. We can isolate particular features—height, hair color, manner of speaking, and so forth, but however long the list, we will still be unable to fully describe the person, because personhood is inevitably tied up with relationships, not data. It is like trying to grasp fog—the moment we stop treating a person as a Thou, then the relationship is one of I-It, and we are left with a set of characteristics, not a living connection.

Put in technical terms, in traditional philosophy, metaphysics has typically preceded ethics. That is, we define a person as a rational being, a pleasure-seeking animal, and so on, and then construct an ethical system around those initial assumptions about human nature. Buber's challenge is to reverse the claim: We start with people in relationships, and only then can we determine what it is to be a fully realized person. The ethical life, in the sense of constantly becoming open and willing to engage in I-Thou relationships, becomes paramount, and the other issues in philosophy are simply derivative of this foundation. For Buber, the fundamental awareness ought to be that our existence is found in dynamic relationships and connections and not in isolated individuals each controlling and affecting others like a set of separate balls on a pool table being knocked by others banging into them. Similarly, employing the I-Thou relation also means that the traditional notions of egoism and altruism—either emphasizing the primacy of one's own interests or those of third parties—no longer apply. By definition these categories already appear to split the world into self and others, something that Buber would maintain gives us a false picture of our existence as states of being rather than in dynamic relationships.

It is difficult to draw easy ethical prescriptions from Buber's work. He witnessed the Nazi Holocaust and the turmoil associated with the founding of Israel, and so was well aware of the presence of evil in the world. He held strong views on the horrors of genocide. It would certainly be wrong, therefore, to consider him an ethical relativist. However, it is clear that his ethical perspective begins from particular situations, not abstract principles, and is grounded in a notion of responsibility. He gets this account of responsibility from the notion of real response implicit in the I-Thou encounter. That is, my encounter with the other as a Thou calls me to respond with responsibility to him or her.

This raises the question of what Buber means by responsibility and response. As we might anticipate, he provides a double answer: We are responsible *for* objects in an I-It relation, and we are responsible *to* those in an I-Thou relation. One of the special features of the I-Thou is that it is dynamic—the other party calls to us and demands a response. A further nuance is that we can actually distance ourselves from our inner or true selves—in effect, treating ourselves as objects. We do this when we think reflectively in the third person, removing our involvement from a decision or memory as if we were visualizing a stranger. Thus ethical action involves (a) being true to ourselves, (b) actively inviting the I-Thou relation, and (c) being attentive to the call to action that the I-Thou presents.

Most of the standard ethical maxims—do not lie, cheat, or steal, for example—would emerge from having a responsible relationship to a Thou. The very idea of an I-Thou dynamic would be broken by lying, it appears, because we inherently disrespect the other party by hiding the truth and thereby treat him or her as an object, or as the I-It. Buber rejected the criticism that his view lapsed into relativism, acknowledging that norms have their place as useful guiding principles but stressing that we can only work out what to do in concrete situations with a given context. Consider an example from the Second World War. Sometimes Nazi soldiers would demand that observant Jews rip up the Torah scroll, the sacred text kept in each synagogue. Some refused at the cost of their lives, while in other cases they complied. Buber's approach would say that a general rule would be inappropriate: Every case has to be considered in its own context and with sympathetic regard for the individuals involved. Arguably, committing sacrilege may have mattered less in some cases than preserving adherents of the religion who would make it possible to carry it on to future generations. Thus while the general norm of honoring the sacred is a reasonable starting place for ethical action, Buber holds that we must find our own direction in each particular encounter.

Buber believed that we are able to discover the mystical in an I-Thou relationship, and thus there is a spiritual element that suffuses and pervades his work. In spite of this religious undertone, as a philosophy his writings challenge us to reconsider what it means to be a person, and suggests that ethics is not an "add-on" element to our existence that can be treated separately.

Rather, fundamentally we have an ethical posture in anything we do: We can choose to treat things and people as objects, or we can open ourselves up to authentic engagement with them. Interestingly, Rousseau felt the only book appropriate for a child's education was *Robinson Crusoe*, the story of a sailor who overcomes adversity when marooned alone on a desert island. In contrast, Buber would note that Crusoe really becomes a person only when he is able to interact with others.

Summary

As we have seen, philosophers have long believed that arriving at an understanding of the nature of the individual might point us to an adequate ethical system, but they have differed greatly on what those features may be. The first two thinkers we discussed in this chapter believed that there is some innate essence, that continues even as we grow and have fresh experiences. Rousseau suggests that we have an innately good nature, which becomes compromised by the political and social environment that communities inevitably foster. Nietzsche considers that our nature is reflected in the strength of our will, and it takes a superior person to see through societal norms that mask as eternal moral truths. Sartre rejects essentialism and thinks there is an authentic self, and thus the moral project is to know ourselves well and act accordingly, not merely in response to external demands. In stark contrast, Buber rejects the notion of an isolated self that exists independently of our shared experiences with others.

The philosophers we have looked at all see that morality is intimately tied to a notion of the self, and what it takes to act morally in a world where we are constantly influenced by outside influences. In various ways, Rousseau, Nietzsche and Sartre want us to actively resist such dynamics and find true morality within, whereas Buber thinks we inevitably engage the world and become our authentic self only through sincere engagement with one another.

The founder of Summerhill said that he would rather his school produce a happy street cleaner than a neurotic scholar. If we value authenticity as a prime virtue, then according to some philosophers it will become all-important to foster self-awareness and personal responsibility from a very young age to develop genuine relationships and behaviors, even if they sometimes lead to discomfort or inefficiencies, as they appear to at Summerhill. The alternative may be to accept a degree of inauthentic behavior for the sake of social ease and productivity.

Nevertheless, if we hold authenticity as paramount, any compromise will be inauthentic by definition. That is, if we suppress our own desires or feelings for the sake of the common good, we are not being true to ourselves. Following some of the thinkers in this chapter we need to consider whether there is a balance between the authentic self and communal living, or if they are two separate conceptual islands without a link between them. Perhaps we have to work out that puzzle individually. Buber's response is to provide a third option by radically questioning our traditional notion of the self as a discrete unit of existence—that is, as distinct people leading separate lives. Whatever view we adopt at the outset will have significant implications for the ways in which we treat one another, and show us the importance of framing a sense of self in the moral endeavor.

6

Utilitarianism

Utilitarianism, an ethical theory, holds that the rightness or wrongness of actions is determined by the results they produce. It is a *consequentialist* theory in that it is less concerned with personal character or motives but looks instead to the consequences of the decisions we make. Utilitarianism is a particular brand of consequentialism. It claims that certain qualities such as happiness or pleasure are good, and that we should work to foster more in the world. Thus if there is a choice about how to behave, we should decide to do things that bring about the overall amount of happiness, or pleasure. So for a utilitarian, an action that results in an improvement of overall human welfare is good, and an action that results in a decline in human welfare is bad.

Economists often use the term *utility* as a measure of the total satisfaction received by consuming a good or service. We all have personal ideas about what provides most satisfaction, but one rough guide is to look at the way various people spend their money, which give us some indication of what makes them happy. Some will entertain themselves or acquire possessions, whereas others may donate to charity. Philosophers have given the term *utilitarianism* to theories that take consequences to be most important and also believe they can be measured in terms of utility. As noted, utility need not be judged just in monetary terms: Another way is to gauge it by how much it contributes to human happiness, welfare, or the common good.

CASE—VACCINATION

In January 2008 a seven-year-old boy returned to San Diego after visiting Switzerland with his family. A week later he had a severe cough and was taken to his local doctor, but was allowed to return to school. A couple of days later his condition worsened and he went to the local hospital. Test results led to a diagnosis of measles. He had not been vaccinated against the highly infectious disease. Eleven more cases quickly developed: The boy's siblings, five children in his school, and four other children who had been to the doctor's office the same day. Additional cases arose from people who had no contact with the boy, but had been around those infected. Three were infants who were under a year old, one of whom travelled on an airplane to Hawaii before its symptoms became fully apparent. The outbreak was contained, but about seventy children who had been exposed were placed under house quarantine because they had not been vaccinated, either because they were too young or because their parents had refused to let them have the injection.

Measles—which is transmitted through respiratory droplets—is a highly communicable viral disease that causes fever, cough, and a body rash, and can remain infectious for several days. Sufferers can develop complications such as encephalitis and pneumonia. It has a 3/1,000 risk of death, and one child in every thousand cases will be left with brain damage. A highly effective vaccine is given to children after their first birthday, although it provides protection only to 95 percent of those who receive it.

California allows parents to opt out of mandatory vaccinations for children based on their personal beliefs. The seven-year-old went to a school where about 10 percent of children were unvaccinated. Large-scale vaccination reduces the chance of infection, but if the level goes below 90 percent, the likelihood of an epidemic increases dramatically. Thus the consequences of non-vaccination will probably affect more than the individual unvaccinated child. Parents who refuse vaccination often do so based on a belief that there is an association between administration of the vaccine and diagnosis of autism, originating from a now discredited study. However, in the words of one parent, "I cannot deny that my child can put someone else at risk… [but] I refuse to sacrifice my children for the greater good."

UTILITARIAN APPROACHES

One formulation of utilitarianism says that we should act to maximize human welfare. Measles can be deadly, and it has significant risks. The benefit of vaccination is that it is inexpensive and gives lifelong immunity from the disease. The downside is that children may experience some discomfort when the vaccine is administered, and 3/10,000 may have a more serious reaction such as swelling in the mouth or a bleeding disorder.

A utilitarian analysis would look at the benefits and harms, not just for the individual parents and patients but also for everyone who may be affected by the decision. It would not be as interested in motives or intentions, but assess the choices on whether they add or subtract to human welfare. Yet at the same time, not all utilitarians would agree that the state should impose mandatory vaccination. To see why, we should look at historical and contemporary approaches to utilitarianism, which is typically associated with its two major English originators, Jeremy Bentham and John Stuart Mill.

BENTHAM

Bentham (1748–1832) was a social reformer at a time when punishments under the English legal system were often arbitrary and extreme—for example, one could be sent to the penal colony of Australia for petty crimes such as poaching or vandalism. In order to create a more just system of punishment, he suggested that a standard be developed to compare and judge the rightness or wrongness of actions overall. His basic formulation is that the measure of right and wrong is discovered by assessing the greatest happiness of the greatest number. Bentham explained his use of the principle of utility by saying we all seek happiness, and we are all ultimately governed by pain and pleasure. We try to avoid pain as much as possible, and work to do things that make us feel good, and when we do, we are happy. These pursuits can be intellectual as well as sensory—for instance, there is satisfaction in a job well done or looking after someone who is ill.

One of the early criticisms of utilitarianism suggested that hedonism essentially means sensuality. In the elegant language of the time, the critics made reference to the Epicureans who supposedly advocated a life of eating, drinking, and sexual indulgence. However, this mischaracterizes utilitarianism in at least two ways: It excessively narrows the definition of pleasure, and it focuses solely on individual rather than the collective good. For instance, in the vaccination case, utilitarians would think of avoiding debilitating disease as happiness, and then would stress that we have to look to the community welfare, instead of thinking purely of ourselves.

The basic idea is straightforward: maximizing the amount of happiness. Happiness, though, is very hard to pin down or quantify, and Bentham felt that we had to include several factors—intensity, duration, certainty, propinquity, fecundity, purity, and extent—when examining total happiness. For example, imagine bungee jumping: The emotions are very intense although relatively short in duration. Certainty refers to predicting if an act will bring happiness: For some, the jump could plausibly generate unpleasant traumatic memories in the future. Propinquity is an archaic term referring to how immediate and available an experience will be. Similarly, fecundity deals with the ability of an experience to produce further pleasure—perhaps the individual takes great joy in reminiscing about or retelling his or her adventures. Purity involves the mix of pleasure and pain—very few of our experiences are exclusively just pleasure or pain—for example, finishing a marathon may bring great personal satisfaction at the expense of physical distress. Extent, also part of the calculus, asks how many people are affected by the act or experience. Taken together, Bentham believes, these factors can combine to assess any particular choice.

Bentham believes that we should look to the total amount of human happiness generated by any human project, that we all count equally, and that our choices are equally valid. Thus no particular individual or human activity would be given a privileged status. If more pleasure was generated overall from trivial video games than the opera, then he believed it would be mere elitist prejudice to condemn the gamers merely on the grounds that their activities don't somehow enhance learning and culture. Similarly, social policy should rely on what will bring about the best outcome for everyone, not just some particular group. Underlying utilitarianism, then, are two important notions: first, we have to integrate considerations about the wider community's welfare into any decision, and second, no one has a privileged ability to tell others what is best for them. Hence in the vaccination case, Bentham would probably look to what is the aggregate benefit by balancing the value of individual freedom against the distress of widespread infection.

MILL

John Stuart Mill (1806–1873) was a child prodigy taught at home by his father. He later became an English civil servant and was for a brief period a Member of Parliament. His father was a friend and follower of Jeremy Bentham, and groomed his son to become a proponent of utilitarianism. Mill suffered a mental breakdown in his early twenties, and describes in his autobiography how he was able to overcome it through the redemptive power of art and literature. He was a strong believer in individual rights and an early advocate of women's suffrage.

Mill's book *Utilitarianism* is a short but powerful statement of the doctrine. We should note that it is consequentialist in that the moral assessment of an action is determined by its results. It is hedonistic, because it takes happiness to be the sum of pleasures. Like Bentham, Mill thought the prime motivation was avoiding pain and creating pleasure. Moreover, he follows Bentham in that the calculation applies to everyone affected by the action, not just the individual. We also can't give ourselves special favorable weighting in the calculation. As he puts it, we have to consider our own actions "as a disinterested and benevolent spectator." Thus, for instance, if someone might benefit himself or herself at a cost to others by understating personal income on a tax return, Mill would say that the person should judge the act as if he or she were a neutral third party with no particular stake in the outcome. Mill argues that if we behaved with community interests in mind, it would lead to a society where everyone is better off.

The most significant distinction between Bentham and Mill is over the nature of pleasure. For Bentham the phrase "greatest happiness" means the greatest quantity. However, Mill believes that some pleasures are *qualitatively* different, too. As an advocate for enhancing the potential of great art, he thought that some experiences were worth more than others. He was an ardent believer in the power of education to improve one's appreciation and enjoyment of life.

Mill did not think that appreciation of "higher" quality experiences precluded enjoying others. To make an analogy, meat-eaters might be content with hamburgers. However, once they have tasted a well-cooked filet mignon, it is likely that all things being equal they would prefer the filet. This is not to say that the experience of eating a hamburger is ruined or it would never be appropriate to eat one again. Rather, once people have been exposed to a range of qualitative experiences, they will be better equipped to make a choice. Similarly, presented with the option of funding opera, unsurprisingly most people would initially choose not to. On the other hand, if we have been educated about opera and taught how we could appreciate it, we might think differently. Mill's point is that we shouldn't treat utilitarian assessments as merely reflecting our naïve preferences. Instead they should be a result of education and experience.

Famously, Mill is remembered for saying "It is better to be a human being dissatisfied than a pig satisfied: better to be Socrates dissatisfied than a fool satisfied."[1] His point is that we would rather be more aware and engaged with the world even if it means we are less content. Generally, we are glad for our intelligence, even if it brings some highs and lows. It would be unusual, for instance, for someone to exchange 20 IQ points for a more even and content outlook on life. The pig or the fool does not know any better, but Mill suggests that it is part of our human makeup to embrace the frustrations that come with greater awareness. Another way of putting this is to distinguish *happiness* from *contentment*. Some may be content by having no ambition or awareness; their basic needs are furnished and they live moment to moment. Yet most of us would rather be conscious of broader ideas and aspirations, even if we can't attain them. They may enrich our lives. Bentham's point of view implies that all experiences are equal as long as they lead to happiness; Mill suggests that some are qualitatively better and we can appreciate them despite the frustrations we might encounter. It might be better, for instance, to play a musical instrument and recognize that no performance will be perfect than to never appreciate music at all, or it might be better to work at a philosophy text and learn from it although the experience involves some hard work along the way than it would be to never encounter the material.

Because higher and lower pleasures matter critically to Mill, knowledge of happiness relies on being able to discern experiences relative to one another. Hence one interesting implication of his analysis might be that when we assess our moral options, we should rely on elders and connoisseurs, that is, people who have lived through more and have greater education than we do.

ACT AND RULE UTILITARIANISM

So far we have generally spoken about a moral act as the subject of the utilitarian analysis. If we imagine a case, for instance, where a rich person drops a $20 bill, and we are aware of an appeal for the victims of a disaster, would it be wrong to pick it up and donate it to a worthy cause? On

---

[1]J. S. Mill, Utilitarianism http://www.gutenberg.org/files/11224/11224-h/11224-h.htm

reflection, we can think of the case in two ways: first, as a snapshot where we look at the immediate circumstances to determine what particular act will bring about the greatest happiness for the greatest number. But, second, we can also see utilitarianism as a way of generating rules for our behavior that would apply more broadly and give us a set of principles most conducive to maximizing happiness overall.

Act utilitarians think of the case in the first way. When faced with a choice, act utilitarians consider the particular situation to determine what individual act would maximize happiness. On the other hand, **rule utilitarians** generate rules or derive guidelines from the greatest happiness principle that look beyond the immediate case and bring in other considerations. Thus the money dropped by the rich man might be appealing to the act utilitarian who would donate it, since the act would probably not harm the owner significantly, and could be used to bring great benefit to people facing distress. But if we shift the focus from the act that maximizes happiness to the rule that will bring it about, we might reach a different answer. For example, it is plausible that maintaining property rights could be a part of generating overall welfare, and thus the principle that governs ought to be whether we should appropriate money that is not ours to use for causes that the owner might disagree with. Thus the rule utilitarian would likely return the money to the person who dropped it.

In both cases, the morality of the action is assessed in terms of the consequences, with the general principle that we should do whatever brings about a net balance of happiness over distress. The distinction between act and rule comes about when the individual looks at just the immediate circumstances or the broader context where the other considerations may alter the balance. Take a routine example such as giving to a homeless person who is begging on the street. If we don't take any other considerations into play, by solely looking at the individual act, giving spare change may seem to help the person and not hurt the donor. Yet, on a broader social scale, rewarding begging may lead to the recipient not getting help from social agencies and possibly promote destructive behaviors such as drug or alcohol abuse.

The act/rule distinction is useful and helps us think through the way that a utilitarian calculus might be applied. Nevertheless, we probably blend elements of both approaches when we make utilitarian decisions; perhaps it is more accurate to say that we initially invoke rules but then modify them if the particular circumstances are extraordinary and pressing. Thus a reasonable utilitarian rule would be to help others if it would produce great benefit at low cost. The default would be to follow the general rule of giving charitably if you can afford it, but in any particular case our judgment will be affected by more sophisticated questions—in our example, for instance: How genuine is the need? Are there more effective ways of helping the person? Will you, in fact, be supporting substance abuse and its deleterious effects? Thus we cannot merely take the balance of happiness to be a simple calculation. In most cases, we must weigh several factors, recalling that utilitarians are centrally concerned with the overall effects on everyone affected.

Mill is a philosophical liberal who wants to allow people maximum choice. At the same time, as he evaluates actions based on aggregate happiness, some individual preferences may be overridden. He looks to a standard of what will be most useful to society, not to what each person would allow. Recreational drug use, for instance, might be tolerated, but only if it genuinely did no harm. If it stimulated a trade that involved crime and suffering that outweighed any individual happiness, Mill would accept that it should be restricted. The vaccination case highlights this tension. There may be considerable value in having a society where individuals can make their own choices and opt out of government programs. However, those choices do not always affect the individual alone, and the risk of a disease epidemic has widespread repercussions. Thus we have developed policies that generally tolerate personal choice up to the point that there is a societal interest in restricting the behavior, and there the overall balance may favor the aggregate interests of everyone potentially affected by either action or, in this case, inaction.

CONTEMPORARY UTILITARIANISM

About a hundred years ago, the philosopher G. E. Moore (1873–1958) took utilitarianism in a different direction by arguing that people strive for multiple goals. Moore's problem with the traditional view of happiness is twofold. First, he thought it is not the single ultimate good; second, he thought the utilitarians had confused the mental state of happiness with the means used to attain it. Recall that seeking overall happiness is the goal of utilitarianism. If we are all seeking overall happiness, then our own actions are the means to something else—let us call it the summum bonum, a Latin phrase meaning the best good.

Moore contends that our own happiness is thus a means to an ultimate end, and therefore utilitarians are confused over happiness as a means, and happiness as an end in itself. As an analogy, let's take the acquisition of money. Unless you are a miser, you acquire money as a means to achieve other ends—perhaps personal comfort, health, or security. Thus getting money is not an end in itself, but rather a means to achieving an end. The question is whether there is a single end for all humans, or multiple possibilities. Some might say that the ultimate end for humans is something like happiness, as Mill and Bentham understood it as attaining pleasure and avoiding pain, while others describe it as human flourishing. On the other hand, Moore felt there were a range of potential things we find valuable.

To make his point, Moore describes a thought experiment, where we have a number of possible worlds. Some, like ours, have a mix of valuable things, such as love, health, sexual gratification, or pleasure. Others have only a single quality; that is, we can imagine a world where there is happiness, but no love; or the only feature is pleasure. He believes that we would always opt for the world with the mix, and hence it is wrong to equate the overall good with just one feature.

Moore believed that Bentham and Mill were mistaken in saying there was a single quality that captures the concept of *good*, which he believed is a "simple, indefinable, unanalysable object of thought."[2] For him, it is an intrinsic property. Although it is not simply defined through linguistic synonyms, he nevertheless thought we know it when we come across it. His view is more understandable if we think of something like beauty. We might think of an artwork or a person as beautiful, and we know it when we see it, but it is hard to define. Moore is open to the charge of social construction, in that some societies have very different views about what constitutes beauty, for example. Nevertheless, for our immediate purposes we can see that we discern qualities that we can't easily describe, and notions of love and what it means to be good may be less sensitive to cultural changes.

Moore claims that in his work *Principia Ethica* (1903) he was clearing the ground by showing the defects of other theories, and he asserts without any other justification, that the two prime qualities are **personal affection** and the **appreciation of beauty** in art and nature. This is perfectly consistent with his analysis in that he believed people of refined sensibilities would be able to discern these qualities. Whatever we make of this, his important legacy is the move from a single hedonistic view of the good to one that is more open to plural notions about its nature.

The second major development is a challenge to the idea that we have to maximize: If we have a moral duty to maximize happiness, then the question is whether we can ever do enough or spend

---

[2]G. E. Moore, *Principia Ethica*, 1903, section 15.

time to ourselves when the potential to increase the general welfare remains. The Nobel Laureate Herbert Simon proposed an alternative, based on **bounded rationality**. He realized that because we have limited knowledge, time, and resources to make decisions, sometimes achieving the best available outcome may be better than the best possible one. Simon gives the example of looking for a needle in a haystack that contains many needles: One way would be to find and examine every needle in order to find the sharpest one (a maximization process). The other would be to search for the first needle sharp enough to do the job at hand. He describes the second process as **satisficing**. If we apply his approach to utilitarian ethics, we recognize the cognitive and other limitations that humans have, and at the same time it releases us from the demand to completely maximize the good, and tells us that we can find an answer that is both sufficient and satisfying (hence satisfice).

Combining these two developments, if we have multiple conceptions of the good and then do not have to maximize the good but satisfice it, what is the gauge for the contemporary utilitarian? One answer has been that we should not seek to maximize happiness in the abstract, but look to individual preferences. The utilitarian still attempts to achieve the best outcomes for all involved, and **preference utilitarianism** suggests that the moral endeavor is to fulfill as many preferences as possible. This could be one definition of happiness, of course, but modern theories tend to avoid the term because of the complications it introduces. Unlike earlier forms, it focuses on individual outcomes, so there we can all have our own unique preferences. It is an **antirealist** position in that what is considered good will completely depend on the interests of people involved, not some external moral standard.

An objection to preference utilitarianism might be that some people have preferences that many would consider odd or negative, for example, someone taking joy in plucking the wings off fruit flies or creating graffiti. Mill's original answer "There is no difficulty in proving any ethical standard whatever to work ill, if we suppose universal idiocy to be conjoined with it" was somewhat abrupt.[3] The more charitable way preference utilitarianism is formulated usually has conditions that mitigate the problem—perhaps that the only genuine preferences are those that would withstand reflective scrutiny or some kind of therapeutic intervention.

Moreover, although these preferences are individual, the people involved will have views about the kind of society that they want to live in, and so social policy will be framed based on the sort of political system that would maximize the preferences of as many as possible. Preference utilitarianism thus answers some of the criticisms, but it depends crucially on us having a solid sense of our preferences and priorities. A sophisticated preference theory will thus also encourage us to make sure that our preferences are authentic and thoughtful, rather than impulses prompted by peer pressure or marketing appeals.

A traditional criticism of utilitarianism is that it suggests a never-ending requirement to increase overall welfare, with the result that many people have dismissed the theory as overly demanding and unrealistic. However, preference utilitarianism, where we believe in satisficing rather than maximizing welfare, significantly reduces the potential burden on each person.

SINGER

The move to personal preferences might be considered as returning to egoism, where everyone acts only on his or her own interests, but it actually brings us full circle to the initial starting point of utilitarianism and its two preconditions of impartiality and sympathy with

[3]Mill, *Utilitarianism*, chapter 2. http://www.gutenberg.org/files/11224/11224-h/11224-h.htm

others. Peter Singer (1946–), a leading proponent of preference utilitarianism, believes that the ethical project has to begin with the belief that we cannot favor ourselves and that our interests are inevitably intertwined with those of others. From this realization, he believes, we must take into account how our actions will touch everyone potentially affected by them for better or worse.[4]

Singer has been influential by reformulating utilitarianism in this way. By some readings of traditional utilitarianism he is not so very far from Bentham and Mill, as they might easily accept that we have personal interests, and in their terms the universal ones will be avoiding pain and enhancing pleasure. We can also see that the impartiality condition will imply that we should treat others as moral equals irrespective of their gender, race, or any other arbitrary features.

Singer's claim is much more modest than that of Bentham or Mill: Simply, he says that if we can benefit others greatly at little costs to ourselves, then that is what we should do. He notes that the amount spent on a bottle of water would feed a starving child for a day and that if the one billion affluent people in the world each gave a single gift of $200, we could achieve the United Nations Millennium Development Goals of reducing by half the population living in extreme poverty and hunger and ensuring primary school education for all children worldwide.[5]

Singer, in *The Life You Can Save*, proposes that people in the developed world should give 5 percent of their income to charitable causes. He also notes that most people in the developed world live better lives than Louis XIV of France did in his day. Admittedly he could order palaces to be built, but he could not live as comfortably as most middle-class Americans, for example, who can eat out-of-season foods routinely, have access to advanced medical care, and travel at will. With the amount of disposable income many Americans and Europeans have at hand, his telling question is whether they would really miss $200, given the amount of good it could do for the needy.

CHALLENGES

A number of issues that point to some difficulties for utilitarianism emerge. Utilitarianism has been criticized on several grounds that tend to cluster around three alleged problems: the utility calculus, challenges to autonomy, and the tenet of impartiality. Let us examine them individually.

Problems with Calculation

Utilitarianism critically relies on its calculus, that is, quantifying the outcomes so they can be assessed. In the traditional articulation of utilitarianism, the calculus applies to all those affected by a decision. Imagine we get a solicitation for a charitable donation to orphans overseas. The calculation would be one of working out how much benefit we would get out of the money if we didn't send it to the charity, contrasted to how much good it would do for the recipients. I might be deprived of a frothy coffee, whereas some children might be given a dose of vitamin A that wards off blindness. The result of the calculus may seem straightforward and imply that donating is the only moral course of action. Yet at the same time, we must think about the total effects of the potential donation. The coffee shop will be less well-off, perhaps. But do we have to expand

---

[4]Peter Singer, 2000. "About Ethics," in *Writings on an Ethical Life*. New York: Harper Collins, pp. 16–17.

[5]Peter Singer, 2009. *The Life You Can Save: Acting Now to End World Poverty*. New York: Random House, p. 143.

the circle of concern even further, maybe even to the coffee farmers and processors? A further difficulty is when we look at people who aren't directly affected, but could have been helped by an alternative act. That is, I may have denied myself the coffee, but donated elsewhere that could have saved a life rather than someone's eyesight—how do we balance those concerns, and have I caused distress by choosing to not help when I could have?

Another criticism of the utility calculus is that it looks at the total quantity—that is, the greatest amount—rather than the distribution. Consider the case where one person could be benefitted tremendously, or lots of people could be mildly better off. In the case of saving someone's life or sight, it is worth a small sacrifice on our part. But in the case of pure enjoyment, our intuition appears to change. For example, a millionaire might buy up famous paintings for his own collection and thereby deprive many other people of seeing them. His happiness could be greater because of his extensive interest in great art and heightened because he takes joy in the fact that he has the exclusive ability to see them.

Utilitarian reasoning could also have the potential of hurting minorities: If the governing principle is to maximize the good for the maximum number, then it seems to imply that a simple majority rule could squelch the interests or rights of the minority. For example, many people could get great happiness at the cost of a single individual suffering very badly. In her short story *The Ones Who Walk Away From Omelas*, Ursula Le Guin describes an affluent society that lives a utopian existence, but at the price of scapegoating one unfortunate child who is kept in utter misery.[6] A modern analogy might be a rich society that enjoys cheap goods, not realizing that part of the savings comes from children laboring in wretched conditions. We might assume that if consumers were aware of the origin of their affluent lifestyle, they might act to redress the injustice. Le Guin isn't so sure: There may be a bargain with the devil, but in her society, at least, people are made aware of the cost of their happiness and simply choose to ignore the fact. In contemporary times, we may decry sweatshops where unskilled workers are often exploited and abused, but at the same time it turns out that few consumers consider the conditions of workers when purchasing their clothes.

Utilitarianism does not always address issues of individual merit or responsibility: Should our obligation to improve the welfare of others—perhaps through a state-paid liver transplant—change if the person is somehow to blame for his or her own distress by, say, a casual attitude about drinking alcohol? Conversely, should we make some people less well-off in order to benefit remote others, regardless of the hard work the affluent may have put in to acquire their wealth? At some point, perhaps, the history and context of each case and its justification may play a part in calculating the utilitarian balance. Here again, these concerns may not derail the utilitarian project, but just give impetus to creating more sophisticated methods of quantifying and justifying human utility. Moreover, critics point out that there has to be a point where we have done enough, and doing more would be going over and above what is morally required. In other words, if we take the requirement of maximizing happiness for the maximum number at face value, then we could never stop working to help others, even when it might significantly diminish our own welfare.

To test our intuitions, let us take two more hypothetical cases: In the first, someone is found to have a natural immunity to HIV. By tapping into some of his organs, scientists can extract a cure for HIV-AIDS sufferers. Unfortunately, doing so involves keeping him in sterile surroundings at all times, and considerable pain when he undergoes the weekly extraction of

---

[6]Ursula K. Le Guin, 1992. *The Ones Who Walk Away From Omelas*. Mankato, MN: Creative Publications.

the appropriate enzymes from his body. Would we be justified in depriving him of a normal life in exchange for saving others? Would the numbers make a difference in this case—would we be more willing to treat him this way if the numbers saved were in the millions than if it were just a few?

In another case, a voyeur gets great happiness from spying on young women in their dorm rooms, while they remain ignorant of what he is doing. It seems in this case that overall happiness is increased and so utilitarianism should actually encourage his behavior. Mill's answer is that the principle of utility must include notions such as trust and respect. Thus, in the AIDS case, millions might potentially benefit, but the cost is that we would be part of a society that might harvest anyone at anytime, something most of us would condemn, even if the price were not providing the cure. In the voyeur example, again if we generalize and think how much less pleasant our lives would be if we constantly worried about being spied on without our consent, the overall diminishment of the quality of life would outweigh any pleasure that the individual voyeur might get.[7]

This certainly makes Mill sound like a rule-utilitarian, and following his line of reasoning we see that for utilitarianism to work the individual must see the paramount tenet to not hurt one another. This will override any immediate or expedient actions that may seem, initially at least, to be more attractive. Another way to put this is to say that Mill endorses a version of rights. They are derivative from the utilitarian calculus, applied in its widest fashion, and favor personal liberty and immunity from harm by others. This will give an answer to the hypothetical cases where utilitarianism would necessitate the greatest happiness overall even at the cost to some minority group. His fundamental notion is that societal happiness should be found in the principle of 'Do No Harm', and if that is violated, then happiness will not be maximized, whatever immediate benefits may come about as a result.

As utilitarianism is based on results, there is an empirical component to Mill's claims. Although it would be hard to think of a way we could scientifically examine his claim that doing no harm is more effective than any other principle and overrides other considerations, his claim could, in effect, be subject to a critical test. Perhaps we have one society that bases its whole government and social policy on maximizing personal liberty and minimizing harm to others, and another, perhaps like the Omelas, which is willing to make a minority suffer in exchange for the majority enjoying a very pleasant life. If it turned out that Mill was wrong, then we could still adopt a utilitarian viewpoint, except it would now allow some injustice as the price of maximizing aggregate happiness.

Autonomy

Another worry is that utilitarianism interferes with an individual's own life plans. In essence, the criticisms of utilitarianism challenge its two main roots: sympathy and impartiality. One line is that we may not care about others to the point that we should alter our life plans, and the other is that although we have some sympathy for others, we don't have to hold their life aspirations or concerns as equal to our own. I may want to devote my life to art or contemplation, and utilitarianism appears to demand that I subordinate my plans to the common good. Thus I may enjoy collecting stamps, and it has become part of my self-identity; to some it may seem frivolous, but it means a lot to me, to the point that I am unwilling to follow the utilitarian's demand that I

---

[7]J. S. Mill, 1863/1901. *Utilitarianism.* New York: Longmans, p. 89.

abandon some of my expensive hobbies to preserve the health and well-being of people I have never met.

This turns out to be a personal version of the concern about oppressing minorities, since the needs of the many seem to interfere with the individual's own desires. Mill was a passionate believer in individual rights, with the qualification that we should be allowed individual liberties up to the point that they interfere with the freedom of others.

It is worth reflecting back on the view of human nature that we bring to moral thinking. In a tribal society, for instance, the unit of consideration may be the tribe, not any particular person. In the Western liberal tradition, roughly since the time of the Enlightenment (about 1700) there has been an emphasis on the individual, whereas here Mill defaults to the common good. It isn't that we can't have our own personal projects and follow our own interests, but the utilitarian may feel it is appropriate to intervene if those seem to detract from the overall welfare of society. For example, if someone has a modest stamp collection that brings him great pleasure, that seems reasonably harmless.

On the other hand, if he becomes obsessed with the collection, not as an investment or cultural artifact that others would enjoy, but merely for the acquisition, then perhaps the resources he expends might be more usefully employed elsewhere. The utilitarian view need not be coercive, and we shouldn't understand it as compelling others to adjust their priorities. Instead, what the theory provides is traction to the argument that in any moral decision, the gauge of right and wrong is whether it brings about more human welfare.

Impartiality

Mill characterizes Bentham as saying that we all "count for one, and none for more than one." Taken at face value, this means we treat ourselves and those we love as equals in the calculus. The wants and needs of those close to us will count just as much as someone we don't know in a remote land. Some say that the impartiality condition is too demanding; others suggest that the idea of improving welfare generally hurts the individual's own right to choose what his or her own priorities should be. The details matter in assessing the theory. If utilitarianism is characterized as little more than cost/benefit analysis, then it is easy to criticize because it would imply that whatever brings happiness to an individual is the right thing to do.

Our intuitions about impartiality are often tested in "trolley problems" and our responses to these problems serve to inform us about a utilitarian calculus, and whether the impartiality condition is too demanding. They are thought experiments where we are to imagine a tram (or trolley) heading toward five innocent workers who are inevitably going to be killed. The driver of the trolley has the option of switching on to a branch of the track where there is only one person.

Philosopher Philippa Foot suggests that a utilitarian driver would necessarily choose to steer toward the one instead of the five.[8] We can tweak the example in many ways: For instance, we can make the five less innocent, but convicted criminals, and the one becomes a cancer researcher. From a social utility perspective, we might think not only about the numbers but also about the value of each to society. We can also ask whether having a relationship with someone matters. For example, if the one turns out to be your mother, you would favor the person you know and love. There are a number of creative versions: If the decision were between one person and a penguin, the natural inclination is to save the human. On the other

---

[8]Philippa Foot, 1978. *The Problem of Abortion and the Doctrine of the Double Effect in Virtues and Vices.* Oxford: Basil Blackwell, p. 23.

hand, what if you knew it were one of the last pair of mating penguins on earth? Alternatively, is there an artifact that would be worth sacrificing human life for, perhaps, the Mona Lisa painting, or some holy relic?

A strict utilitarian will say that we are all moral equals, and therefore we should generally be indifferent about whom we should rescue, at least in the human case, and all other things being equal. However, that need not be the end of the story: Any factor that would either increase or decrease the eventual utility can be brought into play. Thus we could argue that there is utility in family relationships, and that enriches human welfare overall. Hence we should have an expectation that we will favor those we love in these kinds of dilemma.

Looking at overall utility also means that we can consider the contributions that someone might make to society: Perhaps the cancer researcher's ability to add to human welfare will be included in our reasoning. We should also note that utilitarians wouldn't be the only ones who face difficult decisions: Judging dilemmas will be problematic from any moral perspective. Focusing on the results doesn't necessarily make hard problems easy, but the utilitarian will say that at least it gives us a practical process for working out what to do.

It would be wrong to treat utilitarianism as a neat formula where we put in data and it produces a clear solution, and indeed Mill, for one, was aware of the fact that it has to rely on the best possible, but always fallible, human judgment. He says there are always exceptions to blanket rules, and issues have to be worked out depending, as he puts it, "on the intellect and virtue of the individual."

Agency

Another result from trolley problems is that we find people have a psychological resistance to making decisions that bring about harm even if the result is likely to bring about overall benefit. So in one twist on the original example, the trolley is driverless and you are on a bridge overlooking the track. There is a large person leaning over the bridge and you could nudge him so that he falls on the track and diverts the train (as it is a hypothetical example, we can imagine these as certain outcomes). The calculus remains the same—one person dies and the five others survive. Presented in this way, though, many people are horrified that they would have to take a positive action to save the five, even though they would have little problem operating the switch to divert the train.

A very similar psychological effect is found when we think about vaccinating a whole society. As we have seen, at first glance it seems that vaccination is a societal good. But at the same time, some vaccines might cause potentially deadly side effects for some people. For the sake of argument, let us imagine a case where without the vaccine, fifty out of every million will die from a certain disease. Once we administer the vaccine, no one will die from the disease, but it is predictable that six will die from the side effects, but we won't know ahead of time who they are. How should we decide policy in this case? The numbers are compelling—over forty lives will be saved. Yet those who now die will be the victims of human action rather than something "natural." Thus there is an understandable reluctance to be an agent of harm, even though there is a net saving of life. Given the centrality of impartiality for utilitarians, though, the claim of special treatment or exemptions because of personal feelings is not considered sufficiently important to override the common good.

Adaptive Preference Formation

Social psychologists have also identified other ways in which we are not as dispassionately rational as the theory appears to assume. Aesop has a fable in which a fox tries all day to get some grapes off a vine. After considerable time and effort, it abandons the attempt and declares that the grapes were probably sour anyway—leading to the expression **sour grapes** for thwarted ambition. This shows us that our preferences are not fixed, but we often adapt them to our circumstances. Perhaps a student has ambitions to become a medical doctor but then does poorly in an organic chemistry class and learns that he would probably not do well on the standardized entrance test for medical school. After a period of initial disappointment, he reconciles himself to his changed circumstances and sets his sights on becoming a teacher.

In another case, an inspiring instructor tells a first-generation college student who comes from a household with low expectations that she could become a lawyer. The idea had never occurred to her, as she felt it was well beyond her capabilities. She now readjusts her thinking and gears her studies accordingly. The point is that our preferences are not static but are constantly changing. Moreover, our preferences aren't always obvious, even to ourselves. They can also be shaped, both by internal psychological dynamics and by external forces. For example, television advertisers are very adept at persuading us that we need various products for a happy life and we should feel deprived without them.

These dynamics do not undermine utilitarianism, but show that we have to be very careful and precise in articulating our preferences. From this discussion, utilitarianism demands reflection about what will make us happy, but typically in terms of communal happiness considered over the long term, rather than individuals each seeking instant gratification.

Probabilities

A lingering concern is that utilitarianism must always work with probabilities. That is, decisions need to be made about the outcome before we know what the outcome will actually turn out to be. This means we are always making our best guess based on the probabilities. In some cases this is fairly straightforward: If we are weighing the option of enjoying a coffee against the benefits the money may achieve if I give it to a local charity, the balance may be relatively easy to work out. However, things are usually more complex. We don't know what impact we might have on others, or how any particular event will turn out. We have all had episodes in our lives where something emerged from a meeting or event that we didn't expect and it had a profound impact on our lives—how can we build that into our calculations?

We are all constantly faced with making decisions under uncertainty, and have to make the best possible guess about the outcome. Just after the Second World War, for instance, the insecticide DDT held the promise of eradicating tropical diseases such as malaria and was widely used, and one of its proponents was presented with the Nobel Prize in medicine. Just over a decade later, it was found to linger in the soil and have carcinogens that put wildlife at risk, and it was subsequently banned. A utilitarian defense would remind us that this is not necessarily a failing of the theory but a fact of life—we may not know the effects of an act or a product until afterward, and by that time, of course, we don't have the luxury of starting over, we simply have to make the best decision possible given the circumstances at that time.

The way issues are presented also plays into our moral intuitions. When we think of the runaway trolley where one person is at risk on one track and five on the other, we could think of the difference as four more, or alternatively as five times as many. Articulating the problem as a multiple tends to make the case more dramatic and alarming. Moreover, consider how the context matters. If we say the numbers are, perhaps, ten thousand and five versus ten thousand and one, we may not think that the four people are quite as significant and tend to be indifferent between the outcomes (although, in both cases the total deaths remain the same as four more people die in one case rather than the other).

Thus we need to be aware that the way the outcome is framed can have a significant impact on the decisions we make. Casting something in a positive light (e.g., movie theaters give a mid-week discount) is far more likely to motivate us to act than saying the same thing with a negative connotation (e.g., theaters charge a premium on the weekends), even though they describe the same effect. Saying that we save forty-four lives through immunization sounds positive and desirable. However, we might also say that six people will likely die who would otherwise have only had a very small risk of catching the disease. Mill's maxim of do no harm could apply in both interpretations: We are saving forty-four people from harm in the first case, but violate the principle when we concentrate on the unfortunate probable deaths from side effects.

Utilitarianism is forward-looking and therefore projects our best assessment of likely outcomes. However, as is readily apparent, there can be unfortunate or unforeseen consequences. One critic, Elizabeth Anscombe (1919–2001), criticized utilitarianism because it is mainly prescriptive—that is, it tells us what we should do—based on probabilities. In other words, she felt utilitarianism was lacking because it let some actions off the moral hook: If a politician gives money to charitable causes, the utilitarian looks at the result rather than the reasons that brought it about. Anscombe argued that morality is not only about right and wrong, but also about praise and blame, and thus we also have to incorporate motives into the calculus. Thus the politician may have done good, but his actions aren't necessarily morally praiseworthy in her eyes. It was Anscombe who introduced **consequentialism** as a technical term, because she felt that if we talk about consequences, then we must consider all of them, both intended and unintended, and that means we need an account of what prompted the moral action. Accordingly she thought that any adequate moral theory had to incorporate the psychology of motives and intentions.[9]

Defining Happiness

For Bentham and Mill, if we live a life with minimum pain and maximum pleasure, then we will be happy. This might at first appear to be true, but when we look deeper we find cases that give us pause: A rich tycoon may have no material cares and yet feel unhappy; a married couple may constantly squabble and have few luxuries, but declare themselves happy. Let us return to Mill's example of Socrates for a moment. Mill claimed that anyone who had experience of a range of mental states would opt for the highest, even though it would bring about some mental distress. Again, this may be something of an empirical claim. We might ask people whether they would be willing to gain IQ points at the risk of becoming less happy, and although many would assent, it isn't obvious that everyone would make the trade.

Utilitarian theories all say that the good is determined by having something maximized. However, that something has often proved elusive, as it doesn't easily map onto any particular quality. For instance, the concepts of pleasure or happiness don't arise from a simple sensation, but are often mixed with other emotions and are experienced in the context of other emotions. If pleasure were simply the same as the good, then it ought to be straightforward to say that whatever increases pleasure is always good, and, conversely it is always good to increase pleasure, but that doesn't seem to be the case.

Nevertheless many utilitarians believe that given a sufficient refinement of definitions, what is good could be described in other terms—here, pleasure or happiness, and these could be

---

[9]G. E. M. Anscombe, 1958. "Modern Moral Philosophy." *Philosophy* 33: 1–19.

factually tested. We could see if, say, giving to charity leads to the donors becoming more happy or fulfilled (or other more nuanced descriptions), and if so, we might conclude that such giving is good. In this case, "donating to charity is good" is equivalent to "charity makes people more happy and fulfilled." That is, moral claims could potentially always be translated into claims about natural facts, which leads to the expression *ethical naturalism*.

Similarly we might consider analogies with the concepts of humor, friendship, or love. Although elusive, they are hard to tie down. Still, we don't deny their reality. Similarly, a utilitarian might say that *good* is difficult to define, but very real nevertheless, and clearly something that ought to be maximized in the world. The philosopher's task from this point of view is to help us all in working out what we mean when we use the term, and that while not perfect, the notions of happiness, pleasure, or personal preferences give us a head start on that project.

The Expanding Sphere of Moral Concern

Peter Singer has dramatically used utilitarianism to promote the animal welfare movement. The way the two are linked is by focusing on the basic unit of moral consideration as *having interests*, and these lead to preferences. Singer asserts that beings with sentience—sensory awareness—will have interests. Thus animals can feel pain or distress, and have an interest in avoiding those sensations. In making his case, Singer quotes his intellectual ancestor Bentham who thought that the ability to feel pain was common to all people and hence it would be wrong to discriminate on the basis of skin color, gender, or age at a time when slavery and child labor were both legal and condoned by society. Bentham went further, and contended that we would come to realize that all animals are worthy of moral consideration. The common denominator is not the ability to reason, speak, or any other quality unique to humans, but the susceptibility to suffering, which is felt by humans and animals alike.[10]

Whether or not we are persuaded by the argument that moral consideration should be linked to the vulnerability to suffering, we should nevertheless reflect on the historical development of ethics: Moral consideration used to apply only to a select few, but it has developed over time as an expanding circle to include common people, non-landowners, women, children, people of color, and animals.[11] This does not necessarily mean that we could never use animals in medical research, say, or cannot eat meat. Rather, it asks us to consider the balance of suffering involved in each case. Perhaps the potential to cure blindness in humans would outweigh the pain of a rabbit used for research. On the other hand, routinely testing the effects of some cosmetics on monkeys with no constraints on their pain and distress might not be appropriate.

Recall that utilitarians are concerned with decreasing distress and increasing happiness, and many recent theorists believe that the relevant set of those affected by an action is not limited to certain humans, but also future generations or the natural world. If we take those claims seriously, then utilitarianism gives us a strong impulse to choose actions that will promote global sustainability.

[10]Jeremy Bentham, 1780/1907. Chapter XVII, "Of the Limits of the Penal Branch of Jurisprudence," section iv, including footnote 1, in *An Introduction to the Principles of Morals and Legislation*, p. 311.

[11]Peter Singer, 1981. *The Expanding Circle: Ethics and Sociobiology.* New York: Farrar Straus & Giroux.

Summary

There are several advantages to adopting a utilitarian approach: It gives us the possibility of coming to definitive answers to moral questions; it is straightforward and clear; and it relies on results that are open to public scrutiny. If we are presented with a balance of benefits and harms, then the obvious response would seem to be to go with the course of action that will do most good.

Some of its strengths are also its drawbacks: Because it relies on outcomes, it is only as strong as the methods we have to judge them. As we have seen, there are real difficulties in calculating utility functions and trying to weigh them. Utilitarians would not consider these criticisms as mortal blows, however, but rather issues to be worked through.

The knotty problems with utilitarianism reflect deeper concerns about personal identity and societal justice. The theory doesn't assign any special value to particular people, and measures their worth in terms of the welfare they generate. When we think about other people, especially those we love, we tend to see them as more than vehicles for utility functions—we use the language that we cherish them for *who they are* rather than *what they do*.

The demands that utilitarianism makes to treat all people equally and maximize aggregate welfare are challenges that most would feel ask more than regular and decent people can deliver consistently. Psychologically it is also difficult to put the general welfare ahead of one's own interests. The parents who refuse to vaccinate against measles may genuinely believe that doing so would put their own children at risk, and therefore the threshold to override personal choice should probably be a high one.

However, utilitarians will not be persuaded by claims that moral action is difficult to achieve. They believe that utilitarianism provides the most convincing set of arguments for what we *should* do, even if we often fail to live up to those standards. Utilitarianism at least gives an analytical framework that lets us describe and argue for the moral decisions we make and the normative standards we should create. Because they are based on consequences, utilitarian theories require us to justify acts in ways that allow quantitative comparisons, and thus provide a strong basis for individual choice and social policy.

7

Duty-Based Ethics—Deontology

Deontology is an ethical framework that maintains that acts are morally correct insofar as they conform to a principle of duty or obligation (from the Greek: *deon* = "duty"). Duty-based ethical theories usually consider outcomes immaterial or secondary in our moral assessment, and look first to the motives involved. A reasonable way of starting to think about deontology is to consider the phrase that we should "be good for goodness' sake." We should keep promises or fulfill obligations simply because they are promises and obligations, and not because of any particular anticipated outcomes.

There are three key elements to deontology: First, how we arrive at a moral decision is entirely rational, in the sense that we can work out what is the right thing to do just like we can work through a mathematical proof without having to appeal to evidence. Second, the process can be worked out ahead of time. Third, it is based on respect and purity of motives, not on the desirability of the effects or results of actions performed.

CASE—THE STUDY OF AIDS

Acquired immune deficiency syndrome (AIDS), caused by the human immunodeficiency virus (HIV), is typically transmitted through sexual activity or blood transfusions. It is estimated that over thirty-three million people are currently infected, and some twenty-five million people have died from the disease since it was identified in the early 1980s. Annually it kills about three million people, and roughly the same number of people are newly infected each year. Infection rates vary depending on people's natural resistance to the disease. If the resistance factors could be isolated, then medical researchers might be able to develop a vaccine, with the promise of curtailing any new infections. However, conducting a fully scientific study would require some subjects to engage in risky behaviors. If they were fully aware of the risks, they might alter their behavior by practicing safe sex.

In the late 1990s, Cornell Medical College studied the infection rates in couples with one partner being HIV positive. The trial was set in Haiti, one of the poorest countries in the world. The subjects were not receiving the care available in the developed world, and cultural and religious traditions meant that condom use was low. Consequently the uninfected partner would probably have a high chance of exposure to the virus. The study consent form said, "We would like to test your blood because you live in an area where AIDS may be common." It seemed that some of the partners had been infected but then for some reason the disease failed to progress, and these findings were hailed as milestones toward the development of a vaccine.

If the research had been carried out in the United States, the prevailing protocols would have required explicit information that one partner was HIV-positive, counseling about the risks, and treatment using retroviral drugs. In the Haiti study, the partners were offered counseling and free condoms, but there were no written consent forms letting the couples know that one had the virus but that the other did not. The lead doctor felt that anyone who subsequently contracted the disease during the study would only have themselves to blame, since they already had access to information and resources.

The case brings up many moral issues. Should the trial prove successful, then millions might be helped. If the trial had never taken place, the individuals involved would likely have continued being at high risk of infection, and so in a sense they were no worse off because of the study. Yet the scientists were in a position to help people avoid a deadly disease and failed to educate the subjects involved. One way of looking at the case might be to examine the potential outcomes, and balance the eventual benefits and harms. However, duty-based ethics rejects any notion of "all's well that ends well" and instead focuses on the way people are treated. It centrally asks whether a moral act could be universalized—in other words, whether we would agree that everyone deserves equal respect and "do unto others as we would be done by."

Was it appropriate for the scientists to deal with people in the way they did in the hope of making a medical breakthrough? The deontologist would focus on the motives behind the actions, whether the individuals were treated with respect, and if the behavior would survive a critical test of being applied to everyone. For example, if someone knew that an individual was at risk for a life-threatening illness, would it be acceptable to withhold the information and let him or her continue for the sake of scientific research? We will now look at some major figures who believe that respecting the individual and motive matter more than outcomes in moral deliberations.

KANT

The key figure in the history of deontology, Immanuel Kant (1724–1804) attempted to derive a system of ethics that did not depend on religious faith or experience but could be worked out rationally. This would give it the force of a logical proof, as opposed to being contingent on the particular facts of a case. Both his general philosophy and ethics are complex, but they have the elegance of an elaborate mechanism, and if we accept the basic axioms, his conclusions follow in a compelling way. Some of the language he uses is archaic, but here again once we grasp what he is saying, the essential points are fairly straightforward. It is worthwhile to note that he approaches ethics with fascination and curiosity:

> Two things fill the mind with ever new and increasing admiration and awe, the oftener and the more steadily we reflect on them: the starry heavens above and the moral law within.[1]

---

[1]Immanuel Kant, 1788. *Critique of Practical Reason*, conclusion. http://www.gutenberg.org/cache/epub/5683/pg5683.html

The Good Will

Kant believes motive is the key to assessing morality. He believes that our acts are governed by our will whose purity will determine how ethical an act is. He surveys the human character, considers qualities such as courage, wit, resolution, and perseverance, and decides that while they are generally desirable, they can be diverted in various ways depending on the character of the person involved. For instance, wit can be deeply wounding, a thief could be bold, or intelligence could be used for creating a mischievous computer virus. Thus character traits aren't good in themselves but need to be guided in the right way. Kant also believes that we have inclinations and desires as part of our particular nature. Someone with a kindly disposition may naturally want to help out others, whereas another person might be self-absorbed. However, he feels that there is no merit in following our natural inclinations. Morality, he believes, emerges when we do what is morally obligatory.

In a memorable phrase, Kant opens his book by saying "Nothing can possibly be conceived in the world, or even out of it, which can be called good, without qualification, except **a good will**."[2] Take the case of visiting a sick relative. If Kant is correct, then we reason that it is decent to pay the visit out of duty. Kant's moral law imposes a duty that overrides our personal desires: Someone may want to go to the movies instead, but feels that he or she ought to forsake that and do what duty requires. He notes that people may do what is right more or less good-heartedly; in other words, we might cheerfully adopt what duty demands or we may go more begrudgingly. For Kant, it is up to us to align ourselves with what we know we ought to do. Kant says the truly good person will always have motives aligned with the good will; in other words, the ideal case is one where the person realizes that he or she should, say, visit the relative, and subsequently willingly and enthusiastically takes on the obligation, without any reservations or qualifications.

Moreover, Kant feels that actions done without regard for any payoff are better. He also argues that if we rely on results to gauge our moral actions, then our judgments will necessarily vary depending on the outcomes. Kant thinks that this leaves us with the impossible task of working out what is the right thing to do ahead of time when we don't know what will happen afterward. He concludes that the only proper way to determine what is moral is to have a process where we can establish the rule ahead of time (from the Latin **a priori**, "what is before"), so that our judgments do not depend on probabilities or chance. Taking this to its logical conclusion, he thinks that the highest good is done because we see the **intrinsic** value of what we do, that is, doing good for goodness sake, not because we will benefit from it in some way. Consider spending time working with the homeless: We might be wary of a political candidate who did so temporarily amid much publicity, or someone who loudly paraded his charity work to others. These sorts of intuitions might make us think it morally better that someone helps out not because of any potential personal benefit but merely because she thinks it is the right thing to do. In Kant's language, doing good should be an **end-in-itself**, not as a means to some other end such as personal pride or political ambition.

In another example, perhaps someone is faced with potential embarrassment, say, by having an incomplete homework assignment. At that point, the individual has the freedom to choose between telling the truth and lying, maybe claiming the pet dog had eaten it. For Kant, we should not be looking at the potential benefits or harms that might result from what we say. Rather, he

---

[2]Immanuel Kant, *Groundwork for the Metaphysics of Morals*, http://www.earlymoderntexts.com/pdfbits/kgw.html

wants us to realize that in that particular moment we have the choice of doing the right thing by telling the truth, and we should take that path because it is dictated by reason.

The Categorical Imperative

Kant believes that given certain basic principles, we can determine what the moral choice will be. Sometimes his approach is characterized as the so-called Golden Rule, "Do unto others as you would have them do unto you." However, this fails to capture the sophistication of his view. Kant believes when faced with a moral question, we can discern the answer by an appeal to the **Categorical Imperative**. It emerges from a rational decision procedure, which, consistent with his views, can be determined through a thought experiment rather than gathering evidence.

Kant tells us to consider whether a course of action could be made universal, by asking what would happen if everyone did the same. Critically, this is not a test of consequences, but instead a logical question that forces us to confront whether the act would lead to a self-contradiction. It is not so much that the world would be a better or worse place if lying or theft was rampant, but more fundamentally, if everyone stole, then there would be no sense of personal property, or if everyone lied, then truthfulness would lose its meaning. Kant's test is a principle of noncontradiction: If we can universalize our behavior without undermining a central ethical concept, then it will be moral. On the other hand, if it turns out that everyone acting similarly compromises a basic concept, then the act will be immoral. We cannot excuse ourselves based on particular circumstances, and because it applies across different situations it is called *categorical*. Kant also thinks that once we work out what to do, we have a moral obligation to do it, and thus the duties involved are not suggestions, but carry the force of a command, hence the word *imperative*.

Kant formulates the Categorical Imperative in three ways that he thinks amount to the same thing. The common thread is his view of human nature. He believes that we are all rational and free to make choices. Thus when I see another person, I should recognize and respect him or her as a moral agent, someone who is capable of reasoning to a decision. This gives us three strands in developing a moral imperative: that it would apply to all rational beings; that we should respect others insofar as they are human and capable of making independent decisions and, given that we all have the freedom to choose right from wrong, we acknowledge that each individual is responsible for recognizing rational moral choices and acting accordingly.

Kant's first formulation says that a person should always act so that the maxim of his or her actions could rationally be willed as a universal law. This is the **universalization** clause. Note, again, that he is looking at the motive behind the act, not the outcomes. Let's take the case, say, of someone tempted to take office supplies home from his or her workplace. Individually, the minor thefts might not be noticed, but if everyone did it, then the boss might arrive in the morning to find the place empty.

We might take from this that it would be wrong to do anything where the cumulative effects would be bad, or more cynically, that we should do only morally questionable acts as long as everyone else doesn't. But for Kant the actual outcome is not the place where we should make the moral decision. Rather, if everyone stole, then it would mean that the notion of private property would make no sense, and so we can tell that it is inappropriate to steal without even considering the results in any particular case. The **maxim** is a moral principle that will govern the behavior of all reasoning people.

An important note is that the universalization procedure means that we cannot make exceptions for ourselves. For instance, Kant won't allow us to extrapolate along the lines of "any student who is living on financial aid, has pressing needs, and facing the situation I am in now should be allowed to fall behind on his rent." Obviously, with sufficient ingenuity we could craft all sorts of unique rules. Kant is aware of this, and his default is the generic person capable of reasoning: He does not give any slippage room based on our unique circumstances, and his maxims are going to apply without exception.

The second formulation says "So act as to treat humanity, whether in thine own person or in that of any other, in every case as an end withal, never as means only."[3] This tells us that humans have an intrinsic value and dignity, and ought to be treated with respect. We could imagine someone who collects money at a toll booth; a driver has the option of going through a lane with an automatic coin basket or giving money to the person manually. In a very real sense, the person and the machine have the same function, but Kant would argue that we have a moral duty to treat the person with respect only because he or she is a person. Significantly, Kant doesn't say that we can't ever use people for our own ends, and indeed we do this all the time. For instance, an employer may hire people to do a job that will end up making him or her money. In that sense the owner of the firm is enriched, and the employees are being used to generate profit, but this need not be a bad thing.

The key phrase Kant uses is that we may not use people as means *merely,* which tells us that we can interact with people in ways that further our personal interests, but in so doing we must realize we are dealing with humans who have inherent dignity, and hence treat them with respect. If we drive through the manual toll lane, then it is morally appropriate to treat others the way we would like to be treated, and not behave as if they were an organic machine. In business terms, we often hear the phrase "human capital" which has the effect of making us think that employees are resources just like the physical plant or raw materials. Kant's formulation is a constant reminder that people have absolute worth in and of themselves.

The third formulation tells us that ethical people should "always act as both subjects and sovereigns in the kingdom of ends." This condition emphasizes the autonomy of the individual, who both creates the moral law and then is subject to it. For Kant, we come to moral judgments ourselves and therefore we are ultimately responsible for our actions. There may be cases where we have been told what to do by someone else, but he feels that we need to assess them for ourselves, and then internalize them. Thus a priest may tell us that stealing is wrong. Kant would disapprove if we then refrained on the basis of someone else's recommendation instead of reasoning it out personally and following the dictates of our own thought process. The effects may be identical, but for Kant it is critical that we are self-motivated. The consequence is that we cannot shift responsibility for what we do to anyone else. Hence it isn't sufficient that we act according to what duty demands, since that could be unthinking obedience or sheer coincidence. Instead moral actions must be motivated *by* doing duty as well as complying *with* the dictates of duty.

Kant's moral decision procedure thus moves from the individual to a more general level of what everyone should do when faced with a dilemma. One way to think about it is as an arch that gets more abstract and then returns to the practical: We move from one leg where we are deliberating over our personal issue, then it is elevated to the point where it would apply generally and at the apex the issue is transformed into a general moral principle. It then takes on the force of a moral law that will be binding on every rational person. Finally it touches ground again when the moral law tells us how to conduct ourselves in our everyday behavior. Here he means the moral law, in other words, the rules and duties we derive from universalization process, not a legal code.

---

[3]Immanuel Kant, *Groundwork for the Metaphysics of Morals,* section 2. http://www.gutenberg.org/cache/epub/5682/pg5682.html

Kant distinguishes doing good for external reasons from our intrinsic drive to do the right thing. The student might refrain from doing something because he or she was told it is not decent behavior by a parent or other authority figure. Kant calls a self-imposed law an **autonomous** action, or self-directed, whereas if someone else commands it, then it is **heteronomous**, or other-directed. For him, merely following orders, even if they are noble and lead to good results, will never constitute good action. This is not to say we can't agree with those in authority. The point for Kant is that we don't just accept a moral rule because someone else tells us to, but instead we reason it through and then adopt it as our own.

Kant also separates outcome-dependent reasoning from the internal justification that forms the Categorical Imperative. The reasoning involved when we look at outcomes is called **hypothetical** because it relies on "if…then" justifications. For instance, "If I make this donation, then I will please my mother" or "If I act this way, then I will get favorable publicity." The commands that we give to ourselves in these situations will vary by the benefits we are likely to reap as a result. Kant calls these outcome-dependent rules **hypothetical imperatives**, as distinct from those which derive from unsullied motives.

Following this fairly complex analysis, as a way of testing whether our motives are truly moral, we could ask three summary questions:

- Is the motive of the right type? Does it seek goodness for its own sake, or for some ulterior motive?
- Does the motive arise from respect for the natural moral law in that it is applies to everyone and without regard to any particular circumstances?
- Is the motive inevitable, in the sense that the Categorical Imperative shows there is no other possible moral choice but to do the right thing?

As is often the case with Kant, it is best explained by reference to an example. Let's take the case of a professor who leaves the room with the answer key to an upcoming multiple-choice test visible on her desk. A student who is not doing well in the course and is the last person to leave the room sees it lying there and has the opportunity to copy the key and pull up her grade without being discovered. Should she do it?

Kant would reason along these lines: The essential question is whether she should cheat. She should not consider herself specially privileged, so then she should consider whether anyone at all should cheat, in other words, would it be morally acceptable if everyone behaved that way. The answer revolves around the concepts at work: Cheating involves undermining the point of the test, which is administered to provide the students and teacher with accurate feedback about the level of learning in the class. Thus we come to an inconsistency since if everyone cheated then there would be no point in having a test. Put in that way, she should not cheat because the act cannot be *universalized*—applied to everyone—without reaching a contradiction, because a test where everyone cheats is no longer a real test.

It could be that the student is spotted and reported, or sometime later must use the information on the test in a critical situation and fails badly. Alternatively, she could go on to great things. The point is, though, that for the deontologist whether she did right or wrong in deciding to cheat shouldn't depend on those factors: The outcomes are somewhat arbitrary, and what matters most is that in the moment she knows there is a moral choice to make. She cannot know exactly what will come of her actions, but will know that in the moment she had the choice to follow the dictates of rational morality—she should have known what was right and wrong and followed the moral law regardless of the consequences.

The Conflict of Duties

Kant himself believed that if we framed the issues correctly there would never be a clash of principles derived from the Categorical Imperative. Nevertheless, it seems that there are times where we can imagine that we are faced with compromising one maxim or another. For example, in a Biblical story, we are told of a Pharaoh commanding midwives to kill all Israelite boys, but they saved the children by lying to him.[4] Clearly they felt that preserving life mattered more than always telling the truth. We can see the same intuition at work when we think of a promise to meet a friend for coffee, but then witness someone fall and volunteer to take the person to the emergency room. It is wrong to break promises, according to Kant, but there are surely times when one maxim, perhaps "help those in distress," will outweigh a much more trivial obligation like showing up for coffee. Another way of putting this is to imagine someone's reaction if we say that we can't take him or her to the emergency room because we have a prior arrangement to catch up with a friend. The natural reaction is that there is a ranking of duties, perhaps something like life matters more than property, and property more than convenience.

Perfect and Imperfect Duties

Kant's own response to the apparent conflict of duties was to distinguish between **perfect duties** and **imperfect duties**. Perfect duties are generally prohibitions, whereas imperfect duties are those that encourage us to improve, for example, phrases such as "develop your talents" or "help others." The key difference is that we can work out what is a perfect duty by seeing if it leads to a contradiction when we universalize it. Thus the concept of a lie makes sense only if there is a general background of telling the truth and we want to make an exception for ourselves. Given the conceptual contradiction, Kant would say that this means we deduce that there is an absolute prohibition on lying and hence a perfect duty.

On the other hand, if we take the case of not giving to charity and universalize it we would find that the concept would still make sense, just that no one practices it. We can imagine that the world might be a better place when people are charitable, and so we can rationalize that it would be a decent thing to do, but not obligatory, and therefore it is an imperfect duty. Similarly, we have an imperfect duty to forgive: There is nothing contradictory about a world where forgiveness doesn't happen, and the fact that we forgive people doesn't mean that they have a right to forgiveness for past wrongs. At the same time, we might believe it preferable that people forgive those who have hurt them, and we should endorse and encourage this behavior. Nevertheless, for Kant, there would be no reason to *compel* someone to forgive another.

Kant gives four examples where he contrasts perfect and imperfect duties, and duties to the self and duties to others:

1. In the first case, a man contemplates suicide because of unfortunate circumstances. Kant says that committing suicide would be contrary to human nature: Instead of looking at his personal satisfaction, he should ask himself whether suicide is contrary to the natural human desire for survival. Because he shouldn't make an exception for himself, he therefore has a perfect duty to himself to avoid suicide.

2. In the second case, someone needs to borrow money but knows that he won't be able to repay it. The question is whether he should lie to the prospective lender. When he

---

[4]Exodus 1: 16–19.

universalizes the issue, he realizes that the outcome would be self-contradictory, and therefore he has a perfect duty to others not to lie.

3. In the third case, someone has talents that he chooses not to develop, instead choosing a life of personal indulgence. If he universalizes his choice, he could imagine a world where everyone just lazed about, but Kant thinks we have a natural instinct to not let our talents rust. So while it is conceivable that everyone could act indulgently, Kant thinks it wouldn't happen. The failure here is not one of self-contradiction, but that people would not will for that sort of outcome. Hence in this case we have an imperfect duty to oneself.

4. The last case is one of charity, where a wealthy man sees others struggling. He wonders whether he should help them out. Kant again reasons that he could choose to help them but has no obligation to. Kant's view of human rationality is that no one would wish to create a world where everyone simply looks out for him or herself alone, but he acknowledges that it is possible, and hence doesn't involve a self-contradiction, and this deduction leads him to say that we have an imperfect duty of charity to others.

This framework allows Kant to say that a perfect duty will always supersede an imperfect duty. As an example, it appears that along these lines he would condemn Robin Hood, the famous outlaw who supposedly stole from the rich to give to the poor, since stealing is *always* wrong, but charity *depends* on beneficence and is not morally required of us.

The question remains, though, as to whether Kant's solution really works. There are cases we can imagine where someone is literally starving and has the opportunity to steal a crust of bread from a baker who would not miss it.

We need to be careful not to caricature Kant, though. From notes that his students took during his lectures it seems he qualifies some of the more strident claims.[5] For instance, he tells us that some men are malicious, cheats, liars, and wicked, and therefore white lies are forced upon us by necessity. That is, if you are mugged and hand over a wallet, but then the mugger demands to know if you have any other money on you, Kant would believe that it is acceptable to lie. Further, he suggests that deceiving the deceivers is a lie but not an unjust one. So in a bargaining situation, if you firmly believe that the seller has made an unfounded claim, it is fair game to not stick to the literal truth. Kant realizes that we make practical judgments all the time, and so his work tends to include notions of justification as well; that is to say, we have the rules, and there will be clear lines of right and wrong. At the same time, though, Kant acknowledges that moral discussion will also often deal with context and explanations. In those cases, we may realize that what we did was wrong, but then go into a further conversation about how blameworthy or excusable an act was given the circumstances.

MORAL LUCK

The notion of moral luck comes about when factors outside the individual's control alter the outcome. Imagine two people at a party who decide to drive home after they have had several beers. Both have impaired judgment, and the first gets home without incident. As the second drives home, a woman steps into a crosswalk, but he fails to react in time and runs her down.

The question that Kant would pose is whether we should judge people on the motive or the outcome. When we discuss the drunk drivers, they behaved exactly the same, and their positions

---

[5]Immanuel Kant, 2001. *Lectures on Ethics;* J. B. Schneewind, ed., P. Heath, trans, Cambridge: Cambridge University Press, p. 203.

could easily be reversed. We could think about luck in a positive light, too: Imagine two cases where individuals attempt to rescue someone from a burning building. The first finds the victim, whereas the second cannot locate the resident because of thick toxic smoke. The successful rescuer is lionized as a hero, whereas the second gets few accolades for trying, even though both took the same risks and managed to get to the same room in the building.

Kant strongly feels that we shouldn't look at accomplishment; he says that if circumstances are such that someone is not in a position to achieve a goal his or her pure motive or good will nevertheless "like a jewel, it will still shine by its own light." Thus we should judge people by the reasons they do things. An elderly person may devote all the time he or she can to helping out in a soup kitchen, but not accomplish as much as a corporate tycoon could with a single cash donation. Kant believes that we should assess the morality involved by the dedication and commitment rather than on the outcome.

Kant's analysis goes against some of our experience: We tend to condemn the driver who hurts someone more than those who could have, but luckily didn't; we give awards to heroes who rescued others but tend to ignore those who tried and failed, even if the situation was essentially out of their hands. However, we shouldn't confuse **descriptive ethics**, that tell us what people do, with **normative ethics**, that tell us what people ought to do. That is, Kant is more concerned with how we *should* behave and what we should aspire to do than empirical reports of what we actually do. Perhaps we *should* praise trying as much as accomplishment. For Kant, at least, the arbitrariness of our natural gifts and financial wherewithal and the luck we have along the way ought to have no bearing on moral assessments. In essence, his moral system demands that we bracket away those factors we have no control over. On reflection, many of the outcomes from our actions are indeed incidental and we are often overly generous to ourselves in taking credit for a lot of what happens.

As we can see from the discussion of perfect and imperfect duties, Kantians are not completely removed from considering what will make the world a better place. However, Kant's analysis is at a conceptual level of beneficial principles rather than immediate consequences. For example, a deontologist might readily admit that a world where people tell the truth would be preferable to one where people routinely lie, but he or she will not focus on specific outcomes as the way of judging any particular case. Thus for Kant and his followers, recognizing that outcomes are part of the overall moral landscape is not the same as saying we should therefore use them for moral assessment. Furthermore, if we go into just how capricious outcomes can be, the deontologist will maintain that we are on much safer ground making moral judgments by concentrating on notions of duty.

W. D. ROSS

Sir William David Ross (1877–1971) was a **pluralistic deontologist** insofar as he asserted that there is more than one basic principle. So while Kant is adamant that the Categorical Imperative does not allow for exceptions and perfect duties will not clash, Ross thinks that there will inevitably be conflicts and we must find the greatest balance of competing obligations. Suppose, for example, that someone has promised to tutor disadvantaged students, but then knows that her mother is sick in the hospital. One way to construe this might be to say that we have a perfect duty to not break promises, and only an imperfect duty to visit the sick. However, that would strike many as an odd result, as we'd usually think that visiting one's mother would take precedence.

The solution that Ross comes up with in his most influential work *The Right and the Good* (1930) is to say morality is a two-stage process. First, we intuit our general obligations, and second we have to reason to see how they apply in particular situations. He uses the phrase

prima facie obligations to describe and list seven fundamental kinds of duty. *Prima facie,* a Latin term for "first appearance," can be understood as the self-evident raw intuition that strikes us first—like the idea that visiting one's sick mother is a good thing to do. All things being equal, we should obey the prima facie obligation. In the case of conflicting obligations, he believes we have to use reason to see if one obligation will outweigh another, and these will eventually give us **actual obligations**.

Ross accepts that his list may not be exhaustive, and is not really systematic. He also considers the objection that there is no overarching principle at work. He doesn't see this as a critical problem, since each case has to be weighed on its own merits. He is also suspicious of moral theory that seems to go against common sense; he makes the analogy of beauty, and whether people would change their mind about something being beautiful just because they are given an aesthetic theory that conflicts with their own intuitions. He personally believes that general "rules of thumb" tell us, for example, that the demand to do no harm should take precedence over beneficence. He is reluctant, though, to say that these rules apply in any whole-sale way, but rather they always have to be judged in context.

All prima facie obligations are conditional in that we have to supplement them with other considerations, and so none will ever be supreme or absolute. He lists his candidates, but believes that there may be others:

1. Fidelity—the duty to keep promises
2. Reparation for a previous wrong
3. Gratitude for past acts of others
4. Duties of justice—to redress cases where personal happiness is not in accordance with merit
5. Beneficence to others—improving virtue, intelligence, or pleasure
6. Self-improvement—in terms of virtue or intelligence
7. Nonmaleficence—not harming others

There is considerable appeal in a theory that relies on common sense and reasonable intuitions. Ross believed that his provisional list, which would be tested over time, would fit the intuitions of "thoughtful and well-educated" people. Some modern critics suggest that Ross's intuitions may reflect of the conventions of his time. Still, despite the shortcomings in his approach, we cannot entirely discount his view, and it is worth considering if there are any other obvious duties that are readily apparent and cannot be explained other than saying that we know they exist.

THE DOCTRINE OF DOUBLE EFFECT

If we have a moral theory based on intentions alone, we might criticize it on the grounds that some bad effects will inevitably result. The deontologist may not be too concerned about this worry since we are in control only of our personal choices, and otherwise the chips will fall where they may. Kant and his followers would say the consequences can't always be predicted and are often out of our control, whereas we always have the freedom to choose the moral path or not. Thus in the case of unintended harms, the important thing for the deontologist is that bad outcomes were not intentionally willed.

A more significant challenge to the deontologist is that an act may have multiple effects, so that we can't intend for one to happen without realizing that the others will occur as well. For example, a physical therapist working with someone who broke his ankle knows that certain exercises will inevitably cause pain. She is not trying to cause pain, and if she knew of a way to achieve the end result without inflicting it she certainly would choose that instead. Her motive is to try to reduce the suffering of someone in distress, but the means to achieve her end inevitably had predictable side effects, at least in the short term. The pain is a collateral result of the exercise, and hence we often use the term **collateral damage** to describe the phenomenon. The problem of multiple results emerging from a good intention is known technically as **double effect**, and the way it is reconciled as morally acceptable is referred to as the **doctrine of double effect**.

We can see how the analysis applies in several contexts: In a just war, killing enemy combatants is acceptable. The overall aim of the war is to restore peace and justice to a troubled area. Imagine the armed forces have launched missiles with a remarkable 98 percent accuracy rate at strategic enemy installations. However, this still means that two out of every hundred launched will fall outside the target zone, and that innocent civilians will likely be killed or injured. The missile operators know there is a risk to noncombatants, but feel that their overall aim was noble and justified because there are predictable but unfortunate casualties that will result from their actions.

We can also see this at work in the commercial realm: Car manufacturers want to provide affordable and convenient travel options to their customers. They know that they could restrict the speed of their vehicles to four miles an hour and cover them with a foot of foam rubber all around, and these changes would result in far fewer deaths. Yet they compromise by allowing drivers to go faster because of consumer demand, with the predictable result that some people will die because they are unable to control their cars at the high speeds they are capable of reaching. Here again, the justification along these lines is that the makers understood that a very small number of consumers may die owing to the use of their products, but their intention was to provide the best-quality goods at the lowest cost based on consumer preferences.

The issue has been addressed since the time of St. Thomas Aquinas (1225–1274). His solution to the problem of double effect was to make a morally relevant distinction between intended and foreseeable effects. His insights have been developed into a set of conditions that show when well-intended acts with foreseeable but unintended outcomes may be justified.

1. The act itself is not immoral.
2. The agent does not positively will the bad effect.
3. The agent cannot obtain the good effect without the bad effect.
4. The good effect results at least as directly as does the bad effect.
5. The good effect is sufficiently good to offset the bad effect.[6]

Proponents of the doctrine feel that it is much more than a utilitarian balance of benefits against harms, since the whole emphasis is on what the intentions are of the people involved. We can see how this plays out in the case of the physical therapist: First, it is not immoral to assist someone doing exercises after an injury; second, the therapist does not will the harm; third, it is inevitable that the exercises will distress the patient somewhat; fourth, a benefit will emerge from doing the exercises—it is not a remote or haphazard possibility in the face of pain which is obvious and immediate. Last, the proportion of benefits must outweigh the harms. If we take the case of the just war, the analysis becomes more complex: the military would argue that it is not immoral to fire weapons at a dangerous enemy; that other means had been exhausted, and that collateral damage is an unfortunate fact of life in a war zone; destruction of necessary

---

[6]Cf. *The New Catholic Encylopedia*, Vol. IV. Washington D.C.: The Catholic University of America, 1967, p. 1021.

targets is more certain than the loss of life due to targeting mistakes or missile failure; and, all things considered, winning the conflict (and subsequently saving the oppressed or preventing genocide) outweighs the safety of a few noncombatants.

It matters vitally for the deontological argument how the participants formulate their intention and how they explain it. It is undeniable that the therapist deliberately caused the pain, and that the military caused the death of innocent civilians, even if they wish that their actions wouldn't have had those consequences. The therapist might explain that her main aim is to make the patient well again, and the bomb operator might say that the deaths were an unfortunate accident. Similarly, in a famous example to illustrate the power of framing the issues, imagine that five people are in an underground cave while the water is rising. The largest member of the group is wedged in the only exit facing out. The group is equipped with explosives and, having tried everything else, is faced with the question of whether to use them to blow up their leader.[7] If they do and escape, the undeniable fact is that they killed him and he would probably be alive if it hadn't been for their actions. However, members of the group are likely to cast a positive light on their actions, saying they saved themselves the only way they could. His widow might reply that no matter how they describe their intentions, they killed him and are morally responsible for his death. If someone accepts the doctrine of double effect, then the language and distinctions describing the action are really important since the deontologist believes intention matters most and that is where the moral judgment should rest.

CHALLENGES

Deontology has many attractions, and whether we agree with it, it has been hugely influential in framing ethical debates in the last two centuries. The pull of deontology is certainly very strong, yet it has met some significant challenges that have to be confronted.

Kant's system relies not only on rational thinking but also on the presumption that we will all come to the same conclusions. His argument seems fairly straightforward in the way he lays it out—for instance, there would be few who would endorse lying. However, when we expand the analysis, our intuitions may start to vary. Take the case of stealing: If people routinely stole, then it would undermine the idea of property, Kant reasons, and therefore there is an absolute prohibition on theft. But consider how embedded these terms are already. If we had a communal hunter/gatherer tribe, who subsisted off the land and shared their resources, they might fail to grasp the concept of personal property as easily as those of us who have grown up assuming that it is right and proper to acquire and transfer material goods. Without getting into an anthropological debate, the point is that Kant readily assumes that we have uniformly shared understandings about the world that will inevitably lead us to the same conclusions, and we might question whether that is always the case.

The universalizability test is based on the idea that we are moral equals—no one has a special privilege exempting him or her from general moral rules, and reciprocity has been a consistent theme in religious and secular codes of conduct, telling us that we should treat others the way we want to be treated. Kant is clear when he says that we cannot claim a particular immunity based on our life situation or circumstances.

---

[7]See Philippa Foot, 2003. *Virtues and Vices*. New York: Oxford University Press, pp. 22–23.

Additionally, Kant holds personal autonomy paramount because ultimately we are all responsible for our own actions, and we cannot say in defense that someone ordered us to do something or that it wasn't our personal choice. Nevertheless, these excuses point to an important element in our moral decision-making in that we always operate within a certain cultural and institutional framework, and get influenced in significant ways, often by factors we are unaware of at the time. We don't always have the time or luxury to make reasoned choices, especially in times of stress; the truth of the matter is that we rarely enjoy the freedom and immunity from outside influence that his method prizes so highly.

It also seems that the deontologist needs a sophisticated understanding of human psychology. Recall that one of Kant's own examples deals with someone in great personal distress contemplating suicide: Surely the psychological processes at work for the unfortunate man are much more complex and diffuse than he characterizes. The minimal view he presents which focuses solely on the decision processing of a reasonable person relying on a few basic premises may bolster his analysis, but on the other hand its simplistic vision may ultimately detract from the power of the framework he establishes.

Kant also relies on a notion of strict impartiality: We should treat others as moral equals, and not allow any exceptions when we devise the Categorical Imperative. However, when we think about the way we live, our relationships are not impartially between equals, but, as in the case of families, they are often unchosen and between unequals: We would treat those we love differently, and probably favor them if we could. This is not to say that the normative ideal that we *should* treat everyone as if they had no special ties might not be something to strive for. Still, it forces us to reason as if we had no biases, when in fact we do, and this may either be too difficult or too unrealistic for many people.

Let us return to the earlier example of visiting a sick person. When confronted with a couple of relatives she asks, "What brought you here?" Kant is insistent that duty expressed in the good will is the purest motive. How would she react, though, if one replies that he was there because it was his moral duty, based on what everyone should do in similar circumstances, although it meant missing a movie he really wanted to see? The point is that there appears to be something amiss if we rely on impartial duty alone—compare how the sick person would feel to the first answer as opposed to someone who said that he really felt for her and wanted to let her know she was loved and missed. Much the same might be said of the nursing staff—if the patient asked why they took on the work, being told that it was a duty being fulfilled still leaves a gap for other accounts that may include care and dedication to others. The plain fact is that although we may act out of a sense of duty, it limits our motivation to the purely **rational** when there may be much more to be said about other moral factors like compassion or empathy, for example.

Another challenge is that Kant provides us with only a few absolutes such as lying and theft. He thinks they should be clear to any rational person and do not compete with each other. In contrast Ross gives us several principles, but with no means to judge between them. Critics suggest that this leaves us with a few precepts, but the hard work still needs to be done to show how they apply to particular cases and how we judge between rival claims. One response by the deontologist might be to say that ethics is like life—messy, and we are always left to work out the details. In any case, the apparent clarity and simplicity of deontology fails somewhat when we go from abstract principles to actual concrete examples. Indeed, Kant's book is called "groundwork" because his aim was to establish fundamental, but general, ideas about ethics, and so perhaps it is not fair to criticize him for doing what he wanted, and not what we want, in setting out an ethical theory. Still, many of those who oppose the theory do so because it apparently presents a loose set of intuitions rather than a coherent means to deal with real issues.

Summary

Deontology has the strength of putting questions of motive front and center in our moral discussions. Admittedly, motives are often elusive, even to ourselves. Yet this doesn't mean that we should discount motives, only that we have to be discerning when we incorporate them into the moral mix.

The compelling feature of Kantian deontology is that it gives us a way of thinking about ethics that isn't contingent on the accidental features of the world, including the variable consequences of any action. In the moment that we make a decision, we may know right from wrong, but we don't know what the eventual results of our actions will be: Lying might be an expedient means of getting out of an immediate fix, but we can never know how it might come back to haunt us. Because we can never be certain about outcomes, it seems odd to rely on them as the gauge of our morality—it isn't always the case that "all's well that ends well" either—we do care about the means used to achieve those ends.

If we think about an act, perhaps a donation to charity, we don't assess it purely on the outcome. Invariably, part of our thinking is *why* the person did it. For example, some big businesses give large amounts back to the community voluntarily. Many people consider it a form of advertizing, and suggest that they wouldn't act this way unless the donations provided some competitive advantage. That is, we judge these businesses by our perception of their motives, and think that an act is better the more it seems there is no advantage in the agent doing it. It is very natural to ask what prompted people to do what they did; perhaps they visited a sick relative out of guilt, or because there is some promise of a future legacy. Kant posits the simple and compelling view that duty based on good will is the highest motive: We do good things and avoid the bad simply because it is the rational thing to do in a world where we respect others.

A key feature of deontology is the demand that we respect people as people: We should not treat them just as objects to be exploited. Kant extends the notion to embrace our intuition that humans are special and deserve to be treated with dignity because of their intrinsic value. These concepts may be hard to pin down, but give us a basis for honoring the individuality of each person.

Kant and his followers have tried to show that morality can be generated through a sense of doing good for its own sake, and, put that way, there is much to recommend it. This leads to a rule-based system of morality that provides us with ideals that we can aspire to. The danger, though, is that if we are slavishly absolutist—"never lie!"—then it may give us a morality that we can never realistically achieve, with the result that we may abandon the attempt. Furthermore, the paramount stress on reason and duty may effectively sideline some very important features of the morality we operate on in our day-to-day lives such as love and compassion.

Going back to the opening case in Haiti, there is nothing to suggest that the scientists had sinister motives. In fact, they probably saw their research as part of a higher calling to benefit all mankind. Yet the case touches on a number of issues we've covered: Did they think about the welfare of the individuals who were at risk in the study, and would they have acted differently if they had considered that someone might treat them that way too? Did they realize there was likely to be collateral damage, but accept that because they felt their prime objective was an overarching goal, and hence their motives were, in fact, quite noble? Although they didn't lie to the subjects in the study, was nondisclosure of the known risks a morally decent thing to do?

While we may have mixed reactions to the case, it shows the value of incorporating deontological language into moral discussions.

Intentions are often elusive, especially as we have a tendency to change the story over time to color our actions in a more favorable light. Thus we should have a robust notion of how to deal with motives in moral assessment. Nevertheless, the central ideas of respecting the humanity of others in our dealings, and seeing if the universalizability test applies do give us rich ways to think about our actions.

Additionally, as Kant points out, we can never really know how things will turn out: The AIDS research could have resulted in an effective vaccine or it could have been fruitless, and we don't know that ahead of time. Therefore, it may be all important to incorporate a means of predicting the morality of an action beforehand rather than merely trying to justify it after the fact.

Virtue-Based Ethics

Virtue theory is usually associated with the Greek philosopher Aristotle (384–322 BCE), mainly drawn from his *Nichomachean Ethics*, as well as the writings of St. Thomas Aquinas (1225–1274). The Ancient Greeks thought the key issue in ethics is how we should live our lives, and connected individual happiness to human flourishing. For Aristotle's teacher Plato (427–347 BCE), this amounted to living by the dictates of reason; for Aristotle, it meant fulfilling one's function. Later for Aquinas it meant glorifying God by exercising the Christian virtues of faith, hope, and charity. A **virtue theorist**, then, maintains that a person's character demonstrated over time matters most in ethics. Thus although particular acts are significant, we should really judge people only after looking at the entire sweep of their lives.

CASE—BOOKER T. WASHINGTON

Booker T. Washington (1856–1915) was born a slave in Virginia prior to emancipation. His mother was an African slave and his father a white man he never knew.[1] At the age of eleven he was working in salt mines and furnaces, splitting his shifts so that he could attend school during the day. Later he worked as a houseboy and recalled his strict employer, Mrs. Ruffner, who wanted things done methodically and quickly, but above all valued honesty and frankness. When he was seventeen, he started at Hampton Institute in Virginia (now Hampton University), working as a janitor to pay his way. The school's principal, a retired Union general named Samuel Chapman Armstrong, became a model for Washington, who described Chapman as "the most perfect specimen of man, physically, mentally and spiritually." Armstrong thought that a proper education should not only include skill development but also build character by developing habits of self-discipline and hard work. The school was run on military lines, with an early rise, inspections, and exercise.

After graduation Washington became a teacher, later taking over a new school in Tuskegee, Alabama, where he remained for the next thirty-four years. There he used the same model as Hampton, saying "Wherever our graduates go, the changes which soon begin to appear in the buying of land, improving homes, saving money, in education, and in

---

[1]See W. J. Jacobs, 1990. "Booker T. Washington," in *Great Lives: Human Rights*. New York: Macmillan, pp. 119–130.

high moral character are remarkable. Whole communities are fast being revolutionized through the instrumentality of these men and women."[2] Washington was tireless at fund-raising, and he became famous for his oratorical gifts. He maintained that the racial divide would be bridged through education and self-improvement rather than political confrontation. Washington rose to prominence and was invited to the White House by Theodore Roosevelt and later became an advisor to the president. He became a major force in raising funds for education of blacks in the South. His contacts with philanthropists generated support for literally thousands of schools and colleges that would not have existed without private funding. He summed up his vision in a public statement in 1902 where he said "My life work is the promotion of education of my race," including inculcation of "habits of thrift, skill, intelligence, high moral character, and the gaining of the respect and confidence of their neighbors."[3]

VIRTUE-BASED ETHICS

Clearly, the concept of character was central for Booker T. Washington. His approach to ethics was not so much about finding rules that would determine the right action in any particular case but rather about developing his students as upstanding citizens with characteristics that would enable them to live happy and productive lives. Virtue-based theories thus take a very different perspective from utilitarianism and deontology about the ethical enterprise and moral education. Some people resonate with this approach, whereas others find its ideas elusive.

As an initial diagnostic thought experiment, consider the sorts of things you would like said about you at a memorial service. Luckily, people tend to emphasize the good elements over the bad, so for our purposes you can limit yourself to emphasizing positive statements. It seems we often tend to downplay achievements in favor of character traits. Consequently, rather than a list of degrees and promotions, we get general comments such as "she was kind; loving; generous and helped others whenever she could." This phenomenon is philosophically curious: Presumably this is a time when we would like others to encapsulate the most important aspects of who we are and what we did, and yet achievements fall away and character traits come to the fore. In short, it describes how we approached life more than what we did along the way.

Similarly, in some court cases there is a role for a "character witness" particularly in fraud trials when the morality of the individual is questioned. The witness will usually testify about a person's reputation and moral standing based on personal acquaintance. Even in the face of evidence that the defendant actually committed the crime, the witness may describe the event as an aberration or momentary lapse of judgment.

As a third example, consider the way in which many codes of conduct present desirable behaviors. Shell, the oil company, lists honesty, integrity, and respect for people.[4] These are not just corporate approaches, though. In the community, the Boy Scouts of America promote that their members will be "trustworthy, loyal, helpful, friendly, courteous, kind, obedient, cheerful, thrifty, brave, clean, and reverent."[5]

---

[2] B. T. Washington, 2010/1901. *Up from Slavery: An Autobiography.* Gretna, LA: Pelican Publishing, p. 21.
[3] L. Harlan, 1986. *Booker T. Washington: The Wizard of Tuskegee, 1901–1915.* New York: Oxford University Press, p. 10.
[4] Available at http://www.shell.com/home/content/aboutshell/who_we_are/our_values/code_of_conduct/code_of_conduct.html, accessed May 21, 2013.
[5] Available at http://www.scouting.org/scoutsource/BoyScouts.aspx, accessed May 21, 2013.

The point is that many of us think of leading a good life not in terms of formulas for the correct behavior, but as a set of characteristics that describe what we aspire to be. Imagine a person who buys a house, and subsequently parks wrecked cars in the garden, which eventually turns to mud. He has various dogs that he keeps outside and yells at when they howl from hunger or neglect. He builds a barbed wire fence, and hangs signs saying "Beware: Deadly Voltage." Now he may have legal rights to do what he does, and he may have done his own cost/benefit analysis. Yet when we think of him, often our first reaction is simply to ask what kind of person would act that way. Similarly, when corporate or institutional managers let workers go without notice after twenty years of loyal service, the questions raised are typically not about whether the company had a right to act as it did, or whether it was maximizing its efficiency. Rather, the issues tend to focus on the moral character of the individual decision makers.

All these examples demonstrate the way in which we often pitch moral questions less in terms of the motivation behind particular actions, but more about the person involved and his or her persistent nature through time. They focus on the central idea behind virtue ethics, that is, developing characters that will enable us to achieve happiness by living well.

For some, this kind of assessment makes little sense; for instance, they might claim that our lives are made up of individual decisions, and so nothing is aberrant, and there is no real core, only a series of choices that add up to who we are. To sort out the issue, let us return to basic notions of human nature and personal identity. One theory put forward by John Locke (1632–1704) suggests that we are like strands on a rope that constantly overlap but no one strand is continuous from beginning to end. That way we can say that we are continuous with the person we know ourselves to be as a child, but there is nothing constant.

A contrasting theory more amenable to virtue theorists is that we have a core, or essence—the essential you—that persists through time while surface characteristics do change, so that you remember being the same person many years ago, yesterday, and today. This view lends itself to the idea that we are not just vessels for utility, or neutral reasoning agents, but each individual is born with a unique set of gifts and aptitudes which may be applied to moral cases in distinctive ways.

Virtue theorists are less concerned with individual cases and choices than with what it is to be a good person, someone who maintains a moral compass based on solid values. They would say that judging any action in isolation will miss the point, as we ought to be looking at the person's whole life, all things considered. Contrary to deontologists and utilitarians who might say that any person in a given situation will be able to reason to the same conclusion, virtue theorists acknowledge that moral decisions emerge from a purpose-driven life and not just from following moral rules and precepts.

ARISTOTLE

Aristotle's view is that there are three elements in all our ethical decisions. First, the moral agent must have knowledge and awareness; second, there must be a choice involved; and third, as he says "action must proceed from a *firm and unchangeable character*."[6]

To understand his ethical approach it is useful to start by discussing some of his terminology. The first is **telos**, and the derivative term **teleology**. The telos of a thing is its end, purpose, or destiny. The telos of a knife, for example, is that it cuts, and consequently a good knife cuts well. Similarly, the telos of a hunting dog is that it finds his prey, and we can

---

[6]Aristotle, *Nichomachean Ethics*, Book II, Chapter 4. Public Domain.

again distinguish between better and worse hunters by how well they perform their function. Teleology is the doctrine that things have a purpose, and we can discern it by examining their nature. Importantly we should note that things, especially living things, have the innate potential to fulfill their telos: An acorn has the potential to become an oak tree, for instance, or a dog could be trained to bring out its capabilities.

While it is fairly straightforward to say what makes a good knife or clock, it is more difficult to say what makes a good human life. As a rough first stab, we might think that someone who has musical ability but chooses not to develop it misses out on her potential, and has a less fulfilling life than she might otherwise have, and the same logic might apply to a range of human aptitudes. In the case of playing a musical instrument, we can tell what makes a person better or worse in his or her performance, and Aristotle feels we can judge whether a person has truly lived up to his or her potential. Aristotle contends that the distinguishing feature that separates humans from the rest of the animal kingdom is the ability to reason. But it is not just being clever or wily; reason must be directed in a certain way that leads us to the most fulfilling life. Hence it is not enough for us to be alive: We ought to live as well as we possibly can given all the qualities we possess.

Aristotle claimed that the purpose of human life was to achieve **eudaimonia**. Translations vary, but it is usually thought of as *flourishing, happiness,* or *well-being.* In his terms, a person who fulfills his or her potential will achieve eudaimonia. There are two additional factors to consider: Aristotle's point of reference was the Greek city-state, a **polis**, a community created for the common good. Thus it isn't just the individual's happiness or well-being that matters, but their potential for benefitting the community as a whole. Second, eudaimonia isn't a static state, such as contentment; rather, we need to actively strive for it through a continuing motivational dynamic, which he refers to as **energeia**.

The way we work out how to have a life that entails eudaimonia is to manage our **virtues**. We have to be careful to distinguish what Aristotle means by virtues from our more common understanding. In everyday language we tend to think of virtues as positive, so anytime we say someone is virtuous we are automatically praising him or her. Aristotle has a more tempered view. Virtues, or **arête**, are character traits, and we all have them in differing degrees. For instance, people may be more or less courageous, generous, compassionate, or modest. Yet in any given situation, it is not enough to have those traits, as the most important issue is to work out how to apply the virtues we have *correctly*.

For instance, rushing into a burning building to save a pet is certainly heroic, but professional firefighters assess the situation so that they don't take unnecessary risks for themselves or put others in jeopardy. Similarly, it is normally fine to trust someone, but Aristotle notes that we can be too trusting, and turn out to be gullible when the other party isn't acting in good faith, and so trust isn't always good. The same can be said of the other virtues, so in the case of, say, candor, it should be used judiciously. There are times when we are too diplomatic and not straightforward enough, but there are other circumstances where we might want to soften what we say. It is a matter of knowing what virtue is appropriate at the time and in a particular context, and then applying it well. Thus it makes sense to treat Aristotelian virtues as having degrees and the moral agent as knowing the best way to deal with events by applying them intelligently.

For Aristotle, then, the operation of the virtues is not so much an on/off switch, but more a way of navigating between extremes, so we are suitably courageous without being rash or timid, or friendly without being too cloying or too distant. Our job is to find the mean, or the midpoint between extremes, to make an appropriate balance in any given case. As an example, we can imagine that although it may be misguided to always lose your temper when frustrated, there are times when getting angry with someone is the right thing to do: It just has to be done selectively, insofar as we need to make sure that our anger is directed at the right person at the right time and for the right reasons. Aristotle tells us that having a virtue is not just a means to an end: It also involves knowing when the virtue would be appropriate and having the right intentions, emotions, and attitudes. Aristotle's view is that these are all judgment calls, and there will never be a standard or uniform response where one size fits all: We have to assess how much of a virtue is proper all things considered, and here we can contrast his view to philosophers who try to abstract moral judgments from their particular context.

Aristotle suggests there are two kinds of virtues: **virtue of thought** and **virtue of character**. Virtue of thought is also known as **intellectual virtue**, and character virtue is sometimes called **practical virtue**. We can teach intellectual virtue from a book, but he felt that it also has to be routinely enacted. A student may study ethical theory and understand that stealing is wrong from an intellectual standpoint. However, Aristotle felt that we have to experience doing right and avoiding wrong in everyday life and acquire good habits. Moral education would thus also consist of something like service learning, or at least having the student confront significant temptations in order to recognize and deal with ethical dilemmas in very practical terms, and so internalize the temperament to do good. In fact the Greek word for habit, **ethos**, is the root of our English word **ethics**.

Consider the case of the computer hacker: There is no doubt that he is very smart, but we might think his intelligence is misguided. Hence he has the intellectual capacity required to be a good person, but lacks the wisdom to apply it practically. In contrast, a truly good person has the rational ability to know what is good, *intellectual virtue*, combined with a habit of being disposed to doing it, the *practical virtue*.

Consequently Aristotle's version of virtue theory tells us that we learn how to be good in at least two ways: We are first exposed to the actions of those esteemed within the community to be taught what is right, and then we have to practice good deeds. Being good is a skill, like sculpting, that requires instruction and practice. Just as sculptors, football players, or musicians need practice to be good at their skill, those who want to be good must practice the art of being good. So it isn't enough just to learn what doing good is—Aristotle believes that is trying to learn a musical instrument from a book—we have to constantly exercise to improve ourselves and learn from our experiences and from people we respect. The theory also has a sense of moral development: Following the boy scout model, we encourage good deeds, which then become routine, and eventually we internalize the dynamic so it becomes a natural part of who we are. However, the disposition to act correctly isn't just a blind habit, since it involves conscious decisions. One apt analogy would be to eating healthily—we know it is good for us and will enhance our lives, but it requires constant vigilance and effort.

Aristotle contends that we forge our characters only through experience and recognizing the moral choices we face. We have heroes and saints that we can try to be like, but ultimately crafting our character comes through familiarity with ethical dilemmas. If we have never been in danger, it is difficult to imagine what it is like to be courageous or timid, and if we have never faced temptation, it would be hard to project what a moral decision would be like just from abstract theory. Aristotle thinks that there is benefit in exposing children to morally complex situations from a young age, since repeated testing will bring out their strengths and deficiencies, and allow them to develop the habit of doing right.

The Greeks looked to mythology and their history to provide models for their behavior: Heroic deeds of great figures gave the community a sense of how they would ideally want people to act. In much the same way, we have some figures—sometimes people such as Martin Luther

King or Mother Teresa, or sometimes our parents—about whom we say "that is someone I want to be like." For example, Booker T. Washington found a role model in General Armstrong, and emulated the man and the values he stood for.

For Aristotle, the moral choices we face can't have standard answers: The individual has to work out what a person of good character would do when faced with choices in terms of a wider context. Moreover, we find ourselves in different roles in life with diverse demands: Some of the roles are involuntary, such as sibling or child, whereas others are chosen, such as neighbor or employee. Each role may have a different set of appropriate virtues: For instance, obedience may be a good quality in a marine or a nun, but not matter at all among siblings. Similarly, empathy may be appropriate for a nurse, but less appropriate for a farmer. This means unwavering loyalty, for example, is not always appropriate, and has to be judged both at the level of the immediate situation and within the larger framework. A doctor, for example, might be tempted to reveal something told in confidence to the patient's immediate family, but has to consider his or her action not only in terms of the immediate action but also in terms of his or her role in promoting the common good overall.

In another example of someone facing a moral dilemma, an accountant working in-house for a company comes to know that the company is planning to close the plant and relocate its operations to Mexico. If he shares the information with the public, he may warn other employees and allow them to make alternate plans, and the negative publicity might persuade the company to stay. Consequently, he would almost certainly be found out and fired. How should the virtue theorist proceed? One way to make the decision might be to assess the benefits and harms that would likely result, and do whatever is best for everyone affected. Alternatively, he could ask himself what would happen if everyone in his position were to act similarly.

Yet for the virtue theorists, these sorts of calculations fall short, in that they are focused on the individual act, without much regard for the fundamental character of the person faced with the decision. So the accountant may feel that one of his core values is loyalty, and he would be betraying his employer's trust to reveal confidential information. He might navigate between feeling the pull of discretion on one side and candor on the other. Importantly, though, when he makes his decision it will not be independent of his personal discernment of the situation or isolated from his previous personal and professional experience that combined provide him with a kind of sensitive managerial judgment Aristotle calls **phronesis**. Ultimately he may justify his decision on the basis that he "wants to be able to look himself in the mirror in the morning," a phrase reflecting the virtue-theorist's position that is more concerned with his self-worth and moral consistency than following any particular rule.

ALASDAIR MACINTYRE AND "AFTER VIRTUE"

The Enlightenment was a period in Western history, beginning in the mid-1600s, when thinkers such as Isaac Newton (1643–1727) promoted human reason and the scientific method as a means to improve human welfare. Enlightenment philosophers embraced a renewed emphasis on reason instead of faith, and applied it to ethical thinking. Whereas Aristotle had taken reason to be a means to develop our character by balancing the use of virtues judiciously, these philosophers felt that use of the scientific method could develop rules of moral conduct. For instance, the philosopher Immanuel Kant (1724–1804) thought that we could test our moral intuitions through a method that asks whether our actions could either be generalized—for example, "should everyone be permitted to lie?"—or end up in a contradiction of the sort that if everyone lied, then the concept of truth would lose all meaning. Others such as John Stuart Mill (1806–1873) believed that we could create rules for our behavior based on the principle of examining the results to see what would create the greatest happiness for the greatest number. The significant advantage of these kinds of theories is the promise they held for having a standard of behavior that was independent of any particular person, and could be applied in different times and places. Virtue theory was regarded as inevitably tied to limited roles within given cultural contexts, so that what applied to an ancient Greek male living in a city-state could not easily pertain to contemporary times.

Virtue ethics has made a rebound in recent years. The critical insight that has brought that about has been to acknowledge that all moral theory is unavoidably caught up in its own times. If we accept that point, then we don't have to graft Aristotle's particular virtues drawn from an ancient Greek city-state into our personal experience, and instead the ethical project becomes one of working out the best lives we can lead in our current society.

The Scottish philosopher Alasdair MacIntyre (1929–), drawing on earlier work by the English moral philosopher Elizabeth Anscombe (1919–2001), turns the tables on principle-based ethical theories by readily admitting that they are embedded in a historical and cultural context, while at the same time denying that there is anything pernicious about that fact: It is just the way things are. He feels that other theories have been misguided in trying to formulate universal rules, without regard to the society and the trajectory of our personal lives. He claims that we inevitably live in a moral tradition that turns out to be the means we have of making sense of our lives. We do this, he claims, by engaging in practices that enable us to develop our virtues in the here and now.

MacIntyre draws an analogy with science, which we usually think of as a unitary and progressive endeavor. However, science is very much a social construction that emerges from societies that have a stake in the outcome of the research, whether it is for improved social welfare, military success, or the promotion of commerce. The point is that it would be wrong to think of scientific efforts without some understanding of the political and social conditions that encouraged them. Moreover, the most important feature of science may not be how we view ultimate reality, but how successful our theories are in practice. If a society that believes that various personal energies and auras need to be balanced in order to have a happy life, but is ignorant of the nature of atoms, that might be a perfectly reasonable way to live. In short, he maintains that science operates for a purpose, ultimately to improve human welfare, and it is structured and rewarded accordingly.

The same might be true of ethics; the lack of a definitive answer to the nature of ethical truth doesn't necessarily imply that the moral project is flawed; given our collective experience and knowledge, we try to work out things as best we can, while at the same time recognizing that we are limited because we can view things only from the perspective of our own culture and traditions. It follows, MacIntyre says, that moral claims always have to be provisional, since we can't rule out the future possibility of our present beliefs and judgments being inadequate in a variety of ways.[7]

MacIntyre suggests that philosophy became derailed by searching for universal and impartial principles where we distance ourselves from our particular situation. In reality, he says, we humans define ourselves by our multiple relationships: "I confront the world as a member of this family, this household, this clan, this tribe, this city, this nation, this kingdom. There is no 'I' apart from these..."[8] MacIntyre considers that we can frame our

---

[7] Alasdair MacIntyre, 1989. *Whose Justice? Which Rationality?* University of Notre Dame Press, p. 361.

[8] Alasdair MacIntyre, 1981. *After Virtue, A Study in Moral Theory.* South Bend, IN: University of Notre Dame Press, p. 172.

personal stories in terms of our personal experiences, societal institutions, and what he terms *practices*. The practices are where we hone our virtues, and we realize our best potential in a life well lived.

MacIntyre's basic idea is that society creates various institutions that foster such practices. For example, a hospital is an institution that practices medicine; a university is an institution that practices scholarship. Within each practice, specialized forms of behavior are promoted—perhaps the development of diagnostic skills or research skills that indicate excellence in the field. External rewards, such as pay and status, that reward practitioners are not unique to the practice as they can come from other activities. At the same time internal rewards come from conscientious engagement in the practice—perhaps satisfaction from a patient recovering due to the doctor's intervention, or fulfillment for the instructor when students master a particularly tricky passage or problem set. Hence, as MacIntyre sees it, external rewards can come from a variety of experiences, but someone could not be part of a practice without being motivated by the internal goods. As a commonplace example, we can bribe children to take music lessons, but that tactic will be successful only up to a point, and true mastery requires the individual to internalize the challenge and become self-motivated absent other incentives.

MacIntyre's view is that as long as a society has a set of rational standards, then it will develop an internal critique that will, in time, overturn misguided notions. Drawing on the parallel with science again, he would say that the scientific community establishes standards among themselves of what constitutes legitimate, as opposed to bogus, science. So, for instance, a set of findings will have to withstand a critical test, and other parties ought to be able to replicate the results. The same sort of thing would ideally occur in ethics, where there would be sufficient internal discussion about the justification for the state of affairs so that we would move toward ever more refined ideas about what the ideal setup would be for society and the overall good. Thus for MacIntyre, the debates Booker T. Washington faced about whether emancipation should come about through accommodation or confrontation would be healthy challenges to the accepted norms, and he believes that we are rational enough to discern the merits of each argument and accept the better one. The key, of course, is that we agree to rational terms and allow ourselves to be persuaded.

This schema allows MacIntyre to argue that we develop virtues—in his rendering, excellences—within practices. One hallmark of practices is that the individual enters the field and accepts the standards of those already involved, independent of the external rewards. The link from the individual to the practice and institution lets us make sense of our lives, since we can locate our actions in terms of a tradition, whether it is education, farming, science, or the arts. MacIntyre concludes that there still has to be a telos, a sense of destiny or completion, and he characterizes it as an overarching virtue in one's own life, which he calls **integrity** or **constancy**.

What emerges, then, is an Aristotelian virtue theory, but it very explicitly shows that we don't just have a set of excellences without context. They come about when human nature interacts with the set of circumstances in which we find ourselves, whether it is a Greek city-state, America after the Civil War, or our current lives. This means we always have to examine moral claims by reference to a continuing cultural tradition and the standards of rationality it sets. This doesn't imply that we can't judge the Mongol hoards, for example, as wrong when they raped and pillaged in search of conquest, but rather that when we do judge them we must remember that we can only do so from our particular vantage point and not some fictional perspective outside time and context.

CHALLENGES

There is something very appealing about looking to character as an ethical bedrock. It seems to offer a strong basis for a moral life, and it is hard to argue with exhortations to be courageous, honest, friendly, or merciful. Yet, as is often the case, the issues surface when we try to articulate the details of the theory.

First, which virtues count, and do they all count equally? Recall that the virtues espoused by Booker T. Washington included thrift and industry. These terms may seem neutral and harmless, but have sometimes been interpreted as sending a message that blacks should be passive and not adopt attitudes that might pose a threat to the dominant white culture.

The point here is that we don't all agree on what is virtuous, and rather than being some objective standard, it appears to be socially constructed; that is, good is what society deems to be good. This, after all, is what Aristotle saw as the common good, and a necessary part of an ethical life. One ready implication is that those who succeed will do so by following convention and acting in socially acceptable ways. Hence in ancient Sparta, the appropriate virtues were war-like, at least for the men, but differed according to the society one happened to be born into. Following convention need not be a big concern as long as those conventions are, indeed, well founded. On the other hand, we could imagine that if we had lived in the southern states in a time before the American Civil War, the powerful members of society would have endorsed slavery, and there would have been little incentive for them to question their beliefs.

Thus virtue ethics seems to lack an external criterion for self-criticism: If we take virtuous action to be what our elders and paragons do, then it is likely to be self-perpetuating. For example, generations of colonizing Europeans forced native peoples to follow their ways, believing that they were uplifting and civilizing them. We find this in works such as Rudyard Kipling's poem "The White Man's Burden" (1899),[9] which at the time seemed to portray an obligation to enhance the lives of "half devil and half child" peoples, whereas today it represents a patronizing and racist view.

Booker T. Washington was not immune to this line of criticism. Several of his contemporaries, including W. E. B. Du Bois, attacked him for advocating a stance of gradualism, calling him "The Great Accommodator" and labelling Washington's address at the 1895 Atlanta exhibition that accepted the current disparities and worked for the benefit of future generations the "Atlanta Compromise." That is, Washington felt that blacks who demonstrated civic virtues would eventually be recognized and given equal status in society, whereas Du Bois believed that they should be more confrontational and demand equal rights immediately. The rift illustrates the issue with a virtue theory approach in that unless there is some external standard, then virtue appears to be a social construction that favors the status quo.

A related problem is that people might be virtuous in many ways but evil in others. For example, Martin Bormann, Hitler's private secretary and one of the architects of the Holocaust that killed over six million people during the Second World War, was a kind and doting father, a good family man, hard working, diligent, and fiercely loyal, but unfortunately to a horrendously warped cause.[10]

In short, critics contend that the theory can become relativistic because it lacks a basis in principles, rules, or rights. A virtue theorist could respond by turning the table on the critic,

---

[9]Rudyard Kipling, 1899. "The White Man's Burden." *McClure's Magazine*, 12, February.

[10]D. Sanai, February 1, 1999. "The Sins of My Father." *The Independent* (UK). Available at http://www.independent
.co.uk/arts-entertainment/the-sins-of-my-father-1068013.html, accessed May 21, 2010.

pointing out that notions of good character, which are formed from our primal relationships, are foundational. The starting point for the virtue theorist is to conceive of what the best purpose-driven life we can think of would be like, and only subsequently formulate communal rules that would allow it to come about. Thus the individual and common good are integrated at the outset. Principles and rules, under this view, emerge only after we have the vision of the best possible society. Similarly, we would be mistaken, from this perspective, to mix up morality and law, since the language of rights and obligations is legal and can come only after we have established what it is to be moral.[11]

Still, this leaves the problem of the misguided person, or even the evil one who exhibits otherwise virtuous behavior. The contemporary philosopher Rosalind Hursthouse (1943–) has suggested that this attack is based on a fundamental misunderstanding of virtue ethics.[12] She says that when we consider the virtues, they aren't culturally relative; courage, honesty, or trustworthiness are universally acknowledged to be desirable traits, although how they are manifest within societies may alter according to their particular circumstances.

Moreover, if we use the language of virtue and vice, there are never times when society promotes behavior such as laziness, vindictiveness, or arrogance. She says this shows us that there are actually rules already embedded in the language of virtues. It also means that someone who displays any of the vices is not fully virtuous. When we combine these claims, we find that virtue theory actually has action-guiding principles at its core. Furthermore, it means that someone like the loyal Nazi isn't really virtuous: While he may exhibit some good qualities, the fact that he uncritically practices vices such as brutality or indifference shows us that he is not a moral character—as he would see if he took the time to reflect on his own actions.

Hursthouse's analysis may not resolve the dispute between Washington and Du Bois, however. There it seems that two people of goodwill and experience have reached opposing views about the best course of action. Is this sort of impasse a damning criticism of virtue theory? Proponents would argue that it does not, for at least two reasons. First, reaching a moral impasse is not unique to virtue theory: Certainly other moral theories provide good rationales for positions, but often fail to reach a single conclusion that all their adherents would agree to. So, for example, animal rights activists may agree that unnecessary suffering is bad, but then differ on what to do about suffering of animals in the wild or as laboratory specimens. Secondly, we may agree that people ought to be treated with dignity and respect at the end of life, but differ on the appropriate acts that will bring them about. Thus the virtue theorist may say that a person of good character, of experience, and with practical wisdom just has to make the best assessment of a situation and act accordingly, leaving the final judgment to history.

Even if Washington T. Booker may have been mistaken in advocating gradualism, we can't say that his view was out of character, or was not done to further his vision of the best society possible. Moreover, it remains an open question as to whether a different tactic would have worked better. Similarly, the Reverend Martin Luther King promoted nonviolence rather than confrontation in his struggle for racial equality, and the question is whether his strategy was the best available and stood most chance of success. But, of course, this echoes our everyday moral dilemmas, too. We are always working from a position of information paucity, and thus we do the best we can based on our character, judgment, and experience.

---

[11]See, G. E. M. Anscombe,"Modern Moral Philosophy," available at http://www.philosophy.uncc.edu/mleldrid/cmt/mmp.html, accessed May 5, 2013.

[12]R. Hursthouse, 1999. *On Virtue Ethics*. Oxford: Oxford University Press.

Let's take the case where a society has enacted bad values: One solution might be to impose better values by coercion. Thus when the South was defeated in the American Civil War, the North imposed new norms and demanded that they were followed under penalty of law. The idea is that the new norms will become accepted and adopted over time so that they won't have to be legally enforced. While this is historically accurate to some degree, it is ethically troubling. For an example, just reverse the preceding case: If the South had won, slavery would not only have become legal but would also have been accepted as appropriate within a few generations. That is, we should not allow the idea that it is right to force people to adopt new standards just because they happen to coincide with our current ideas of right, since the system would likely work just as well if an immoral system were imposed instead.

Perhaps the case of a Confederate officer after the defeat of the South will help us to reflect on our own experience of what it takes to alter our perceptions. Rarely does change come about from rules being imposed from above. Rather, it is usually a mix of increased awareness and practical experience. Perhaps the officer never had the opportunity to deal with black people who were not slaves and might come to realize that they deserve full and equal treatment once he engaged with them on a much more personal level. Alternatively he might read some literature—for example, *Uncle Tom's Cabin* by Harriet Beecher Stowe was hugely influential in promoting the antislavery movement when it was published in 1852, just before the American Civil War—or he might encounter some philosophical or political works that change his views. In short, modifying our ethical positions is most likely a mix of internal influences, such as personal experience, and external influences, such as argument or persuasion.

The example shows us that some discussion of character and virtues is going to be a necessary component in ethical decisions. Traits such as integrity, courage, loyalty, empathy, guilt, shame, and remorse are unavoidable in talking about human actions, and how they make sense in the arc of our individual lives. By the same token, though, it appears that a full moral theory cannot rely on issues of character alone: There is also room for the language of rights, obligations, and social welfare.

One other issue not traditionally well addressed by virtue theory is worth mentioning. Because it is human-centered, it tends to ignore issues of other animals and the environment. These are ever more pressing in contemporary society, and ought to be discussed. As we have seen, virtue theory looks mainly at what it is to be a good person within the polis, or culture. Yet issues like global climate change and acid rain are worldwide in scope, and management will require international discourse. One advantage of the language of rule-based ethics is that it aspires to provide moral prescriptions that aren't bound by the context of a particular society or its prevailing norms by looking to an external independent standard such as rights or obligations. This is not to say that virtue theory is unable to address environmental and animal issues, but rather that the current discourse on the topics is largely dominated by other ethical approaches.

Summary

One of the critical elements in virtue theory is the demand that we address the question of what it is to live a good life. Perhaps this is an unrealistically difficult requirement, as many people struggle from one moment to the next without constructing an idea of what the overall arc of their lives should be, or what purpose drives them. Nevertheless, it is worth reflecting on what propels our routine actions—are we doing what society tells us is appropriate when we go to college or get married, or are they things that we have determined as conducive to being the best individuals we can possibly be? Certainly it requires us to repeatedly ask why we are doing what we do, but the payoff is that striving for personal flourishing given the talents we have will give structure and a unity of purpose to our actions, both big and small.

Virtue theory also stimulates questions about moral education. The ancient Greeks looked to mythological and historical characters, and felt that young people should look to their elders as exemplars. In contemporary society we have few role models who are universally lionized, and we are often encouraged to question the status quo. Celebrity often takes the place of heroism, and some of the hero figures we have are frequently shown to have flaws.

Booker T. Washington thought that education that provided both instruction and role models would result in responsible individual ambition. He created schools with strict codes of conduct, and thought that people would respond to inspiring role models in the way he did. Moreover, he thought that those with power in society would come to respect those who emulated their values. At the same time, however, there is a risk in uncritically assuming the prevailing conventions and morality: It may leave little room for reassessment of our values or progress. Thus it is still up for debate if Washington's approach would have led to full and equal rights.

The moral projects of rule-based and virtue-based moral theories are distinct. Instead of treating virtue theory as competing with, say, utilitarianism and deontology, the apparently competing approaches are perhaps best thought of as a gestalt cube such as the one below (Figure 8.1).

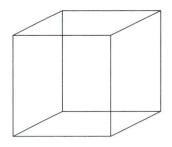

FIGURE 8.1

Some viewers will think that the front face of the cube is in the bottom left of the diagram, whereas others will see it as the square in the top right. It is a matter of perspective, and with practice we can switch from one to the other. Nevertheless, it is impossible to see both at the same time. Virtue theory presents us with a similar challenge, where we can see the ethical endeavor in a different way from rule-based theories. They all deal with how we ought to live our lives, and we can adopt one or the other, but not both at once. They both have a place in our moral thinking, but it would be a mistake to assert that one sort is superior to the other. A more appropriate view might be to think of them as useful for particular ends, so that the strength of rule-based theories is giving us ways to judge particular principles and actions, whereas the power of virtue theories is their ability to take a step back and look to the overall character in a purpose-driven life.

9

Rights and Justice

Human rights are entitlements or immunities that are used to justify and codify moral behavior. They often form the basis of legal systems and may protect people from unwarranted interference. Some believe we have rights by virtue of being human, and hence everyone is entitled to them unconditionally. Others see rights as a function of human society, because they are intimately connected with the legal system, which will differ from country to country depending on the nature and scope of its laws.

Talk about rights is a relatively recent historical development. In times when the king or lord could treat his subjects however he wanted, rights talk would not have made much sense. Famously in 1215 in England, however, disgruntled barons surrounded King John and forced him to sign the first rights charter, the *Magna Carta*, with the significant clause that people could not be imprisoned unlawfully, a right known as habeas corpus ("you have the body").

Rights talk became more common during the French and American revolutions, when individuals were attempting to justify rebelling against the tyranny of the state. For examples, look at the 1776 *Declaration of Independence*, the French Declaration of the Rights of Man, and the American *Bill of Rights*. The Declaration of Independence states, "All men are created equal" and endowed with "unalienable Rights," including life, liberty and the pursuit of happiness. A core set of rights are found in many different societies, such as immunity from unjustified imprisonment or punishment, slavery, or the maintenance of bodily integrity. Just after the Second World War, the United Nations issued its Universal Declaration of Human Rights, which lists further rights, including adequate nutrition, medical care, and equal rights for men and women, freedom to travel, housing, clothing, elementary education, and provisions for rest and leisure.

Classical ethical theories can support many fundamental rights: For instance, a deontologist, consequentialist, and virtue theorist could all give sound reasons for abolishing slavery. Accordingly, some suggest that there is no need to develop a special theory of rights apart from the ethical theories which are used to justify certain asserted rights. Nevertheless, it is useful to clarify the various ways we talk about rights.

The discussion of rights is best considered in association with the background concepts of **justice**. Paintings or statues frequently portray justice with a set of scales, and it is useful to imagine that the figure is balancing **rights** to restore justice, whether in the form of property rights, rights violated by negligence or crime, or simply rights to fair treatment. Philosophers have been wrestling with the concept of justice for two thousand years, since the time of Plato and Aristotle. Broadly speaking, the concept of justice is about establishing what is right and fair, then working out how to put it into practice.

Generally talk about justice comes into play when something is amiss and needs to be balanced or redressed, typically by a higher authority. For example, a parent may insist that a child who is hoarding toys share them with siblings, a court may impose fines or punishment on someone who has harmed others, or society may attempt to reallocate personal wealth through taxation. Thus the notion of justice is typically appealed to when there is dissatisfaction with the status quo, followed by some form of judgment about unfairness, and intervention designed to rectify the situation. For example, when we talk about people who have been harmed, the question becomes what will compensate them appropriately. Similarly, we frequently discuss justice in terms of allocating—or reallocating—societal resources.

CASE—E-WASTE IN CHINA

Guiyu is a small town in China's Guangdong Province—relatively close to the port of Hong Kong—where over one hundred truckloads of electronic components are disposed of every day, amounting to a million metric tons annually.

The electronics industry thrives on software upgrades and the limited life span of hardware products such as cell phones, computers, and monitors. Some estimates suggest that Americans trash more than 350,000 cell phones and 130,000 computers *every day*.[1] Many developed nations deal with the disposal of e-waste by collecting and shipping it to China for recycling. Although the Chinese government controls the transport of e-waste, a significant tonnage is smuggled past authorities and dumped in large piles at mainland sites.

These discarded electronic goods contain considerable amounts of precious metals and materials, which are difficult to retrieve. For example, copper wires are covered in plastic, and many other parts are soldered onto circuit boards. A cathode-ray computer monitor may contain up to three pounds of lead, and circuit boards contain small amounts of gold. Because retrieval is labor intensive and does not need much skill, component recycling is attractive to poor areas with a large population. Local people are paid to sift through the piles of electronics and scavenge valuable metals. The workers take the components home, dismantle them and then burn off the plastic and solder from wiring and circuit boards using small coal fires or baths of acid, while they hunch over them and pick them apart. This means those workers are breathing fumes and touching toxins, including PCBs and mercury, for most of the day. Typically, the pay for recycling work is less than 30 cents an hour, and no protective gear is provided by the metal brokers.

The chemicals used in the recycling process are leached into the groundwater, so that drinking water has to be carried in. Once the components are stripped, the leftover waste is buried in landfills or burned in the open, releasing smoke and chemicals into the air. Women in Guiyu are six times more likely to experience miscarriage than the general Chinese population. Breast-fed infants were found to have more than twenty-five times the World Health Organization's recommended levels of dioxins. Lead dust is thirty times more concentrated in the tiny workshops than in electronics recycling plants in India, and levels in the downtown

---

[1]Bryan Walsh, 2009, "E-Waste Not," *Time Magazine*, Available at http://www.time.com/time/magazine /article/0,9171,1870485,00.html Accessed May 29, 2013.

area are over 370 times higher than in surrounding towns. A study discovered that 82 percent of Guiyu children had enough lead in their bloodstream to put them at risk of neurological damage, including mental impairment and nerve problems.[2]

Do people have a right to well water that is not so acidic as to melt coins and to air that won't poison them? While it may be noble to offer people jobs, should these be jobs where they don't have to put their health and safety at risk in order to scrape a subsistence living? One way to assess such questions is to use the language of human rights and justice. When we talk about situations like these, it seems that traditional ethical principles saying we should maximize welfare or treat others the way we want to be treated fall short if only because they may be too abstract: We need the conceptual apparatus that allows us to claim people are entitled to clean water and clean air. Thus it is valuable to develop a philosophical framework that will help us sort out some of these issues.

RIGHTS

Rights are often invoked as a measure of the injustices in a particular case. For instance, e-waste provokes reactions that something is wrong and needs to be remedied. In the Western world in particular, the language of rights has been used to refine our concerns as we attempt to persuade others of the injustices involved.

In international affairs, countries often criticize one another on the basis of rights violations, since the language implies justification that goes beyond national or cultural boundaries. If the point of comparison is the humanity of those involved, not their nationality, it would be wrong to expose someone to harmful chemicals in America or anywhere else on the basis of a person's right to immunity from unwitting harm. Thus rights talk is hugely important when we discuss how we should be treated, especially in terms of threshold levels of personal liberty and overall justice. It is also immensely powerful in moral arguments as it can act like a *trump card* that ends the argument and forestalls any further discussion.

Although the power of rights language might seem appropriate at first glance, it isn't as obvious that rights will always trump other claims, or that they bar any future disagreement. After all, states have the right to enlist citizens into the military, demand that individuals are inoculated against some diseases, or require medical tests for couples before marriage. Thus rights may not be as absolute or influential as they initially appear, since society often balances them against utilitarian considerations.

In the United States of America, when arresting someone, the police recite the **Miranda warning**—certain rights the individual can claim—before taking the person into custody. Part of the warning typically goes:

> You have the right to remain silent. Anything you say can and will be used against you in a court of law. You have the right to an attorney. If you cannot afford an attorney, one will be appointed to you. Do you understand these rights as they have been read to you?

Importantly, this warning involves two kinds of rights. The first is the right to remain silent. No one has to do anything; instead it is a protection, a cloak or shield against coerced

---

[2]"Lead Levels in Children Linked to Rise in E-Waste Profits," *China Daily*, 2011, Available at http://www.chinadaily .com.cn/cndy/2011-11/16/content_14101761.htm accessed May 29th 2013.

confessions. Second, the Miranda warning tells the person he or she is entitled to an attorney. This is not a shield but an entitlement, since it requires someone to take action to take advantage of the benefits. The first part of that warning, where nothing needs to be done, is called a **negative right**, whereas the second part that requires action is called a **positive right**.

Thus in discussions about, say, adequate health care or decent housing, some might take the starting point that people are entitled to them, whereas others might focus on not allowing the government or some other entity to take certain rights away unjustly.

In addition to distinguishing between positive and negative rights, philosophers often distinguish between human rights and **privileges**. A human right, sometimes referred to as a **fundamental right**, a **natural right**, or a **basic right**, says that we have certain rights by virtue of being born. Potential lists of basic rights often consist of the dignity and worth of the individual: life, liberty, the pursuit of happiness, ownership of property, self-determination, freedom of religion, free speech, privacy, and freedom of conscience. Advocates assert these rights will be both absolute and universal: We are entitled to them without having to make demands, and they apply equally to everyone on the planet. The right to free speech, they would contend, is not governed by authorities that may choose to grant or deny a license. It is an entitlement, and asserts immunity from outside interference. Using our terminology, then, it is a negative right—as no one has to take action to enforce it—and a fundamental right.

In contrast, a *privilege* is a granted right. Some claim that certain rights emerge only from a system of laws, so unless the right is granted by the state, it doesn't exist. In most countries, for example, the right to drive is conditional. Aspiring drivers have to take a test and get licensed before they are allowed to drive legally. In certain cases, such as drunk driving, the government may revoke the right. People thus do not have a natural entitlement to drive. Thus the "right to drive" is a privilege that emerges within the context of a specific legal system.

The idea that we have natural rights apart from a social structure that endows them has struck many scholars as plainly mistaken. The English philosopher Jeremy Bentham (1748–1832) was particularly scathing about natural rights, declaring them to be "nonsense upon stilts."[3] Importantly, Bentham does not dismiss the idea of rights. As a lawyer by training, he felt they were a necessary part of ethical and political discourse. He believes that there are no automatic or necessary rights possessed by people, but they come through the workings of legal systems.

Consider again the case of the right to decent housing. Using the preceding framework, we can see how it will mean different things to different people. Some will think of decent housing as something that ought to be provided to people if they don't have it (a positive right), whereas others see the right much more in terms of something that we shouldn't be deprived of, at least without appropriate compensation (a negative right). Along the other axis of debate, some people will see decent housing as a right for all humans, whatever the circumstances they find themselves in (a basic right), while others will see the right deriving from the particular government that exists where people live (a privilege).

There may also be some question about whether decent housing is a right at all, or merely a worthy aspiration that is given more force if proponents label it as a right. That is, few people would dispute everyone's desire to having a roof over his or her head, but if we call decent housing a right, it assumes a lot more rhetorical power than if we say it is a goal that would improve society. Once it is considered a positive right, those without housing can then assert it as an

[3]Jeremy Bentham, 1843. *Anarchical Fallacies*, The Works of Jeremy Bentham, vol. .2, ed. J. Bowring. Edinburg: William Tait.

entitlement and demand that action be taken. Thus we should be aware that people who use the language of rights may start with very different conceptual assumptions which will significantly shape subsequent debate.

Wholesale denial of the possibility of fundamental or natural rights, in the way that Bentham does, leads to a difficult position when it comes to cross-cultural assessments. Many rights strike us as not a mere benefit granted by our society, but ones that should apply to people across borders. Thus the rights of employees to not have to work in conditions that jeopardize their health or safety without their knowledge—such as handling asbestos without protective gear—appear to be rights that apply universally.

The issues at stake can literally be issues of life and death, so these distinctions are highly significant. For example, one right often discussed is freedom of association, which may include the right to form unions. However, in many parts of the world, unionization is discouraged, to the point of violent, sometimes lethal, suppression of strikes. Hence it matters a lot whether forming unions is a fundamental right, which everyone, anywhere and at any time, is entitled to. If it is, then the activity ought to be tolerated and protected. On the other hand, if it is a function of a particular society, then our posture to the way a given government handles fledgling unions becomes a matter of societal judgment, rather than a rights abuse that warrants action.

Some cultures view the right to bear children as fundamental. Other societies might believe that people, especially young people, may not be able to accurately judge what is in their own best interest, and therefore the state should interfere with their personal liberty, perhaps by mandatory birth control. When we consider the burdens that child rearing imposes on both the parents and society in general, it is interesting that the state does not have a greater say in our personal lives. In this instance, traditional rights are held to be more precious than social utility. However, the reverse case is also true, as in China's "one child" policy introduced in 1979; it strongly encouraged a decline in population on the grounds that this would benefit the common good.

A functional middle ground might be to accept that a few basic human rights do exist, while saying that most turn out to be privileges that can be rescinded. Moreover, as contemporary philosopher Tom Donaldson (1945–) suggests along these lines, fulfilling some rights is dependent on the nature of the society. If drug lords run a country, it would be naïve to demand free secondary education: The society has to be secure and economically viable to be in a position to grant rights.

In given instances, society routinely takes away some rights. Felons or the mentally incompetent are not allowed to vote. Driver's licenses are revoked for acts such as drunk driving. Searches are conducted of private property when a warrant has been issued. These rights may be taken away by authorities, as in the case of licenses, where the right-grantor withdraws the right. This indicates that these are conditional rights, or privileges. Alternatively, a person may forfeit a right by virtue of his or her actions. For example, a patient is routinely given a guarantee of confidentiality by a doctor, but there are situations where what the patient says may end the right, for instance, if there are admissions of child abuse or neglect.

Further complicating the analysis, it is also clearly possible to have rights that are ignored or suppressed, whether rights are natural or legal privileges. A regime might torture suspects, or force them to recant their religious beliefs whatever the status of their rights. While it may be of little consolation to those who suffer, such abuse of rights may still be grounds for external criticism. Not surprisingly, if a government chooses to regulate free speech by censoring newspapers, the complaint that it is violating rights might be met with dismissive rebuttals by officials claiming that no such rights exist, demonstrated by the fact that they are able to censor at will. However, suppression by itself doesn't prove that the rights don't exist, only that they are often ignored. Similarly, a regime may ignore its own laws when it suits them, but that doesn't nullify the rights granted by the laws. Thus an administration may take to imprisoning political activists without trial, even if there are rights of habeas corpus in its constitution. The fact that a right is ignored, however, does not, by itself, mean the right doesn't exist.

We should also note that rights advocates fight for others who are able to demand their rights: for example, children and the mentally ill. Recently advocates have suggested that animals have rights—such as to not undergo unnecessary suffering, perhaps inflicted by research that could be done in other ways. For others, the environment itself can be thought of as a right holder, perhaps, in the sense that any interference needs to be justified before harms are allowed.

NONHUMAN RIGHTS

Rights are typically referred to as human rights. This brings out the question of what is so special about *humanity*. Are we, as humans, exclusively entitled to be treated in certain ways, for example, not to be enslaved? The author Desmond Stewart wrote a short story titled *The Limits of Trooghaft* in which he envisioned the earth being invaded by extraterrestrial beings called Troogs with intellectual and physical powers that enabled them to treat us the way we now treat animals.[4]

The puzzle the story poses is whether the Troogs should limit their behavior in their use of humans for sport, as pets, and hunting them for food. If we treat animals as we do by virtue of being on the top of the food chain and having power over them, then presumably the Trooghaftian answer is that there would be nothing to stop a superior species treating us as they wish: In effect, might makes rights.

Another line of argument asserts that there are rights involved—rights not to suffer unnecessarily, or be unnaturally caged, in short, to be treated *humanely*. However, can we then prove that there is indeed something special about humans that means we should be spared some of the bad treatment we deliberately inflict on animals? It could be our ability to reason, or communicate, or some other feature. Yet to counter the Troog challenge, we have to show not only that we can do these things, but also our abilities are sufficiently special and superior to warrant distinctive treatment, even though in the eyes of the Troogs we seem little more than monkeys do to us now.

Stewart's story is important because it confronts the circular reasoning we often use in rights arguments: That we have special rights because we are human, and our humanity entitles us to them. Stewart wants us to articulate what is distinctive about our species to grant us unique rights, above and beyond reiterating that we are human. If it is our reasoning power, then we perhaps ought to consider recognizing that any species with reasoning should have some rights. If it is our ability to communicate, then similarly we ought to acknowledge that all sentient beings with that quality should be granted rights, at least in some degree.

Alternatively, if we use some other criterion than our humanity, then to be consistent any correlative rights may not apply just to humans. For instance, if it is our rationality or the ability to communicate that entitles us to rights, then we ought to consider other species that exhibit those qualities. They may not have those qualities fully or to the same degree as we would, but it would perhaps mean that some primates, whales, and dolphins might be right-bearers. Peter

---

[4]D. Stewart, 1972. "The Limits of Trooghaft," *Encounter Magazine*, February. Available at http://www.animal-rights-library.com/texts-m/stewart01.htm, accessed July 18, 2013.

Singer (1946–) has claimed that rights arise out of sentience—the capacity to feel sensations, especially pain. As a utilitarian, he believes that we ought to minimize unnecessary pain wherever possible, and maintains that distinguishing by species (e.g., humans and apes) may be less important than the amount of suffering involved.

Let us summarize our discussion of rights so far:

First, rights either require action to be taken to benefit the right holder (positive rights or claim rights) or shield the right holder from outside interference (negative rights).

Second, rights can be thought of as automatically belonging to humans by virtue of their existence (natural rights), or emerging from a legal system (privileges or civil rights). The legal system will typically be based on basic principles of justice that are moral in nature, such as concepts of equal opportunities or merit.

Third, there is likely to be a hierarchy of rights, since some will depend on others, such as the right of a government to create laws, which will then allow it to create more rights.

Fourth, some rights may be taken away by legal means by forfeiture, for example, when someone violates the traffic rules and has his or her right to drive revoked.

Fifth, the fact that rights are not always recognized does not necessarily mean that they do not exist and should not be honored.

Sixth, rights claims may conflict. What if someone's right to free speech interferes with another's right to privacy? What if the right to subsidized health care clashes with a general right to keep what we each have earned? In these cases, we need to develop a conceptual framework that can arbitrate between rights—for example, deciding that rights to life matter more than rights to property. This leads us to look at the background principles described in theories of justice.

CHALLENGES TO RIGHTS

There are three main lines of criticism about philosophical rights. First, the **communitarian challenge** suggests that an emphasis on individual rights without correlative responsibilities, especially to a wider community, is misguided. Second, there are alternate perspectives presented by **East Asian philosophy**. Third, there are **pragmatic critiques**, which encourage us to give up the search for the exact nature of rights to concentrate instead on practical ways the words we use and the narratives we create can be employed to enhance human welfare.

Importantly, none of these groups dismiss rights talk completely. As we have seen, rights talk developed after the Enlightenment period, from about 1700 onwards. It emerged at the same time as philosophies that stressed the importance of the individual and personal choice, and clearly the concept of rights is linked to the idea that each person is the prime unit of moral consideration.

Communitarian approaches reevaluate where the focus of moral assessment ought to be, and want to shift the emphasis away from the individual and look more to the family or society in general. We have seen that the right to bear children is often held as a sacred individual choice, but we can imagine that holding personal life plans as paramount could harm the overall welfare of a community, for instance if the children become a burden on the state. The same might be said of care of the elderly, which is typically thought of as a binding obligation in many Eastern societies, where families take on this duty instead of letting it fall to community welfare programs.

Similarly, contemporary communitarians such as Amitai Etzioni (1929–) note that we ordinarily think about privacy as a principal individual right. However, there may be times where the community is under threat, say, from individuals who trade child pornography from their computers, or plan terrorist acts. When there is a sufficient threat, communitarians would argue the balance should change so that the welfare of society as a whole is taken into account and in some cases may matter more than individual rights.

The Western liberal view takes the individual to be in tension with the state, with negative rights that protect the private sphere from outside interference. However, some philosophers have pointed out that individuals are not the only ones in society who hold rights; rights are granted to corporations and institutions as well. Michael Walzer (1935–) thinks the theoretical split between state and individual sets up a false dichotomy. He believes that there are a number of spheres, including corporations, the Church, and the welfare state, and he contends the key issue is not so much about rights, as it is about *power*.

Hence Walzer contends that the proper function of the state is to balance the various institutions to equalize their power. From his perspective, it means that the military, corporations, or the Church should not dominate civic life, as they did in some periods in history. His insight is that while we may think of ourselves as autonomous individuals acting without outside influence, the truth is that we are always caught up in communities and institutions that effectively shape our lives and sway our decisions. Rights, in his view, are the mechanism the state should use to equalize the institutions that compete for power.

Thus Walzer contends most rights come about as a function of communities, and, in fact, many of the worst things humans encounter such as genocide and unnatural famines also reflect communities where power is out of balance. The basic human rights he argues for are quite minimal in the sense that they are only those required to have a decent life: Life, liberty, and subsistence, and only violations of these very basic rights will justify international intervention. Beyond those he feels each community will develop its own conception of the nature and scope of individual rights: Some states might stress welfare rights, whereas others will emphasize individual opportunity. We should recognize that Walzer is not casting off the vocabulary of rights entirely, but sees them in context of wider discussions about aggregate human welfare.

The difficulty that Walzer's work demonstrates is that if we take rights to just apply to individuals that we treat as independent atoms each working alone to further his or her own life plans, then we may disregard some of the sociological facts about humans and the way we organize our societies. If we take his wider perspective, then rights are still important, but as a force that works to equalize the various spheres of influence on our lives.

East Asian cultures, especially those from the Confucian tradition, have customarily stressed the welfare of the community over that of the individual. Daryl Koehn (1955–), a contemporary ethicist, points out that obligations do not get their ethical force from the fact that a rational person would make demands based on rights. Instead, it comes from the awareness on the part of individuals that their place in the web of human relationships requires them to act a certain way if they are to exhibit true-heartedness (**makoto**). Thus fulfilling an obligation without sincerity—so-called lip service—would not be ethically good. The downside of this approach is that it puts great power in the hands of judges and other officials with discretionary power. If a judge acts without *makoto*, then there is little structure or process to allow redress on the basis of infringed rights, as so much rests on the wisdom of the judge.

For example, consider the case of someone who has been accused of stealing a chicken. Tradition requires that the judge look beyond individual property rights, to find out the reasons the fowl was stolen and the impact it has on the larger community. Perhaps there was an earlier grievance, or the person was impoverished and desperate. The judge then takes the various interests into account, and looks to whatever will most benefit the community going forward: He or she could award a simple punishment, or encourage restorative activities such as apologies or labor in return. Given the emphasis on the wide perspective, it ought not to surprise us that Eastern cultures are somewhat baffled by complaints about human rights violations based on individual entitlements and protections without much reference to the overall context.

Clearly, there is still considerable debate over the nature and scope of rights. The language of rights tends to treat them as entities, that is, as things, which can be assembled, ranked, or traded in much the same way as any other resource such as personal wealth. Hence we are comfortable talking about exchanging a certain amount of personal liberty for convenience—for example, access to a social networking site. Yet this approach falls short when the individual is not the main locus of moral discussions. If rights aren't like personal property, then this model becomes confusing and won't be understood in ways that will help bring about change.

When we talk about sweatshop working conditions, for example, Western discourse often starts with the presumption of individual rights, rather than what is best for the family or community. That is not to say that workers are not entitled to fair and safe working conditions, only that we need to use language that is couched in concepts that are widely understood by the audience involved.

An alternative approach is to think of rights talk as not so much about entities, as if they are commodities that can be bought or exchanged, but as a means of framing a narrative. The philosopher Richard Rorty (1931–2007) suggested that pronouncements such as the U.S. Bill of Rights or the Helsinki Declaration of Human Rights are best regarded as bullet points; they stimulate a larger story that enables us to make sense of our world. This is a *pragmatic view*. Perhaps what matters is not so much the ultimate nature of rights, but whether the talk of rights is effective in making the world a better place.

Thus the questions should not be about the nature of rights themselves, but more about whether we can help frame the worldview of others by drawing on the language of rights. We may be misguided if we assume that rights exist in the same way as tables and chairs exist, and then demand that others accept our view. Rather, using a common framework to capture reasonable first assumptions will be one way of viewing the world. If it is effective, then we should certainly endorse the attempt.

Seeing rights in this way might be useful as it necessarily embeds them in a historical context. The voices of the Enlightenment raged against oppressive monarchies, and the language of rights gave them common cause. Bentham may have been correct in saying that there are no natural rights—like there are natural flora and fauna—but wrong in dismissing them outright, since rights language became a rallying cry for the repressed. Similarly the U.N. Declaration can be viewed as a reaction to the regimes that provoked the Second World War, and the language involved resonated with people who had suffered and fought for the cause of freedom.

Perhaps the best way to understand rights is to treat them as a dynamic and useful tool, helping us develop a common worldview that will lead to improved welfare overall. If so, we are actually asking the wrong question if we ponder whether the right to association is better described as a human right or privilege and if it is positive or negative. A better way would be to think of the language as fundamentally pragmatic. If we can frame the issues of unionization and worker welfare most effectively in terms of rights, perhaps it is more important to examine how people use this kind of language than to search for its exact meaning.

It also implies that we need to do more work than simply assert rights as if they are readily evident and discoverable entities. Instead, we have to see them as part of a worldview that we have adopted, one that we need to explain to other cultures. Thus rights as we see them are not always obvious but part and parcel of a Western cultural approach that values the individual. This is by no means wrong or mistaken, but we should recognize that it may not be universally accepted. If we are able to use such rights talk as a means of furthering a dialogue about the best way that people should be treated, all the better.

Talk about rights can be invaluable in facilitating arguments about justice and how to pursue it, but it does require that the participants find some common ground to agree on the nature and scope of the rights under discussion. Those who begin the discussion with a strong notion of rights often take them to be self-evident, universal, and absolute, believing that invoking them will have the effect of foreclosing any further argument. But we cannot assume that the people we address will automatically understand what we mean by rights. We need to be prepared to give some supplementary explanation of what those rights are, how they arise, and how they apply in a given situation.

JUSTICE

Societies are able to assert, allocate, or distribute rights, and a fair distribution of rights is regarded as just. Aristotle (384–322 BCE) discussed problems of justice in his *Nicomachean Ethics*, in which he asserted that equals should be treated equally. In his words the unfair distribution of goods *"is the very source of all the quarrelling and wrangling in the world."*[5]

Ensuring equality is not easily resolved. Some have had advantages that enable them to get on well in contemporary society, whereas others have faced considerable barriers to education and opportunity. Each person has different talents, intelligence, and emotional makeup. How should equality be defined, given such differences?

Even if we were to grant equality among persons, equal treatment is also hard to pin down—it could be treating all sides the same without favoritism, or taking no side at all. A parent who sends two fighting brothers to their rooms, for example, may be treating both identically but often the one who didn't start the squabble will feel the treatment was unfair. Thus philosophers have looked at both who should count as a right-holder and the process of allocating rights in society.

RETRIBUTIVE AND RESTORATIVE JUSTICE

In contemporary philosophical literature, the issue of justice has been divided into several areas of concern. In **retributive** justice we look at how to comfort the victim who has been harmed, or what punishment would be appropriate for the perpetrator. For example, in the ancient world the principle of "an eye for an eye" allowed an injured party to claim exact retribution in kind. In the relatively recent subdisciplines of **restorative** and **reparative** justice, practitioners attempt to find ways to restore relationships that allow people who have been harmed to heal and move on. Thus once South Africa relinquished the racist system of apartheid, a state-sponsored Truth and Reconciliation Commission set up systems of truth-telling and amnesty that provided a way for the country to start healing.

---

[5] Aristotle, *Nicomachean Ethics*, Book V ch 3.

To distinguish between retributive and restorative justice, imagine a person who has been robbed on the street. Retributive justice deals mainly with working out the appropriate punishment. An ancient principle would be "an eye for an eye" where the punishment mimics the crime, or now a days a prison sentence is considered appropriate. A traditional legal notion is that any victim of criminal or negligent harm needs to be "made whole again." This might mean that the victim is reimbursed for any losses, including monetary damages for pain and suffering. However, we can see immediately that in many cases being made whole may not be adequately dealt with through monetary damages: If a laptop is stolen, merely being compensated what it is worth doesn't make up for the feeling of threat and violation that goes along with being robbed.

On the other hand, restorative justice attempts to look beyond the immediate incident. For example, we should also be concerned about the mental welfare of the victims, who are perhaps left wondering whether they somehow invited the crime. Some forms of restorative justice attempt to have criminals and victims meet in a mediated setting so they fully understand the event and its repercussions.

DISTRIBUTIVE JUSTICE

The third major area of study in philosophical discussion of justice, and the one we will focus on, is **distributive justice**. Societies typically try to redistribute goods and services among their members for the common good. If we lived on some mythical South Seas islands and were content to eat the bounty of the land without any ambition for more, then there would be no competition for goods or services, and subsequently no feeling that some have the right to make claims on others. However, in the real world of limited resources, there are issues about how they should be used, allocated, or shared. When entitlement claims are made, they typically fall into one of three categories: **equity**, **equality**, and **need**.[6]

In an example, imagine that three people are hired by a homeowner to do some yard work. The homeowner might decide to pay them based on their individual contributions. One is naturally strong and does more work, one is average in performing the work, and one is weaker and hard working but nevertheless fails to do as much.

However merit is judged, the employer feels that he should pay more to the one who deserves it more; this is an equity-based system. Merit in this case might be judged by the amount of work accomplished. In an equal-opportunity process where we paid park workers by the amount of trash they collected during the day, the system tells us how they will be treated, but doesn't govern their individual pay, as they are rewarded according to their productivity. Alternatively, the homeowner may realize that he can't decide between the workers, and pay all of them the same amount, regardless of effort or what they did: Here equality is the governing principle. Finally, the employer could note that one of the workers is supporting an ailing parent and is the only one bringing in income, and decide to pay that person more: a need-based solution.

In contrast, another approach would look to *end states*, in so far as it aims for a given outcome, such as geographic diversity in an incoming college class, or making sure that everyone in a society takes home a minimum wage, which might override other considerations.

With these initial factors at play, we can look at two main theories of distributive justice, **libertarianism** and **egalitarianism**.

---

[6]M. Deutsch, 1975. "Equity, Equality and Need: What Determines Which Value Will Be Used as the Basis of Distributive Justice?" *Journal of Social Issues*, 31, 3, pp. 135–150.

LIBERTARIANISM

Libertarians see the foundation of their approach as maximizing personal liberty. This conforms to theories arising from John Locke (1632–1704) and John Stuart Mill (1806–1873), who would have used the term **liberal**, although that term has taken on different connotations since their time. The basic idea is that the individual is in the best position to know what is best for him or her and should be allowed to make choices without undue outside interference. In other words each person has to decide what is in his or her best interest, and the government should not interfere with personal decisions, especially in the redistribution of wealth or rights.

Libertarians believe in what is sometimes termed **pure justice**. It is *pure* as it sets up a system that provides open opportunities to all, and because of that, deduces that *any* resulting distribution will necessarily be fair. For instance, consider a lottery that is drawn at random: As long as the system is fair, no one can complain about the outcome. If a millionaire paid for a ticket and won, then we shouldn't object on the grounds that he doesn't need the prize or that others are somehow more deserving. In the same way, libertarians promote systems that they feel will give everyone a fair chance, and then any resulting inequalities will be acceptable, whether they are the result of hard work, applied intelligence, or even luck.

Hence in libertarian thinking, it will be unfair if a well-paid doctor is heavily taxed, especially if those taxes are directed to causes that he or she doesn't support. Supporters often make strong correlations to capitalism as an economic system that allows everyone to maximize his or her personal choices—and feel that taxation and regulations often hinder the smooth working of the market. If people wish to buy pet rocks or pay to go to monster truck pulls, it is a matter of personal choice. It would be wrong, according to libertarians, to interfere with individuals allocating their wealth as they wish. They would not want to see the money in the form of involuntary taxes being redirected, say, into subsidizing unprofitable enterprises such as ballet dancing or symphony orchestras.

Nozick

A contemporary libertarian advocate is Robert Nozick (1938–2002). In his book *Anarchy, State, and Utopia*, he promotes what he terms a *night watchman state* that only serves to defend the country, maintain order, and keep transactions honest and legal. All other functions would be left to individual discretion. Nozick gives the example of a popular basketball player who becomes rich because a very large number of individuals are willing to pay to see him on the court. Nozick believes that this is perfectly fair, and the state should not seize the player's earnings and redistribute them in ways it believes more beneficial, perhaps to programs for the poor, or in subsidies to farmers, because the player's worth can be determined exactly by seeing how much people were voluntarily willing to pay him.

If those same people wanted their money to go to other programs, according to Nozick's approach to libertarianism, then they would have put less of their money toward the player and more to alternate causes. He felt that taxation or other forced redistribution of resources is like the state compelling citizens to engage in forced labor, in that they have to work to earn money which is then taken from them against their will for causes they may not believe in or support. He is opposed to what he calls **patterning**, which occurs when a state justifies formulaic distributions based on some predetermined principle such as the communist notion of *from* each according to ability and *to* each according to their needs. He thinks that any attempt to insert values such as ability, need, intelligence, or merit is doomed to failure. Thus we should abandon any imposed redistribution system in favor of personal choice. Ideally for Nozick, the individual has control of his or her property, and can acquire, transfer, and dispose of it at will, without the state determining what is fair, and how much of his or her property should be given over to its control. Nozick boils down his claims to a simple sentence: "From each as they choose, to each as they are chosen."

Market Morality

In the views presented by Nozick we can see what might be called **market morality** at work. Nozick uses the free market to show what people prefer, witnessed by their purchasing decisions. Our real values, he would argue, are reflected in market choices where the consumer is sovereign. Despite our best rhetoric, if we say we care about a clean environment but drive a car that drips oil constantly, or claim to care about recycling but won't pay more for recycled or "green" goods, then our purchasing decisions act as an acid test of our true feelings. As a corollary, we shouldn't say things are unfair or unjust in the market—it just reflects our individual decisions accurately. If no one patronizes the art gallery, we shouldn't lament if it closes since we don't value high art.

This approach would also inform how we deal with issues such as the situation of those who could not be active in the market, for example, people with disabilities. In these cases, if we care about their plight, we would have the option to contribute to their welfare (as we couldn't rely on the state). This would be an imperfect duty, in Kantian terms, since we might have a duty to help out, but there would be no reciprocal sense of entitlement.

It would become an empirical question to observe if people were given a tax break equivalent to the amount spent on social services whether they would then voluntarily donate that amount to equivalent causes rather than, say, buying a new television. There is some evidence that when government services are reduced, individuals fail to make voluntary donations to bridge the spending gaps. Any subsequent suffering wouldn't necessarily be a problem for Nozick, though: It would simply point out that people have different values from the government, and if they choose to acquire material goods rather than donate to charity, ultimately they should be able to make that choice based on their personal preferences.

EGALITARIANISM

The egalitarian starts from a different place than the libertarian. The point of departure is that we all share in one another's fate, and so we have obligations to others. The talents and intelligence we have are not what we earned but they came to us through a genetic lottery. Thus it is great that someone is very bright and excels at math, but we shouldn't think of that as a personal achievement so much as a lucky draw. Conversely, someone who is not blessed with many marketable talents should not be punished for something that was beyond his or her control. Putting these two key insights together, an egalitarian thinks that personal achievements are not merely a function of our own making, and we cannot abdicate our duties to others.

Rawls

The chief proponent of egalitarianism in modern times has been John Rawls (1921–2002). In his major 1972 book, *A Theory of Justice*, Rawls asserts that we are better off through social cooperation than living alone by our own efforts. One of his key claims is that "no one should be advantaged or disadvantaged by natural fortune or social circumstance."

Rawls also feels that we need to avoid skewing our intuitions by favoring our own situation in life. He proposes an armchair exercise in which we know the facts of the world—for example, how many people are there, the proportion of people of color and those with disabilities—but nothing about our particular place in the world. Rawls claims that if we didn't know who we were, but could design society behind this "**veil of ignorance**" we would minimize our own risks by giving everyone the best possible opportunities, regardless their social standing, race, or whatever else might currently impair their fulfillment.

It is critical when reading Rawls to realize that he is *not* advocating social equality, but rather **equal opportunities** for all. Imagine, for instance, that a society has different quality elementary schools, generally correlated to the income level of the community. One-third are in affluent areas, and two-thirds are not. Additionally, let us suppose there is evidence that the nature of elementary education has a direct bearing on success in later life, both in school and beyond.

According to Rawls's *veil of ignorance* proposition, if people did not know ahead of time what their place in life would be and how well they could provide for their children, then it would seem reasonable that they would want to avoid the challenges that come about if they ended up in a poorer school district. Instead, they would strive to design a system where all the elementary schools were good (organizing school funding so that all were as good as the better ones in the current system). That way, it would not matter where people found themselves when the veil is lifted, because they are assured that all children will have an equal academic opportunity.

Rawls believes that his thought experiment will show that rational people will agree on two central principles. The first says everyone has an equal right to the most extensive liberty compatible with a similar liberty for others. Thus we all have an equal right to choose what we want, with the proviso that our liberty will be limited when it conflicts with what others want. The second principle says that social arrangements should be constructed so they are to everyone's advantage, and open to all. Again, we should emphasize this is *not* enforcing equality, but instead he wants to get rid of unequal opportunities that are often the result of accidents of birth. Rawls argues that society may rightfully redistribute what he refers to as **primary goods**, including rights, liberties, powers, opportunities, income, and wealth.

Consider a family that has inherited its wealth. Currently they are able to send their children to the best schools, provide tutoring, and assure them that they will be able to attend college without debts. They live in pleasant surroundings and do not worry much about the safety of the neighborhood. One parent, in this case the mother, chooses not to work, and spends her time looking after the children's needs. Their lives are enriched by art, music, and travel. Now by itself there is nothing very objectionable about this kind of life—these are things many of us would like and strive for. Yet we can see why Rawls might consider it appropriate to reallocate some of their wealth to the less fortunate by contrasting it to a nonnuclear family that is living from paycheck to paycheck working for low wages. The children may go to a school with fewer resources, and there is little disposable income to spend on enhancement activities.

Rawls would ask us to put ourselves in the place of the children in each case—did they do anything to deserve their lot in life, and consequently should we think it fair that they receive different treatment? It certainly seems that the wealthier children will have greater opportunities unless there is some sort of redress mechanism in place. Perhaps the wealthy are taxed, and those resources are used to enhance schooling in poor areas. Perhaps college admissions offices decide that a student who has overcome significant obstacles to achieve equal test scores to other more advantaged entrants may deserve admission and even financial aid.

Rawls explicitly endorses what he terms the **difference principle**. Under it, inequalities may arise after we implement equality of opportunity—perhaps some will take on more challenges or apply their natural talents more than others. He does not have a problem with such inequalities, as long as they benefit everyone, including the least advantaged, and make no one worse off. Perhaps it is necessary to give potential doctors greater educational resources and then pay them relatively more on graduation—but this would be justified on the grounds that everyone in society benefits from having qualified doctors. The difference principle would not necessarily preclude business executives from earning vast amounts, as long as it could be argued that everyone benefits from the enterprises that he or she runs and that paying them like that is the best way to operate a successful company.

CHALLENGES

In general terms libertarians advocate a **meritocracy** where people get what they deserve based on merit. Merit is initially an attractive basis for distinguishing rewards, but is a very difficult concept to grasp in practice: Market terminology may be useful, but as we have seen it does so by putting a price on everything. Notice, too, that the concept of merit will necessarily be considered within a certain societal context. For example, a doctor may be an excellent diagnostician, but have a poor bedside manner. An architect may have a refined aesthetic taste but ignore the traditional nature of the surrounding neighborhood in designing a new building. Additionally, consider some of the highest paid people; many of them are sports or television personalities. While they undoubtedly attract wide audiences and bring in advertising revenue, that may not be a true measure of their value to society.

Other kinds of assessment are no less problematic; it is hard to achieve a level of objectivity that is not tainted by social and cultural biases. For instance, in academic achievement, standardized test scores often have implicit prejudice. An analogy test that asks a student to match "yacht: regatta" with "pony: gymkhana" assumes that those being tested are familiar with sailing events and horse shows, and will penalize those who are not. In addition, many private tutoring institutions guarantee that their paid course will increase test scores, thus favoring those able to pay or willing to borrow the fees. Moreover, "objective" scores alone do not reflect effort; two students who get the same score on a test may come from very different situations, perhaps where one has worked her way through school while the other has benefitted from independent funding and greater leisure time.

Many libertarians believe that a free and open market best reflects societal values. At some point, though, it seems that the market will fail whenever it encounters the kinds of values it cannot deal with well: Perhaps looking after people incapable of looking after themselves is a matter of human rights and decency, and not just a matter of their value in contributing to the market. Additionally, there may be cases, such as selling one's kidneys, where we could imagine that there would be an active market, but one that disproportionately attracts the desperately poor who have no other assets.

Another issue is that we can't always rely on the simple matter of parties having agreed to contracts as a clear demonstration that justice has been served. To get a fully rounded picture, we have to think of the power structure involved. In the earlier case of the three people hired to do yard work, what if one of the workers is well-off and has just been told by his parents to do something during his vacation, whereas another is struggling to feed herself and her family? Obviously, the workers don't all have the same power in the deal. If the richer one could walk away from the job without any repercussions, he has much more bargaining leverage than some-one who desperately needs every penny. Similarly, in many parts of the world, the only options are often for workers to agree to certain marginal terms or starve. This strains the notion of voluntariness. Therefore when we talk about distributive justice, the particular situation and relationships will matter. Perhaps the state will decide to act as the agent of justice, for instance, by imposing a minimum wage to protect those without negotiating power from being exploited, but in a full analysis, the role and level of intervention of regulatory bodies also need to be taken into account.

Objections to the Rawlsian approach to justice tend to come in two forms: first to the nature of the principles he invokes and then claims about the impracticality of some of his sug-gestions. The doubts about his principles arise from the nature of the thought experiment and his views of human nature. How practical, for example, is it for us to bracket out our knowledge of our place in the world and put ourselves in a neutral space where we can develop abstract prin-ciples? He suggests, for instance, that we would all be rational and risk averse, since we would want to maximize our opportunities whoever we turned out to be. However, experience suggests that some people are more risk seeking and entrepreneurial, especially given financial and other incentives.

In the earlier example, we considered a family that had inherited its wealth. If we change that to one where the earners in the family get well paid because society has deemed them valu-able, and it is consequently acceptable under Rawls's difference principle for them to get a larger share for their work, it would be natural for the parents to spend some of that wealth to help their children. Yet such partiality and benefit seems to be precluded under his redistribution to ensure equal opportunity for the upcoming generation. If we extrapolate from the example, using the family wealth to support their children by providing more comfortable surroundings, travel, or extra-curricular activities could all be considered unfair advantages. Hence there are some really practical issues in implementing justified rewards and then limiting how they might be used.

Recall, too, that Rawls says that our talents arise out of happy accidents of birth. A person capable of becoming a medical doctor is blessed with intelligence and a good memory, say. Rawls suggests that even the capacity to work hard is a function of our genetic makeup, so that the effort we put into learning is a result of our DNA and the family circumstances we are born into, which the potential doctor can't take credit for and shouldn't therefore derive any benefit from. Rawls's view of psychology could be correct in that many people are motivated to apply them-selves without any extrinsic rewards. On the other hand, there are others who, faced with the choice of applying themselves or being lazy, prefer an easy life.

Rawls appears to minimize the role incentives factor into our decisions. In contrast, a libertarian would probably claim that we usually work because we are promised some remunera-tion in anticipation that we deserve to keep and do with it as we wish. For instance if someone chooses to not develop his singing talent, that seems to be an individual choice, not one dictated by genetics. On the other hand, if he were to become an acclaimed star, he might expect that the rewards society allows him to keep ought to reflect the energy, time, and effort put into years of study and practice.

Moreover, there are both conceptual and practical issues when it comes to redistribu-tion of the opportunities and goods in society: Who decides how much is appropriate and the means for allocation? Rawls says that he is only developing an abstract set of principles, not a policy blueprint. Nevertheless, we can see real issues that could arise from considerations of intergenerational fairness, for instance, or claims that people need **rectification** for historical discrimination. Imagine that a society has a group that has been marginalized in some way, such as blacks in America. Slavery and its aftermath has limited past generations' access to education and opportunity in such a way that it would be wrong to say that everyone now starts life on a level-playing field. How would we best achieve that? For Rawls, it seems, there needs to be a constant monitoring of society to ensure equal opportunities for everyone, and then constant readjustment to ensure fairness.

Nozick briefly mentions his own principle of *rectification*. This amounts to making our best guess of how things would have been had, say, blacks been fully emancipated after the Civil War, then readjusting things to the way they would have been without the injustice. It is hard to see how that would happen in practice, as we would have to have all claimants make a case for reparations based on hypothetical possible worlds that might have come about but for a set of unjust circumstances. Then it seems there would have to be a one-time payout that would make amends for the wrongs, after which no further claims would be allowed.

The difficulty in reconciling different approaches to justice, and the weighty policy considerations that ensue in terms of government spending, social and racial equality, distribution of health care and other resources, to name a few, have led some philosophers to declare the conflict intractable. Alasdair MacIntyre (1923–) argues that the debates are not rationally based, but function to further particular ideologies. He reasons that if it were simply a question of logic, then we could reach resolution, but when it comes to competing ideologies, there is little hope of reconciliation.

MacIntyre's view suggests that we lack a universal rationality, so we are bound to fail in seeking a unified set of concepts about justice. An alternative approach, however, would suggest that perhaps we could admit that there are competing notions of justice at work, but that they don't have to cohere completely. For instance, we might consider various approaches to be like gears on a bicycle: Some may be more appropriate in certain situations but not others. This would still demand discussion and argument, but retain the hope that we can reach broad consensus on many issues while allowing that there will never be universal agreement on all.

Summary

The case of e-waste in China may crystallize some of the difficult issues in rights and justice. In this situation, the Chinese government has regulations to protect the workers, although they are often unenforced. As we have seen, rights are often said to apply either to all humans across the world without regard to time or place or as a function of a legal system. No matter what the exact nature of rights, though, there seem to be certain threshold standards that most people agree should exist to allow people to lead minimally decent lives. Even if different cultures do not typically use the same conceptual language, the rights discussion serves to draw attention to ethical problems. For example, if we take the right to life as a negative right that provides immunity from outside interference, it follows that people should not have to put their lives in jeopardy involuntarily. In dealing with e-waste they should not be forced to work with toxic materials without access to protective clothing. The same principle might hold for the right to make a living, or the right to minimally clean air and water. Having said that, if we want to move beyond a very minimal core set of rights, proponents may have to provide additional explanations about the role of the individual with respect to the state in order to justify arguments for providing various protections and entitlements.

The philosophical issues have changed somewhat in the last fifty years, from bluntly asserting individual rights that society is then supposed to uphold, to using rights talk as shorthand or bullet points, a means to highlight the fact that something is ethically amiss and ought to be rectified. This opens the door to further debate about relative power balances within and between communities, the relationship of the individual to the state, and the rights and correlative responsibilities of all the involved stakeholders. Subsequently, discussions about rights are today less likely to be about their exact nature (positive/negative, basic/privilege), and more about how they can be used to point out injustices and show a way that they might be remedied.

The case also highlights some of the differences between the two versions of distributive justice: libertarian and egalitarian. For the libertarian view, we are entitled to what we earn or what we are given, and then we create value by making market exchanges. In contrast, the egalitarian looks to equality of opportunity that serves to improve overall welfare.

It appears the workers in Guangdong Province find the prospect of working to dismantle electronic goods more attractive than peasant farming, and to many their employment may simply be a matter of a market exchange of work for pay. Egalitarians, on the other hand, are more likely to say that the situation shows that the initial state of affairs is already unfair: If we followed Rawls's thought experiment and designed societal policies as if we had a random chance of being in their situation, then very few of us would likely accept the lack of education and advancement opportunities that those e-waste workers face. We would probably want to alter things so if we found ourselves in their shoes, there would be institutional structures in place that would provide the maximum liberty and prospects for everyone.

Discussions about rights and justice can appear complex and daunting. At the same time, people have literally put their lives on the line fighting against repression and injustice. The principles involved strike at the very heart of everything we do from international relations and creating social policy, to the way we deal with one another on a personal level. The child who loudly protests that "It isn't fair!" appeals to some of our most basic intuitions and demands things be put right, and demonstrates that from an early age we strongly believe in equal treatment and the redress of power imbalances. Consequently, it has become essential that when we bring these concepts into play we are fully aware of their meaning and broader implications.

Feminist Insights

Feminism is a collective term that covers a spectrum of philosophical, social, and political movements that are unified by asserting equality for women. Feminist insights can help us approach ethical theory in three broad ways. First, women have been marginalized and unempowered for much of history, and thus the scope of moral consideration ought to be widened to include women's insights, experiences, and issues. Second, it could be that men and women have equal but differing natures. Thus women may see the world more in terms of relationships and care than men generally do and so women's experience of, say, nurturing, ought to figure into any ethical theory just as much as a rational method that examines dilemmas and imposes general duties. Third, some philosophers argue that the systematic repression of women represents the politics of oppression in general. They suggest the undergirding social structures have been dominated by men with a gender bias which has systematically delegitimized certain kinds of response, whereas in fact there may be a real benefit in drawing on insights from both men and women. Feminists often claim that we all tend to accept norms relating to gender that are not natural or necessary, and perpetuating them may repress or harm all people.

The literature in this area distinguishes the concept of **gender** from **sex**. Sex refers to the biological features that distinguish men from women, whereas gender refers to the associations and ways of life that are socially learned or chosen. In this chapter we will consider two major approaches to the nature of gender, *equality* and *essentialism*, as well as a few of the major contemporary theories that have offered feminist insights and made important contributions to moral theory.

CASE—MARGARET HOSSACK

In 1900, John Hossack, a farmer from Iowa, was attacked while asleep at home. He suffered two massive blows to the head with an axe. After his death, Hossack was described as "a God fearing and church-going man" who had no real enemies. But after talking to his neighbors, the local paper soon exposed a different side. Hossack was characterized as violent and abusive, and neighbors said that his wife, Margaret, had often sought help from them when her husband was in one of his rages. Just after the graveside service, she was arrested for murder. The evidence from her neighbors about her fear of her husband served to solidify the case against her.

If we take Margaret's experiences as a morally relevant feature of the case, we see that she had been married for thirty-three years to a man who was physically and emotionally abusive. She was trapped for several reasons. She had no resources, as all the property belonged to her husband. Conventional wisdom at that time was that a woman's role was to love and support her family, no matter what. When it came to the trial, the fact that she had endured years of psychological, emotional, and even physical torment did not fit the all-male jury's picture of the world. From their perspective, John was an upright and respectable member of the community, and Margaret an unloving wife. She was quickly convicted of first-degree murder of her husband, and received a life sentence of hard labor.

One of the reporters of the case was a budding author, Susan Glaspell, who later used the case as the basis for her short story *A Jury of Her Peers*. In it, Glaspell shows women neighbors empathizing with the accused wife, Minnie. As in the Hossack case, the fictional husband is described as someone who was sober, kept his word, and paid his debts, whereas his wife Minnie is criticized as a poor housekeeper. The women are well aware that the men investigating the case will only look at the immediate facts, viewing any evidence of abuse only as a motive that informs them of Minnie's guilt. As a result, when the women discover vital evidence that might indict Minnie, they discretely hide it from the investigating sheriff.

We can see why the neighbors might feel that all the cards are stacked against women in general and Minnie in particular. Women at the beginning of the twentieth century generally lacked the legal and social power and influence that came with money and property. They lived in a world that discounted a woman's perspective as irrational, emotional, or sometimes uppity, and expected them to be compliant and subservient to the prevailing norms. It is not surprising, then, that the women aided Minnie, even though it seems she had committed a horrible deed and they became accessories after the fact.

The stories of the original crime and its fictional adaptation reveal two important interpretations of the case. First, some see it as an illustration of the need for enlightenment and liberation, noting that *if* the women had more power and an equal voice that would be heard and validated by the moral community, then they could make the authorities more aware of the true situation of oppression and abuse that existed, perhaps to the point of mitigating the killing. That is, one answer for the unempowered women would be to give them a full and equal place in any moral discussion.

The second point of view, especially in the fictional version, is that even given their marginalized status, the women had special insights and ways of knowing that were unavailable to the men. They are portrayed as considering incidents in terms of relationships, whereas the male perspective tended to view them as individual acts isolated from context. It isn't that the women hide the evidence because they don't understand the facts—the abused wife is obviously the killer. Instead, they realize that there is perhaps more to the story, and looking at the facts and rules without regard to any other information seems unfair or unjust.

To be clear, this is not to say that *all* men and *all* women reason in these ways, or that these various ways of reasoning are necessarily innate to the sexes, as they may well be products of our upbringing. Nevertheless, whatever its origin, diverse behavior exists based on gender. Research suggests that in playground games, boys take longer because they take time out to argue about the rules, whereas girls are keener to get on with the game. This might be evidence that women and men have distinct psychological hardwiring. Alternatively, it could be the case that women are socialized to place the priority of maintaining relationships over sticking to contractual obligations.

We can rephrase the overall question by considering whether the varying intuitions are a function of human nature or, alternatively, our upbringing. Perhaps we become socialized into different roles through various experiences that channel our reactions in a particular way, giving each gender special emphasis on certain insights and different priorities. So, for instance, some writers have suggested that the unique social practices of women—such as motherhood—have allowed them to develop a special set of values. Whatever the truth of the matter, the female emphasis on relationship-oriented morality seems consistent across cultures.

ESSENTIALISM AND EQUALITY

Ethical theory is often based on notions of human nature. For example, if we think that people are fundamentally self-interested, we will develop a different idea of right and wrong than if we believe that most people are generous and altruistic. **Essentialism** will acknowledge that women may have a distinct nature which may involve a more emotional and intuitive component. This view has been used to justify discrimination. However, while feminist-friendly essentialists accept that there are innate differences they deny that these qualities imply inferiority.

In contrast, an **equality** perspective would challenge the claim that there is any basic disparity in men's and women's natures and argue that any apparent dissimilarity is a function of the way women are socialized. Thus if we were able to avoid inculcating different values in boys and girls those believing in equality would suggest that there would be nothing to indicate that men and women would have differing values and ethical responses.

The essentialist/equality debate goes back a long time. The French philosopher Jean-Jacques Rousseau (1712–1778) claimed in his work *Emile* that boys and girls should get distinct kinds of education suited to their different talents and aptitudes. This view becomes antifeminist when pejorative social stigmas are attached to those traits considered "feminine," whereas those traits considered "masculine" are hailed and reverenced. Rousseau describes how a girl ought to be taught to do needlework, housekeeping, and music. He maintains that women are naturally submissive to men, even when treated injustly. On the other hand, he thinks boys would never tolerate injustice and would rebel against it anytime they found themselves in such a situation.

In response, Mary Wollstonecraft (1759–1797) took Rousseau to task in her 1792 book, *Vindication of the Rights of Woman*. She defends the inherent rationality of women, condemning men for promoting female graces and reinforcing a childlike dependence and sensitivity. From her perspective traits such as graciousness and emotionality are socially constructed forms of weakness that belittle and unempower women. Wollstonecraft takes reasoning to be a gender-neutral talent that both sexes are capable of doing well, and she rejects the idea that men are somehow automatically better at critical assessment. Her view that both genders have equal capabilities makes her a **gender egalitarian**.

Both essentialism and egalitarianism are broad categories, and the research of Carol Gilligan (1936–) has gone some way to clarify concepts of gendered moral thinking. Following her work on gender and ethics, many scholars accept that men and women may generally have divergent intuitions about moral issues, and take the real moral project to be working out how those views may be integrated or reconciled. In her 1982 book *In a Different Voice*, Gilligan suggests that *different* need not mean *lesser*: Women may think differently than men, but their insights may be complementary rather than less significant. That is, she ultimately defends a feminist-friendly essentialism, which emerged from work with her colleague Lawrence Kohlberg.

Kohlberg (1927–1987), a psychologist, studied moral development in children. In one experiment, he presented his research subjects, boys and girls, with a series of hypothetical moral dilemmas. In one case given to the children for consideration, an extremely ill woman needed a drug she couldn't afford. Her husband went to a pharmacist who refused to donate it or give him a discount. The subjects were asked to discuss how they felt about the possibility of the husband stealing the drug. Kohlberg then took the responses and assessed them based on the reasons the subjects gave according to a three-leveled moral development scale.

In what he called the *pre-moral level,* children would resolve the dilemma through considering threat of punishment and the pleasure associated with reward. In the second stage of *conventional role-conformity,* children would resolve the dilemma by obeying societal conventions and aligning their behavior to the appropriate moral authority. And in the final stage of moral maturity, *self-accepted moral principles,* children would demonstrate that the moral principles they rested their decision on were an integrated part of their moral perspective.

Typically females rated lower on Kohlberg's scales than males. This was sometimes taken to show that men have higher levels of moral reasoning than women. Carol Gilligan, who taught with Kohlberg, challenged the research, suggesting that it had a bias toward what she described as the "male voice." She pointed to her own findings that compared masculine and feminine ways of moral reasoning as evidence that Kohlberg had smuggled the assumption that male moral reasoning was superior into the moral development scale he used to evaluate children. It is important to emphasize that the differences Gilligan found were not exclusively along biological lines, and hence she is careful to talk about the "voice" her subjects used rather than just identifying them as male or female.

Gilligan's own research showed that in moral reasoning, broadly speaking, men looked to legalistic justifications, for example, what the rules were in any given case, and they tended to use language based on justice, respect, rights, and impartiality. Gilligan maintained that those with the "female voice" were very concerned about isolation and abandonment, which led to focus on interpersonal issues and the welfare of the community in their moral reasoning. Because of this, they were evaluated somewhat lower on Kohlberg's scale. Yet the female voice, Gilligan maintains, necessarily includes foundational values of care, trust, attentiveness, and love for others. In this way, we might reassess many of Kohlberg's female subjects as having demonstrated an integrated self-acceptance of what might be considered more feminine values, thereby meeting a similarly high and mature level of moral development, although it is manifested in a different way than the boys.

Thus we can add a third dimension to the traditional ways of approaching the apparent distinctions between men's and women's moral perceptions. We might believe the *equality* view, as Wollstonecraft did, that the issue comes down to the way that women are socialized. Alternatively, we could say that women's nature is essentially different, but less ethically discerning, because they are less inclined to be rational and distanced from the particulars of any situation, as Rousseau might claim. As noted, Rousseau's view is *antifeminist essentialism,* since it claims that women have a different nature or essence that is necessarily inferior to that of men, resulting in the suppression of women's perspectives. The third view, a *profeminist essentialist view,* emerges from Gilligan's work. While it might admit that those with the "female" voice may approach moral issues in a dissimilar way, the distinction itself does not imply lesser or wrong. It contends that such views are completely legitimate and just as applicable as traditional male ways of examining ethical questions.

THE ETHICS OF CARE

Gilligan's findings, coupled with work by philosophers such as Nel Noddings (1923–), have been an important contribution to moral philosophy, initiating a theory of ethics based on the notion of *care.* The starting point for most ethics of care is in the *relationship* we have with the other party in a moral encounter. This can be contrasted with deference to law and principle emphasized on the justice approach. As with family and friends, relationships may be partial, interdependent, and involved. Thus we may favor those we know and like, we may have various kinds of reciprocal relationships, and we are often be enmeshed in their lives.

A prime question for a care approach is to ask why we develop rules and laws at all. The answer could be that they are to keep social order, perhaps. However, the response from a feminist ethics of care is that the primary function of justice is to repair, restore, and maintain human relationships. As Noddings articulates her theory, then, care is the foundation of justice. She says that we wouldn't be concerned with justice in the first place unless there was some relationship that we needed to build or mend. As she explains it, a moral theory based on justice claims alone stresses detachment from emotional influences in moral reasoning, and evaluates acts on the basis of laws and codes. She points to this as the traditional conception of moral reasoning associated with the masculine perspective. In contrast, Noddings sets up moral reasoning that emphasizes sensitivity to particular issues, relatedness, and responsiveness to the needs of others, traits more commonly associated with feminine viewpoints.

Care need not be thought of as tender-heartedness, though. The proponents of the care approach still believe we will face tough decisions, but these will, and should, be informed by humane concern. If we take the family as our model, there will be numerous examples where we get involved and expend effort because we care about others, even though the encounters may be fractious or difficult. A parent may intervene when her child becomes involved with recreational drugs or is constantly fighting with his siblings. The motive behind her action is probably not that she knows the child is breaking rules or violating social norms, but rather that she deeply cares about the child's welfare and will do whatever it takes to rebuild their relationship.

In another case, a single mother at work is forced to take time off to look after her child with medical problems. The manager has to make reasoned and defensible choices about whether the woman should be allowed to pass her obligations on to her coworkers. There may come a time when her employment is unsustainable for the company. A care ethicist would not automatically claim that the manager should give the woman complete freedom from her job duties: after all, he or she has to be concerned about productivity and the welfare of the other employees as well. A care approach will say, though, that the manager has to be compassionate when it comes to making difficult decisions, which may mean stretching beyond strictly contractual relations or softening the blow as much as possible.

ETHICS AND PATRIARCHY

At this point, let us return to the case of Margaret Hossack. Imagine that the jury consisted of both women and men. They might hear evidence that mitigates Margaret's actions, and understand that she was abused. Yet importantly, as long as they are bound by the rules of the trial and the prevailing law, those insights would do little to change the outcome: Margaret would be found guilty of intentional homicide with very little latitude in the sentencing. Similarly, in Glaspell's story, the women who concealed the evidence would be guilty of a crime, however understandable their actions might be. In short, institutional policies that have been established rule our actions in everyday life. An important contribution of feminist scholars is to note that care and similar views will have little traction if the prevailing social structures nevertheless force us into certain behaviors. They draw attention to the ways in which patriarchal assumptions can be built into the very practices we often view as unbiased, ordinary and objective.

A useful analogy can be made by considering the Olympic Games. In traditional Olympic sports, the record holders are almost universally male. That is, men as a general class can run quicker, jump higher and longer, and lift heavier weights than women. Males appear to be superior to females in many fields.

The solution in recent decades has been to segregate the games for men and women. Certainly, all men are not capable of outperforming all women, but the best performers in those original events are men. Yet if we reflect on this even further, we may see that the games themselves are based around skills that were needed for warriors in ancient times: running fast, hurling objects, feats of strength, and so forth. Thus the games as originally constructed have an inbuilt bias about what individual games are the most representative of human athletic excellence. We rarely think about this, since it seems natural to think of physical prowess in masculine terms.

However, if we were to change the original assumptions and modify the games to be *truly* equal, we might choose a wider variety of athletic endeavors in which women might perform better and hold more world records. For instance, we might have contests that involved balance, elegance, and stamina such as dance and beam exercises and open them to both sexes. Because men largely designed the games to showcase skills they are naturally good at, such as upper body strength, it is not surprising that they excel and outshine women in those contests. Once we realize that there is nothing sacred about the nature of the events, it doesn't have to be the case that women have to conform to men's challenges where they will inevitably fall short due to biological and physical differences.

Adapting the analogy, many feminists suggest that patriarchal assumptions are built into our own social and institutional arrangements. They point out that these lead to unjust power disparities which are accepted as normal and natural although they merely reflect ancient prejudices. Moreover, feminists highlight ways in which our failure to recognize these norms as social constructions results in patterns of behavior which then reinforce and perpetuate the cycle of prejudice. For example, one criticism of Wollstonecraft and the related philosophical view of gender egalitarianism is that it wrongfully condemns the feminine and associates it with weakness. That is, women must live up to male-established standards which appear to delegitimize traits such as emotional responsiveness and sensitivity.

Feminists also reveal that women are often asked to conform to a male template of normality. Ironically, just as men often assume physical superiority because they think of it in terms of strength rather than, say, endurance, those in power see the state of the world as natural and normal rather than reflecting any sort of repression. Consider the world of work: It frequently echoes a societal assumption of a working father and stay-at-home mother, so that a young professional woman may still find a number of hurdles in trying to balance parenting and work. Sociologists point out that working women still tend to do more than half of all housework when both parents are fully employed. Despite recent changes in many businesses, the structures for promotion and success rarely fully accommodate the challenges of childbearing and rearing. In order to do well, women have to adjust to the standards set for men in terms of hours and achievements.

Several approaches have been put forward to address the issue of the male-oriented societal structures automatically being seen as natural. Echoing our earlier discussion, one way would be to make our social institutions truly gender-neutral by removing discrimination and helping women develop their potential and achieve appropriate recognition. This might involve, among other things, ensuring access to equal education, equal opportunities in hiring and promotion, and equal pay for equal work.

However, other commentators believe that simply removing barriers isn't sufficient, since they believe the problems are deeper and more systemic. Thus the notion of gender neutrality is interpreted by some as ignoring the realities of women's lives if the result is to force women to adjust to social institutions such as work that are geared to the male experience of the world.

Feminist philosophers have questioned and challenged various institutions such as the workplace or schools and colleges. A traditional liberal response has been to acknowledge that there were barriers but that they have subsequently been identified and removed. The contemporary feminist Alison Jaggar (1943–) describes this approach as "add women and stir." That is, greater access without any other systemic changes may not alter the reality of women's lives in any meaningful way while still expecting them to conform to long established societal norms. The problem to the "add women and stir" approach is that the culture may itself be hostile to women's identity, and only those who are willing or able to adapt will survive. We can see this dynamic of a male-dominated work culture in that business is still rife with sports and war metaphors, and the language reflects male attitudes of aggression and competition as the model for success. At base, the feminist challenge asks us to consider the fundamental assumptions we make about our relationships with others on a personal, institutional, and communal level, and examine whether these arrangements treat women as fully empowered people.

Another issue feminists point out is not just one of access to the boardroom or college classroom, but also one of validating feminine insights and overcoming barriers in a male-dominated environment. For example, when it comes to ethical theory, one obvious fact is that the canonical figures are typically male, and often come from a privileged background. This isn't surprising, as it is true in many academic fields. In the study of ethics, the historical reality is that women's philosophical perspectives were rarely encouraged and recorded. More recently, the emergence of the women's movement has sought to address this issue in terms of critiquing classic texts and developing alternative philosophical approaches that are more respectful of contributions women have to offer.

For example, historically several philosophical dichotomies describe human nature: mind/body, reason/emotion, permanent/changeable. These have been dominant and highly influential in philosophy and ethics. In most cases, the first in each pair has been associated with the masculine and considered preferable. Thus, for instance, reason is prized in philosophical discourse, and emotional or intuitive responses largely discounted. Feminist teaching reminds us that our psychological makeup will inevitably color the norms we establish and what we consider to be fair and just. For most of human history, men considered that they had the edge on women when it came to reasoning. This view isn't always explicit, but we can see it, for example, when the philosopher R. M. Hare (1919–2002) talks about moral reasoning. Here he distinguishes between the intuitive "prole" and the super rational "archangel." He comments approvingly that

> Aristotle…says the relation of the intellect to the character…has to be a paternal one: it is because [men] "listen to reason as to a father."[1]

Hence if we were to take a traditional philosophical approach, much emphasis is placed on reason. We just don't hear much about the emotional factor. Yet in Glaspell's short story *A Jury of Her Peers,* it is hard to understand why the local wives would conceal incriminating evidence unless we bring in notions of compassion and empathy.

---

[1] R. M. Hare, 1981. *Moral Thinking.* Oxford: Clarendon, p. 46.

SEPARATIST FEMINISM

Given a growing awareness of gendered social hierarchies and discrimination, some feminists have promoted various forms of separatism. The separatist charge is that societal institutions have a male bias, and women who aspire to play by their rules will find themselves subject to a double standard. For example, assertiveness in the workplace is often applauded when practiced by men, but seen as aberrant if women act similarly. Men who put career ahead of families are often seen as go-getters, whereas women who do the same thing might be described as neglectful.

Separatism need not mean exclusive communities that ban men, but it does emphasize the potentially important role of establishing safe places where women can verbalize their familiarity with marginalization, gain validation from other women similarly situated, and explore methods of resolution and resistance to the subordination of women both in their own experiences and in the lives of women more generally. For example, research suggests that men tend to be more active and noisy participants in college classrooms and get more attention because of it. The effect may be detrimental to the education of women, and so a separatist would argue that there may be a place for gender exclusive colleges. One important qualification is that separatist communities are rarely established and maintained as an ends in themselves, but are rather viewed as a means for establishing such things as personal and communal growth, liberty, community, health, or safety.

The point is that male-dominated societies where men make most of the decisions in most of the institutions will, consciously or unconsciously, operate in ways that reflect a male point of view and typically favor men. An example might be the health care debate, where most of the legislators are men, and they speak on behalf of women. The men might be well meaning, but the separatist movement seeks to reclaim the power of women to make decisions for themselves. Hence separatists think that there are valid reasons for women to set themselves apart from male influence in certain circumstances. In that sense the move is an attempt to avoid external forces that shape women's lives so as to promote and establish an authentic female voice and identity.

Practically speaking, the majority of women cannot opt out of social institutions, and therefore we are left with questions on how best to deal with prevailing patriarchal systems. The puzzle we all face is whether it is better to try to alter things from within the system or alternatively distance ourselves and set up new models.

CHALLENGES

The main challenges leveled at feminist theory are a lack of systemization and a charge of relativism in the absence of general principles. As we have seen, an ethics of care aims to focus our attention in moral reasoning away from the distanced application of overarching principles and rules to the contextualized exploration of maintaining immediate and personal relationships. The focus on individual relationships may raise questions as to whether the approach can be generalized into a universal moral theory. If everyone were to act only on emotional intuitions, is there any way of judging between better and worse behavior, or condemning those who might react differently? Moreover, if the central focus of a moral theory is on personal relationships, can it give us a means of deciding what is appropriate when thinking of remote and unknown people?

Recall that Noddings's approach suggests that being taken care of is a universal human experience. Yet if we extend the claim to say something like the uniquely female experience of motherhood provides a basis for ethical relationships, it is difficult to account for the experiences of women who are not mothers and explain the commonalities between, say, the nature of motherhood in suburban America and in an African village. Ultimately, there may be very little in common that could form the basis for a consistent moral theory. To its critics, a generalized recommendation to care has little substance unless it is supplemented by a more formal framework. Otherwise we run the risk of the theory not giving us enough information to actually use. For instance, perhaps Margaret Hossack cared for her husband John, but paradoxically the fact that she cared so much may have enabled continued domination and entitlement on his part. Thus we may need to supplement an account of care with some guidelines for what would be appropriate levels of care, to whom, and in what circumstances.

There are several lines of response. First it would be wrong to characterize feminist views as completely abandoning rationality. It is not that they replace rational thinking or critical analysis with intuition or personal feeling. Rather, the argument is that the head/heart dichotomy often creates a false picture since it would be perfectly appropriate to use both head *and* heart. Recent research in psychology, economics, and decision theory bears this out. Apparently people with some forms of traumatic brain injury cannot access their emotions but remain rational. While this might make it seem that they would be more capable of making decisions, it turns out that they are often paralyzed between competing rational arguments and become incapable of making simple choices, even to the extent of which color socks to wear.[2] It also turns out that many of our day-to-day decisions are rooted in our emotional impulses. This does not mean that those decisions are less pure in some sense, or that reason has been displaced. Instead, it gives us a picture of rich processes at work that blend both rational and emotional factors.

Feminist theories can be as intellectually rigorous as any others; the fact that they take intuitive and emotional elements into account does not mean that they cannot be scrutinized and critically assessed, only that they accept certain concepts that have traditionally been neglected. Feminists could point out that the difficulties facing an ethics of care and other forms of feminist ethics are common to all theories, and none of the classic theories can claim that they have unproblematic prescriptions when they try to deal with the thorny problems we confront in everyday life. Thus placing the foundation of moral response on, say, caring relationships is comparable to canonical traditions asserting that we should seek human flourishing, happiness, or personal autonomy, and is no less legitimate because it includes an emotional element. Furthermore, feminism has emerged only recently as an academic discipline, and hence it has not been subject to the hundreds (or thousands) of years of intellectual refinement of its competitors.

There are considerable difficulties in working out whether women's differing moral intuitions arise from nature or from upbringing. It would be hard to establish the essentialist claim that women have inherently differing ethical insights unless we could do a side-by-side comparison between a community where women were truly emancipated and one that is not. The particular experiences of women may nevertheless offer critiques of the male-dominated public sphere. For example, a profeminist essentialist might start thinking about this by imagining a world where the activities and concerns traditionally associated with women were given equal value, and asking whether the moral and social priorities of society would be radically different from what we have now. Thus if the nurturing and care involved in elementary teaching was given the prestige and rewards of stock broking, or if working in a nursing home was seen as more valuable than truck driving, it is possible that the impulses that drive our moral intuitions might alter accordingly.

---

[2]Antonio Damasio,1995. *Descartes' Error: Emotion, Reason, and the Human Brain.* New York: Harper.

In the end, though, it may be less important to resolve the nature/nurture question than to deal with its implications. For instance, it is empirically true that women face discrimination in the workplace, tend to be paid less for comparable work, and carry the majority burden of domestic duties such as housework and child rearing. These facts go a long way in supporting the claim that in current society there are significant disadvantages to being born a woman. As a result it would not be surprising to find that women in general have different ethical perspectives than men.

Summary

Feminist theory is an umbrella term for approaches that are still developing and have taken many forms. One early slogan said that "feminism is the radical notion that women are people" and in the words of Mary Wollstonecraft from 1792, "I do not wish [women] to have power over men, but over themselves."[3] Clearly equality and empowerment are important issues not only in ethical theory but in the social and political realms as well. Recent advances have addressed issues in epistemology and metaphysics, and integrated feminism with existentialism, discourse ethics, and other postmodernist views. Hence the rise of feminism has added an important voice to ethical debates and challenges us to question not only whether our assumptions about behavioral norms are gendered, but also if the gender biases we can now detect in more dated writing might lead us to suspect that there are other lingering biases in the areas of race, religion, culture, and social and economic status.

Feminist approaches draw attention to the ways in which assumptions about human nature are inevitably a part of our moral theorizing, and that they can have pernicious implications. Feminist critiques also have the very clear strength of broadening the ways in which we conceive of value and moral reasoning, and challenge us to reconsider the features of life we consider morally relevant. For instance, care ethics appeals to our real experience of values such as relationships, compassion, and nurturing as an integral part of our ethical lives. If we think of someone visiting us in the hospital, it is intuitively more appropriate to say that they come because they care about us rather than, say, that their motive was one of duty or maximizing happiness.

There may be alternatives to the primacy of reason, and there may be times when intuition or following one's heart takes precedence. While this seems heretical to many academic endeavors, consider how some of life's major decisions, such as which college to attend, who to marry, and whether to have children, aren't usually worked out with rational choice procedures. Similarly, some of the areas that are overlooked by traditional moral theory might include consideration of the perspectives of the marginalized, the emotional life, sensitivity to the context of our decisions, and attention to human relationships. The upshot is that we ought to view various modes of thinking such as reason and emotion not as polar opposites that compete against one another, but more like different aspects of our nature: more like various tools in a toolbox rather than as stacked in a strict hierarchy with reason at the apex.

Feminism has also had a major impact on areas of applied ethics such as issues in medicine, the environment, and business where it presents a useful alternative to the abstractions of traditional theory and gives

---

[3]Mary Wollstonecraft, 1792/2004. *A Vindication of the Rights of Woman*. Harmondsworth: Penguin, p. 81.

a robust intellectual defense for some of the strong intuitions we feel in difficult cases. For example, when a family has to deal with end-of-life issues, the concept of care resonates much more readily with many people than arguments based on duty or utility. Moreover, it may be that in such complex moral cases, we cannot find overarching universal principles that apply to all cases and we need to focus our decision making on the more specific features of individual cases.

Importantly, although feminist approaches have highlighted the fact that women in particular have been marginalized in classical ethical theory, they are, in effect, the precursor for a wider discussion that deals more broadly with the ethics of oppression. The reactions we have to Margaret Hossack's situation could be based on the fact that she is a woman in a male-dominated society. On the other hand, they may also reflect more general insights about what it means to be oppressed: Studies have shown, for example, that individuals in power tend to take recourse in the language of rights and the law, if only because it reinforces the language and social systems that perpetuate their status. In contrast, people who are oppressed are often less capable of advocating for themselves using legal rules and rights, and are more likely to use the language of care, compassion, and solidarity in their moral thinking and justifications for their actions. Seen in this light, feminist insights are also invaluable when they initiate discussions about oppression in general.

11

Postmodern Critiques

Modernism refers to a view that progress is possible through the application of scientific principles. At the end of the nineteenth century, scientists and engineers had shown that we could control natural forces by harnessing energy through steam power, for example, or by building bridges and dams, and that science could explain and predict natural phenomena. There was also an overriding confidence that we could obtain certain knowledge once we adopted the right method. In ethical terms, classical principle-based approaches posed methods to resolve ethical issues that focused on the application of their respective theory's principles to actual cases. Immanuel Kant (1724–1804) believed that ethical norms could be established by a rational decision procedure, based on individual motivation, which could then be applied universally. The utilitarian philosopher John Stuart Mill (1806–1873) asserted that we should seek outcomes that maximize aggregate happiness for the greatest number, positing a mechanistic system in which initial assumptions are established and then ethics becomes an endeavor to constantly refine the ways it is applied.

In contrast, **postmodernists** react against claims of certainty and propose a more radical reevaluation of the ways we view and understand the world. Their language—drawing on the insights and methodologies of a range of disciplines and employing specialized jargon—is at times obscure to general readers. However, their insights may be invaluable when we consider ethics. They explain that the nature of our language and our social institutions often trap us into certain ways of thinking, many times without us realizing it. They contend that only by stepping back and looking at both the judgments that ethics makes and the frameworks that support those conclusions can we ever make ethical progress. As there are considerable differences in their viewpoints and approaches, it would be more accurate to describe postmodernism as a sensibility, or disposition to certain lines of inquiry, than a specific theory or cohesive school of thought.

CASE—THE HERALD DISASTER

To illustrate a postmodern approach in a practical way, consider the disaster that transpired when a ferry operating between Belgium and England left port with its bow door open to the sea. The *Herald of Free Enterprise* was a multilevel car and passenger vessel that left Zeebrugge fully loaded on March 6, 1987. The crewman in charge of closing the door failed to do so because he was asleep in his cabin. As it left the dock, the ship built up speed and tons of seawater flowed in. This destabilized the ship, causing it to rock and capsize onto a sandbank just half a mile from the shore. Fortunately, rescue ships were near at hand. Nevertheless, 193 of the 539 people on board died.

At first glance, the story seems to be one of simple negligence. It seems obvious to claim that the ship would not have capsized if the bosun had not left the door open, and that became the prevailing single explanation presented in the media after the disaster. We all tend to resolve stories by finding a single explanatory cause, and then move on. However, it became clear to researchers studying the accident that many other factors were at play that night as well. For one thing, the company had recently been taken over, and management was trying hard to cut costs. This downsizing included requiring some crewmembers to pull double shifts. Thus one reason the bosun was asleep could have been that he was completely exhausted. The constant changing of shifts also could have meant that the body rhythms of the crew created conditions where they were unable to concentrate on crucial tasks.

Another way of looking at the case is to think about the design of the ferry: Essentially it was a floating platform for cars, which meant it saved time because it did not have to maneuver to turn around for loading or unloading. However, it was susceptible to instability and concerns had previously been raised about the security of the doors in transit.

The disaster was the largest British sea tragedy since the sinking of the *Titanic*. Just as in 1912, questions were raised about whether the prevailing governmental regulations were too lax. The local Member of Parliament for Dover announced that the accident ought to be seen as a complete anomaly in the context of the vast number of safe crossings, implying that the sea corridor for trade was still commercially viable. Some workers' unions viewed that the behavior of the individual crewmembers was less significant than the system of employment that put people under significant strain to maximize returns to investors.

Because a constellation of causes culminated in the one event that led to the disaster, the explanation could be framed in many ways. Additionally, societal systems set up the conditions that allowed those events to occur. In other words, although it is often assumed there is only one story about what happened, we can in fact see the case from multiple perspectives, and all of them can make claims to the truth. Thus we might say that there is no single truth in the narrative, but rather many truths.

Postmodern philosophers emphasize that we constantly tell ourselves and each other stories to variously explain the world around us and our place in it. The technical term they often use is *narrative*. Think about the way we discuss our lives with our confidants: The origin of the term *confidential* is from the Latin, and it means to "keep faith with" someone. The point is that a person who really understood our thinking and actions would be able to relate to our situation more fully. The key element is that they see our narrative arc—how things came to be that way, and what prompted our subsequent actions. Simply put, they *get* the story we are telling. However, as the *Herald* case shows, there are always multiple stories at work, and so postmodernists reject a simple correspondence of the person and an objective, unchanging reality. Rather, the individual is never truly independent or impartial. We are always going to be part of the story in some way, since we participate in events even when we interpret what we hear to make sense of it ourselves, or use certain language when we tell it to others.

Note, for instance, that when telling the story of the *Herald*, we may have highlighted or downplayed certain events, and the reader will typically react to the story with a personal point of view that already exhibits a set of assumptions about the world. Some may respond to the case as simply a design flaw that needed to be rectified, and reject the claim that the disaster was, in part, due to corporate pressures to increase economic efficiency. Others may interpret it as a case of someone failing to perform his or her duties properly. But however we react, we are not coming from a neutral stance—we already have beliefs about the way the world works, and how things should be.

Inevitably, we shape the stories we encounter to fit our views, and, in turn, the stories will alter the way we see the world. Thus it is not as if we come upon a set of facts to be assimilated, where everyone will see the same thing and view it in the same way. It is much more like a dynamic interchange, where we influence the world, and vice versa. The postmodernist challenge is to recognize these dynamics, and break down some of the traditional dichotomies that beguile us into thinking that there is a one-to-one correspondence of perception and reality: For example, think of the ways that the dualistic language of opposites frames the way we conceive of the world: subject/object, mind/body, fact/value, reason/emotion. Indeed, even right/wrong, fair/unfair, just/unjust are, in the view of postmodernists, functions of social constructions dependent on time and place.

It is important to recognize that the postmodernist project is not to present a theory that competes with others. If we make an analogy to science, Einstein's theory of relativity has supplanted Newtonian physics. The change has come about because of the superior explanatory power of Einstein's initial assumptions about the phenomena that we encounter. Scientific hypotheses—for instance that nothing can travel at greater than the speed of light—make predictions that can be tested, and competing theories can be adjudicated on their relative merits. The postmodernists are not looking for a superior theory in philosophy, though. Rather they ask what conditions allow some theories to become dominant, and how they operate in our communities. Once we see the forces at work that incline us to one theory or another, it will help us be self-conscious of the often-embedded assumptions that we make. Returning to the *Herald* case, the stories involved will differ depending on the background conditions: If we are looking to preventing a future disaster, we may concentrate on the design flaws, whereas if the point is to find compensation for survivors and their relatives, then we may look more at issues arising from legal liability. Alternatively, others may have an interest in preserving commercial activity or improving worker's rights. The point is that there may not be a specific universally accepted hypothesis of the causes involved.

MODERNIST ETHICS

There may be different ways of framing an ethical issue, all of which make sense to certain audiences. For example, all moral theories will condemn slavery, yet the sorts of reasons they appeal to may diverge significantly. As a deontologist, Immanuel Kant and his followers would start with human motivation and autonomy, whereas Utilitarians such as John Stuart Mill would look to aggregate happiness. Unlike science, there don't seem to be systematic experiments that could adjudicate between rival explanations. This is a significant problem for philosophers with a modernist temperament, since they see their project as mimicking the scientific method. G. E. Moore (1873–1958) felt that the answer was to continually improve the methods within a particular theory. He believed that ever refining our ethical intuitions and sensibilities through education would eventually lead to the emergence of a superior model. While that approach has some appeal, no single theory has surfaced as a clear winner, and each generation of philosophers appears to furnish champions of rival theories.

Another kind of response that modernists have made is to hold science as the paradigm we should aspire to and subsequently try to redraft philosophy to conform to a more scientific model. Influenced by philosophers associated with the so-called logical positivist school, A. J. Ayer (1910–1989) rejected any attempt to provide a theoretical basis for ethics. Ayer maintained that the only meaningful propositions were verifiable ones, by which he meant that all statements potentially ought to be subject to empirical tests which would show them to be true or false. Thus if we claim that iron expands when heated, the statement can be given a truth value by testing. Even a false statement "The moon is made of cheese" could, in principle, be tested, and therefore is meaningful (but in this case, false). However, Ayer claimed there were no such tests for truth available for religious and ethical propositions, which by his view are literally *non-sense*, and therefore something we can't discuss rationally. The positivists didn't dismiss the fact that we use ethical language, of course, but explained our use of ethical language as the expression of opinions or personal preferences, which, unlike scientific hypotheses, cannot be tested or validated as known truths. Hence they held up science as the gold standard of discourse, and rejected language that failed to meet their criteria. According to the positivists this meant that significant parts of our human experience, including ethics and spiritual concerns, ought to be excluded from philosophical inquiry.

Thus Ayer and others valorized the deductive power of logic and the primacy of positive factual statements about the world (hence logical positivism). An alternative approach would be to reverse the initial assumptions, by recognizing ethics as having an important function and questioning the paramount status of the scientific method. The moderns took the model of science and imposed it on all realms of human life: No one would contest that the scientific method has been hugely successful in understanding and controlling natural forces but the open question is whether that same approach ought to apply to other, more complex or uncertain areas of our lives.

Significantly, the postmodernists do *not* want to discard critical reasoning and logic. Instead they want to broaden our understanding to embrace discourse that cannot always be reduced to true/false statements or subjected to the scientific method. They suggest that there may not always be a single, identifiable best explanation and predictive theory, but many rival and competing theories that offer various interpretations. Moreover, they hold that the discourse between competing views is quite meaningful, and that we can actually learn from the dissonance. Thus they are not posing that there is a super-theory that would resolve issues between, say, deontology and consequentialism; rather they accept that there will be inevitable conflicts in ethical, cultural, and religious discourse, and seek to find what we can learn from them.

The modernists and postmodernists would likely agree that problems arising from language make it very difficult to talk about ethics in a meaningful, accurate, or clear way. The difference is that the postmodernists wouldn't necessarily see the imprecision of language as a failing, but a basic feature of the way we interact with one another. Ludwig Wittgenstein (1889–1951) coined the phrase "language games" to convey the idea that fluid linguistic meanings are dependent on their context and use. Thus, we describe chess, football, and solitaire as games although the activities are very different—some are physical, some competitive, and so on. Similarly, he observes that we use language in a wide variety of ways, such as play-acting, guessing riddles, making a joke, translating, asking, thanking, cursing, greeting, or praying. It may be hard to say exactly what qualities are shared, and perhaps the best we can do is give various examples of the way we use it.

Similarly the postmodernists argue that language use is fluid and multiform, and so it is shortsighted of the positivists and others to rely solely on a view that statements have to be true or false as the paradigm of meaningful discourse in philosophy and ethics. Doing so would be like claiming that children skipping in a playground are not playing a game because there aren't two sides and a point system. Wittgenstein would say that rather than using a single definition for meaningful language, we should realize that it is malleable to the various uses we have for it. Following this insight, it would be mistaken to attempt to demand that all ethical statements must be verifiable, but instead we should examine how they are used to praise, blame, excuse, explain, exhort, shame, and so forth. That is, the language of ethics takes place in a societal context and instead of trying to find out what a word such as *good* means (as if it meant the same thing in all times, places, and contexts), we would be better off examining how it is used.

The postmodernists also believe that language reflects the ways in which we have created societal institutions. Take, for example, what initially might seem a straightforwardly good act where someone donates to a charity. The person might be motivated by concern for others, or feel that the world would be a better place if the money were used for cancer research rather than using it to buy a fancy meal at a restaurant. The postmodernist would ask us to step back and analyze the case in broader terms. They might ask what brings about charities in the first place— is it that the community relies on private rather than public funding, or is there an implication that their various causes are societal luxuries rather than necessities? Are there state institutions, such as the tax code, that promote certain actions and discourage others? Why do we accept that monetary donation is preferable to political agitation or spending time helping others? For the postmodernist, nothing is taken for granted, all assumptions may be doubted, and they invite us to constantly reimagine how things could be different.

In the next section, we will look at some major figures in the postmodernist movement, and explore how they might critique traditional ethical theory.

HABERMAS

The German thinker Jurgen Habermas (1929–) trained both as a sociologist and as a philosopher. Habermas recognizes that we cannot make judgments from a dispassionate and impartial perspective: We are always embedded in our own worldview. Thus, unlike Kant, we do not take our own moral intuitions and generalize them, because we then effectively impose our narrow viewpoint. Rather, we have to share our intuitions and test them to see if they are more widely acceptable. We do not try to suppress or hide our interests or worldviews, but make them visible to all participants: We should critique others while also being open to critique. He notes that unlike the positivist approach, humans share many cultural and ethical experiences, which are welcomed as legitimate features of any discussion.

Habermas has tried to develop an alternative view of rationality and open up debates about what should count as knowledge. Instead of looking for truth conditions that would tell us whether a claim is true or false (e.g., "giving to charity is a good thing to do"), his approach, sometimes called *discourse ethics*, looks at the nature of the communications, the forms of justification presented in ethical dilemmas, and examines the *communicative action* involved. Thus he is looking beyond the ethical claim itself and wants to put it in the context of its presentation as well as the rules about what counts as a valid exchange.

In looking at ethical issues, Habermas believes that we can't examine them in isolation from the justificatory norms of argument and the social structures in which they take place. Consider a student debate on a controversial topic such as abortion: In a formal setting rules structure the kinds of arguments that must be presented, and how students score. Habermas's project asks us to look not only at the content of ethical discussions but also at the way society legitimizes some types of argument (e.g., a debate) and condemns others such as emotional speech. Hence he wants us to examine both the terms used in the arguments and how they are articulated; the overall communication, including nonverbal gestures; and especially how the norms about what constitutes valid discourse have been set up.

At its best, communicative action produces a situation where each participant presents a claim, and the background assumption is that each will be able to provide reasons that underwrite his or her claim. All parties are then welcome to criticize the reasons. He terms this an *ideal speech situation*. Habermas describes genuine communicative action as *purposive-rational action*, which he contrasts favorably to *strategic action*, where a powerful individual imposes his or her view through coercion or manipulation, motivated by self-interest.

Habermas suggests that we cannot come to moral judgments individually but have to engage in deliberate and reflective discourse with others. In German we find the phrase *argumentativer Veständigung* used as the term for deliberation. It would apply in this context because the term implies both understanding and consensus, even in the absence of a shared ethos. In brief, each perspective has to be applied to the practical problem at hand, open to critique by other parties up to the point that objections are exhausted, and only then are the reasons presented considered acceptable. Moreover, the emphasis on good reasons acts to moderate the effects of power imbalances inherent in debates.

Discourse ethics—and Habermas in particular—can appear to be notoriously obscure and idealistic. However, as a theoretical approach it benefits from the demand that we consider parties traditionally excluded from decision making, and seek consensus of basic understandings among parties who may have widely differing values.

Discourse ethics also tells us that any practical ethics needs to take social realities and concrete practices of all stakeholders into account. For example, in talking about environmental movements affecting the developing world, Vandana Shiva, an environmental activist who is sympathetic to Habermas's approach, says:

> We are now on the threshold of the third phase of colonization [after "civilizing" and "developing"], in which the white man's burden is to protect the environment—and this too, involves taking control of rights and resources....The North's prescription for the South's salvation has always created new burdens and new bondages, and the salvation of the environment cannot be achieved through the old colonial order based on the white man's burden. The two are ethically, economically and epistemologically incongruent.[1]

Shiva argues that the Western world may have framed solutions to the environmental crisis in a paternal fashion, ready to impose those plans in much the same way they colonized two centuries earlier. She points to the fact that although the developed countries believe they are helping out, if we step back and look at the broader picture, they are, in fact, treating other countries in the same colonial fashion that they did a century ago. That is, the subject matter may have changed over time, from setting up political administration to environmental concerns, but the underlying dynamic has remained the same, with the developed countries telling the less developed what is in their own best interest. The benefit of using a discourse approach is that it forces us to look at the broader ethical picture and insists that the voices of all concerned are incorporated into the discussion, so that their values and opinions are heard and assessed on the same grounds that govern all other participants.

---

[1]"Decolonizing the North" in Mies, M. and Vandana, S. eds. 1993. *Ecofeminism*. London: Zed Books, pp. 264–279.

FOUCAULT

Michel Foucault (1926–1984), a French philosopher, wrote extensively on the nature of power and communication. He is significant for contemporary ethics largely because of his original insights on the nature of human freedom. Foucault is sometimes intimidatingly difficult to understand in his original writing. Nevertheless, his work on the relationships between the individual and human institutions provides a useful counterpoint to thinkers who have assumed that we are able to make our own decisions. The French existentialist philosopher Jean-Paul Sartre (1905–1980) felt that we can make independent decisions and hence we cannot blame God, fate, or others for our personal choices. In contrast Foucault draws on literature, psychology, and the social sciences to argue that we aren't as free as we might initially believe: Inevitably we make unconscious choices under the influence of language, stories that shape our understanding of how things are in the world, and various power structures in society.

Although Foucault's work can be interpreted as a response to Sartre's radical freedom, another main target in his writings is the historical determinism of Karl Marx (1818–1883). Marx thought that societies would predictably follow particular patterns of development and struggle between social classes, in the same way that science can trace the necessary link between cause and effect. In his expansive critiques of modern thought, Foucault questioned whether science in general was as objective as it seems, especially in the social realm. He described in detail the way that the social context shapes and legitimates certain practices and suppresses others. Consequently he denied there was any unique progression in science, and questioned Marx's determinist view that things would necessarily evolve in a certain way. From Foucault's critique, novel analyses about the way communities work became prominent and have been widely adopted in both science and the humanities.

Foucault's writing is often historical in nature, since he maintained that he was not looking for formal structures with universal value but rather was conducting an "investigation into the events that have led us to constitute ourselves and to recognize ourselves as subjects of what we are doing, thinking, saying."[2] For example, in his book *Madness and Civilization* (1961), he looked at how humans have treated insanity over time: Centuries ago those deemed "mad" were considered to have special sensitivity to the mysteries of the universe, whereas later they were treated as sick. In Europe before the seventeenth century they were often allowed to be free, but after leprosy declined and institutional space became available, the mad were typically confined and separated from society. The point Foucault makes is that although in our present culture we may feel it is a scientific fact that insanity is a form of sickness, the way we approach madness and treat people is largely a function of the prevailing social norms. Thus he concludes that it is necessary to consider ethics in light of dominant power relations and the societal structures we have developed.

Power is a central concept in Foucault's analysis. He felt that power was a neglected factor in philosophical reasoning. However, he doesn't think of power as a property, like a commodity, that can be accumulated and spent. He sees it at work through various mechanisms, for example, in the way space is organized, the way populations are managed, and the way bureaucracies are set up. He describes these as forms of *regimentation*. Foucault suggested that power and knowledge are dual aspects of a web of relations that shape our actions, and used a combined word *power/knowledge* to express the connection. This is because he felt the two were intertwined—those with

[2]M. Foucault, 1986. "What Is Enlightenment?" In P. Rabinow, ed. *The Foucault Reader*. Penguin: Harmondsworth, p. 46.

power in society help define what is acceptable as knowledge, and those possessing knowledge achieve power over others. As individuals, we cannot escape what he terms the *architecture* of society, the underlying web of power relations that govern our lives, since we are born into them, and we constantly work within them. Rather, his project is to make them more transparent, so we can better exercise our freedom by charting our own course within these power relations.

Foucault explained that one of the manifestations of power is the way social discourse frames our actions. In most cases, it is not as if any single force is imposing its view. Instead it is more like certain kinds of language are more acceptable than others. As an example (not one of his), think of the way certain holidays are treated in the United States. Consumers spend vast amounts on gifts, such as candy for Halloween, Christmas, and St. Valentine's Day. The way these practices have emerged, and the language that surrounds them, encourages consumerism and often equates interpersonal regard with the amount spent. Foucault would have us scrutinize the societal forces at work that support and promote these attitudes, and the way they are sanctioned and unconsciously accepted by most people.

In studying language and its effects, Foucault uses the term *regimes of truth* to describe the linguistic context which we inhabit. One of his own studies looked at sexuality and how views have changed historically. He concludes that society apparently uses scientific means to distinguish *normal* from *deviant* behavior, and then imposes these standards by condoning certain language use. For our analysis, it is significant that ethics uses many accepted terms, whereas Foucault reminds us that their meanings are not universal, obvious, or permanent, but reflect power relations in society that are often used to make individuals conform. As a contemporary example of the power of language, many gay and lesbian people have adopted the word *queer*, which historically has had a demeaning connotation. They believe that recapturing the language is powerful, since a term that used to be used derisively can now be given overtones of strength and pride.

Foucault takes the central question of ethics to be how a person should act. Given his view of society, he says we cannot think of ourselves as independent and autonomous, but instead as in relationship to others who may be seeking to influence us and the cultural space that we occupy in various ways. Individuality, he says, can be achieved only in relation to others and to disciplinary and governmental regimes that shape our lives. He believes there is value in reflection, appreciation of the modes of subjection we encounter, aspirations for the self, and deciding which practices are ethical. For Kant and Mill the notion of the person as a reflective being was hardly touched in ethical analysis: Kant provides rules for behavior, and Mill puts forward the *Greatest Happiness Principle*. In contrast, Foucault believes that the ethical life requires significant self-examination, in effect, seeing ourselves as others might see us.

Ethical practice for Foucault means developing an "aesthetics of existence" where the self is not a fixed subject, but always in a process of redefinition where we "monitor, test, improve and transform" ourselves. As he writes, we decide on certain modes of being that serve as our overall goal, and we have to assess moral precepts that we will follow, always recognizing the power and influence of the dominant institutions within society.

RORTY

The American philosopher Richard Rorty (1931–2007) was a professor of philosophy at Princeton, and later taught comparative literature at Stanford University. In his academic career he moved from being a classical analytic philosopher to one who rejected standard justifications for knowledge claims—that is, he disputed that knowledge amounts to making statements that correspond to some kind of objective reality. He has been called a *postmodern pragmatist*. He is postmodern in his desire to examine not just the internal workings of philosophical theory, but also the very practice itself. He is a pragmatist, since, as he puts it, is "The right question is not 'what is real?' nor 'what is rational?' but 'what is useful to talk about?'"

Critically, Rorty also charged that ethical theorists are simply wrong in how they frame everyday moral thinking: We often think of principled action as if we reflect on ethical theory, work out the right thing to do, and then act accordingly. Rorty argues that this defies common experience. He says we first have moral intuitions, and then we use the theory to rationalize those initial thoughts. Rorty is very skeptical of the view that we somehow reflect rationally on our own morality and assess it against any sort of eternal truth. Consider how contemporary society condemns slavery but is entirely ambiguous about industrial farming of livestock, for example. He would claim that converting, say, to a vegetarian lifestyle is not a function of reflective thinking and conscientious choice; otherwise, there would be pretty much universal agreement about messy moral issues. The more likely course is that we each have an emotional awakening that puts us in one camp or another, and we subsequently invent reasons to support our reaction.

Take the case of the abolition of slavery in America. The question is whether influential people in society were persuaded by good reasoning to support abolition, or, if once exposed to the true horrors of the practice, they recoiled from what they found and then constructed arguments to justify their reactions. As an example of the latter, Harriet Beecher Stowe's 1852 novel *Uncle Tom's Cabin* describes the conditions for slaves on a plantation as including routine whippings and beatings, as well as the breaking up of slave families when individuals were sold to different owners. Certainly there were abolitionist speakers who, hoping to influence society through reason, appealed to universal rights before the publication of her book, but Rorty's pragmatic question remains—what works best to create a better society? If it is literature, including fiction, then he maintains that we should acknowledge its power, and realize that there is nothing unique about philosophical reasoning: It is just one means among many to raise our awareness and lead us to imagine new possibilities.

Consequently, Rorty says that when we frame the argument as saying that slavery was right for one culture and wrong for the other, it denies the fact that we have to make judgments within our own social and political realities: It is not as if we could transport Aristotle into contemporary times, explain the error of his slave-owning ways in terms he would understand, have him undergo an enlightening experience, and then transport him back with a fresh outlook. Rather, we have to realize that in the context of all of his other beliefs, he was probably justified in accepting a false theory.

Rorty does not say that the ancients were absolutely wrong and now we are absolutely right, as inevitably every judgment is made within a specific historic and cultural context. Instead of contrasting complete relativism with rigorous absolutism, he wants to abandon the quest for certainty and say that we do the best with the information we have. We are lucky to live today in the age of antibiotics, should we contract an infection, but then again unfortunate if we contract a disease for which no cure is available today. Similarly, Rorty thinks we are lucky now to have certain beliefs and can do the right thing in ways that were unavailable in the past. He is correspondingly optimistic about the future of morality—the more we know, and the more we are aware, he feels, the more we are likely to progress.

Science, for Rorty, is necessarily fallible and time-bound: He maintains that justification is always made in the context of a wealth of other beliefs and the information available at the time. We may look back at doctors in the Middle Ages who may have been badly mistaken about the nature of infection and disease. Yet at the same time we should acknowledge that they were working in a web of beliefs that led them to the views they held. We now have much more information, and a legacy of knowledge that we can use to justify our current views, and in many ways they are more practical—we cure more diseases, for example. Yet most scientists would acknowledge that their working assumptions are hypotheses that might have to be reframed in light of further investigation and the greater explanatory power of a rival theory.

Applying the analogy to ethics, Rorty contends the key to moral advancement is through our imaginative and empathetic abilities. As a pragmatist, the issue is not about discovering what was there all along, waiting to be uncovered by rational philosophers. Rather, he maintains that we are faced with the question of what makes a good life, and what actions will bring it about. He is less concerned with foundational questions and more focused on whether the discourse is beneficial. If talking about gravity is more useful to us than language about spirits within objects causing them to move, then we should adopt that world view. Similarly, it may not matter that heaven really exists or that we can prove the origin of human rights. The most important factor is not whether these beliefs correspond to some objective reality, but whether our belief in them will change our behavior in ways that enhance our welfare.

LEVINAS

Emmanuel Levinas (1906–1995) was born in Lithuania, and studied in France. He was a prisoner of war during the Second World War, but many of his family members were deported and killed during the Holocaust. After the fall of the Nazi regime, he returned to France where he taught at the Sorbonne.

Levinas challenges traditional ethics in a radical way, minimizing the role of reason and justification in favor of the brute reality of interpersonal encounter. He believes that ethics begins at the point where we recognize other people as beings like ourselves. Levinas's work is sometimes termed *phenomenological.* That is, he takes the phenomena we experience and puts that ahead of rational systems or principles. Most classical philosophers start with a concept of the person as an individual who perceives the world, analyzes his or her situation, and determines the appropriate behavior in those circumstances. In stark contrast, Levinas believes what matters most is our immediate response to others, and he examines closely the phenomena we experience in our daily lives. Because of his far-reaching shift in assumptions from traditional approaches, his work is sometimes treated with suspicion by analytically trained philosophers. However, his supporters would say that his work points to shortcomings in the way Western philosophy has developed as a discipline, and that it will take a radical alteration in philosophy's customary categories and expressions to confront the presumptions it takes for granted.

Levinas is famous for saying morality is not a branch of philosophy, but first philosophy. He thinks that it is wrong to think of philosophy as a method that carves off separate spheres of inquiry that look into metaphysical issues of being. The fundamental truth for Levinas is that we live in an intersubjective world, where the self is not center stage as in most traditional theories. He asserts that the awareness of oneself is less important than becoming aware of the other person, and in that awareness there is an ethical awakening. Knowledge for Levinas always derives from an encounter that is external to the self. Unlike the seventeenth-century thinker Descartes who believed that we are more sure of ourselves than anything else (hence his famous claim "I think therefore I am"), Levinas maintains that it is our experience of the external that verifies our existence. The "Other" as he terms it using a capital *O*, calls to us, addresses us, and by doing so makes us recognize our responsibility to him or her.

The idea of "face" (in French, *le visage*) is critical for Levinas. Typically we think of ourselves as independent thinkers, capable of discerning the world. The face presents us with a puzzle: It is strange, often disquieting, and is not easily reduced to *my* memories, thoughts, and feelings. The face always belongs to the Other. It has expressions that are at once both meaningful and elusive, showing us that we cannot ever fully capture the nature of the Other and treat it as some idea of our own.

Such claims are perplexing to many Western philosophers. Yet they have a basis in psychology, where one of the first things a baby notices is the face. The face has a compelling presence—it tells us there are others, and invites us to address the Other. It is not just the physical features of the face, though, but also its unique ability to communicate, even prelinguistically. Levinas also says we can read ethical commands from the face. It tells us "Thou shalt not kill," "Thou shalt do all that thou canst to help the other," "Love thy neighbor as thyself." These demands are made on us simply by recognizing the Other. That is, ethics is not a reciprocal relationship where we operate from self-interest or maxims. Ethics originates in and through the human fact of sociability. It operates before self-awareness or reason, and manifests itself as continuous *obligation* to others.

To give an everyday example, imagine a person who witnesses an accident and sees someone in pain. The first reaction is often to help him or her. Two linked points are vital to understanding Levinas in this situation. First, the encounter is a dynamic between persons. Traditional theories might present a picture of a discrete individual as seeing the injured person, determining the right thing to do in such a situation, and then acting accordingly. For Levinas there is no separate individual that exists apart from his or her social experiences with others. For him, the encounter is not the meeting of two discrete individuals, but two people sharing an experience and being in relation to each other. Therefore for Levinas we never make isolated decisions. It is not as if we could abstract ourselves from any situation and our interaction with others because we live in a web of encounters with people much like us.

Second, our reaction to the Other is prerational. Any encounter is immediate—that is, there are no intervening steps. We just see the Other, and are instantly able to put ourselves in their position and become aware of his or her needs. This is perhaps most obvious when looking into someone's eyes perhaps, but Levinas does not always literally mean we have to gaze into their eyes or face; rather what matters is that we are able to acknowledge the Other, in the same way we use the phrase to *face another* or meeting *face-to-face*. Similarly, although he often uses the word *proximity* to describe the relationship of one with another, we should not regard that as meaning we care only about those nearby—it is more like the English phrase of *closeness*, which implies care and love.

Additionally, Levinas believes that reason only comes into ethical discourse after the fact, and will inevitably be less than the lived encounter. Again, an analogy might be helpful: When we listen to certain kinds of music, the value is the experience, which at its best can connect us to things beyond ourselves. Yet most of us, even if we can read music, cannot have the same kind of connection merely by looking at the notes. Levinas takes ethics to be a series of transient glimpses of the infinite through experiencing the call of others who are people like us but are always ultimately mysterious and imperceptible.

In any situation Levinas believes we are *responsible* to the Other. The very social nature of humans means that we will always be in the midst of others, and discover that our prime obligation is to them, not to ourselves. He thinks of this as a fundamental duty, not as some kind of contract or exchange that requires some payback. Importantly, the call may not always arise because people are in significant distress. It may be that we see someone who merely needs a friend, and he believes we immediately perceive the need and are called to respond to it.

Another means to think about Levinas's approach is to reflect on the social and family roles that we are immersed in. That is, we are not just individuals, but parents, siblings, children, students, employees, friends, or community members. These are all relationships, to be sure, but they also imply that we are *obligated to* the other. Thus in a voluntary role as a friend for example, although we will certainly get something from it, when we meet our friends, the encounter prompts sincere questions about what is in their welfare and what we can do for them. Similarly parents constantly put the well-being of their children before their own.

In various occupations as well there are many times where personal interests are subsumed to those of the patient, victim, or client. Levinas does not interpret this as an individual making a decision to become altruistic. Instead, the agent feels that the initial and overwhelming call of the Other. In effect, when we put our own interests first, he believes we are denying that original call, one which we are constantly trying to evade and ignore. Thus he believes that the moral call is more than treating others as we treat ourselves—rather, we care for others, and in taking responsibility for them we are discharging the *only* moral duty we have.

One effect of Levinas's approach is that the call of the Other can never be fully satisfied or our ethical duties fully discharged. Once we face the gaze of the Other, there is always more to be done. For him, doing something for the Other and the act of giving are the hallmarks of our humanity and spirituality.

Many see Levinas's claims to be abstract and impractical. Nevertheless, it is worth examining the merits of his view. It is important to see the implications of what he would see as contemporary ego-based ethics. Virtues, rules, principles and, of course, self-interest are, to Levinas, expressions of the beliefs of the speaker, and whatever dressing we put on them, they ultimately reflect our personal preferences. Moreover, responsibility is not a case of being held accountable for our causally related actions since it is a much richer feature of our social and moral identity. Responsibility is the individual's response to the world, and in that sense, it effectively creates who the person is.

CHALLENGES

There are three standard lines of objection to postmodern approaches. The first is the charge of relativism: If there are many narratives but no means to adjudicate between them, they all seem equally valid. In short, anything would be allowed and no ethical position would be superior to any other. Second, as there is no consistent theory, the postmodern viewpoints seem vague and arbitrary to many people. Third, the postmodernists often start with a view of human nature that may not be universally accepted.

The general line of response by postmodernists to these challenges is that they are involved in broad projects that look to the very foundations of ethics, and so it may be unfair to judge them by the standards we would apply to traditional moral theories. As an alternative, they suggest we perhaps should first be as sympathetic to their general approach with an open mind and then subsequently reexamine our original thinking.

Initially the charge of relativism appears to be strong. Importantly, though, postmodernism does not necessarily imply that there should be no rules and that everything is allowed. Habermas, for example, argues that the counter to wholesale ethical relativism is to agree ahead of time to impose rules about the structure of the discourse on ourselves to prevent every case of consensus from being regarded as knowledge: All parties are regarded as moral equals, and coercion and force forbidden. The parties agree to be persuaded by the legitimacy of the best rational argument. The participants will bring only empirical evidence that all can access, and they will only accept norms consensually. Significantly, this is not a case of majority rule, where a minority is left voiceless and oppressed. Habermas explicitly endorses the view that those affected by the decisions freely assent to them based on the persuasiveness of the arguments presented. These aims may seem idealistic, but here again he is not presenting a model for immediate practical use, but a set of conditions he believes are necessary to make ethical talk possible in the first place.

Levinas lived through the Holocaust and was well aware of the dangers of a completely relativistic ethics. His rejoinder is to say that basic claims such as *Do not kill* are primal, immediate, and prerational, and resist formal systemization. His critics suggest that he cannot offer much prescriptive advice other than sweeping demands to respond to apparently vague, limitless, and unrestricted demands of the Other. However, followers might say that we should realize that ethics, as formulated in its traditional systematization, *is* unreasonable—the reality of the ethical life is destroyed once we impose rational boundaries or try to translate it into codes of conduct.

There is also a philosophically important distinction between relativism, where all individual claims are equally valid, and an *intersubjective* view taken by many postmodernists that stresses agreement between people. Thus moral agreement will not be empirically verifiable, but more like a group agreeing on a historical claim, say, that the American Declaration of Independence was signed in Philadelphia. The ultimate historical fact may be less important than the fact that there is an inclusive discussion and decision-making process which leads to agreement. The natural response might be that *agreement is not truth*, since a group could easily be collectively mistaken. However, saying that already presumes, as we often do, that there is a single and identifiable truth that we can discern. For example, how do we know with absolute certainty about historical facts or scientific hypotheses? Foucault points out that we reinterpret the world around us by the social constructs in place—thus astrology is not considered scientific in our contemporary world, and yet we believe in indiscernible subatomic particles. Similarly, Rorty suggests that whether or not there might be some objective truth, how we interpret the data we have for human benefit matters most.

Levinas prompts us to reflect on our core intuitions as a source of moral guidance. Like other postmodernist writers, he might say that the point of ethical inquiry may not be to create elaborate systems or guidelines. Instead, his project presents us with a metaphorical way of looking at the world, one that offers to make sense of the narrative we construct for ourselves. From this perspective, an ethical theory such as utilitarianism or deontology should not be thought of as a definitive set of instructions, but more like a *literary genre*. It captures a story in a certain way, creating its own narrative arc that will resonate with some more than others. Philosophers such as Levinas help describe common phenomena, and then offer a means for people to interpret them in ways that help them make sense of their lives and shape their behavior.

Thus the shift that the postmodernists make is not one from principled action to unprincipled action, but more a question of where our ethical intuitions originate, and whether principles lead or follow. Rorty explains that it is the latter: He believes we imagine a better world, and then create the appropriate principles. "Rational argumentation about moral issues" he says, "always lags behind. Reason can only follow paths that the imagination has broken."[3] Nevertheless, although Rorty is on point when he says we have more information and experience available to justify certain moral views and condemn others, there may still be a need to provide a means for people to differentiate between positions and favor some on principled grounds. In effect, some justifications are going to be more persuasive than others. Even in

---

[3]Richard Rorty, 2006. "Is Philosophy Relevant to Applied Ethics?" *Business Ethics Quarterly*, 16(3): 369–380 at 378.

Rorty's world of justification based on what works best, it seems there may still be a place for rational argument based on foundational principles of equality, freedom, and justice. Thus it appears that no philosophical movement, including postmodernism, fully abandons principles or rationality, and philosophers still have plenty of work to do, whatever school of thought they subscribe to.

As we've seen, the postmodernists put great stress on narrative, which has three parts: the storyteller, the story, and the audience. Rorty relies on the audience to be discerning enough to embrace stories that best capture our reality and justify our actions. As Foucault points out, though, this may deny the power structures at work in society, and how certain narratives are privileged and propagated while others are suppressed. In the American political arena, for instance, one popular belief is that there is equal opportunity for all, and hard work and intelligence will routinely lead to success. Whether this is true, it has dominated the discourse, is widely repeated in the media when the focus is on success stories, and is held out to inspire the younger generation. At the same time, competing narratives may be discouraged. Similarly, it was easier for many to accept that the *Herald of Free Enterprise* disaster was the result of one lax crewmember rather than looking to wider and more systematic explanations, such as the company putting profits before safety and cutting corners wherever they could.

Nevertheless, the reliance on narrative may still leave us wondering if there is a higher-level analysis required. Take Rorty's example of Stowe's *Uncle Tom*, which sensitized its audience to the realities of slavery, and allowed them to imaginatively put themselves in their place. Rorty asserts that this kind of imaginative exercise leads to greater empathy, and is our main hope for moral enlightenment. But consider that Stowe's work also presented caricatures of some of its characters—including Topsy and Sambo—that perpetuated racist attitudes. While we applaud the move to abolitionism, we should note the narrative also has the power to inspire the imagination to create unrealistic and negative connotations. Since we employ the same imaginative faculty to develop our moral outlook, the challenge will be how we should discern positive empathy from other potentially negative associations.

Postmodernists often rely on background assumptions about human nature. Habermas sees us as open to rational persuasion. Rorty eschews notions of human essences, and yet he consistently portrays humans as naturally compassionate. That is, he believes that if someone in a privileged position imaginatively puts himself or herself in the position of an oppressed person, it will spark empathy for the underdog, and subsequently motivate social change. Levinas suggests that we actually do feel the obligation to others as the paramount duty in our lives. His work anticipates that we would deny it, not because it is wrong, but because we want to avoid it. However, there is little room for debate at this level, since each party is appealing to fundamental intuitions that are hard to verify. In short, we might question some of the postmodernists own presumptions about how people are disposed to behave. In their own terms, these axiomatic beliefs ought to be subject to the same radical review that they impose on other ethical perspectives.

Summary

Levinas, Habermas, Rorty, and others challenge the dominant discourses that we take for granted, and instead want us to step back and reflect on our intuitions and how we put them to use. One of the factors they have in common is their rejection of the idea that ethical theory comes first, and that we then frame our behavior accordingly. They turn this on its head and make our moral intuitions foundational, and the rationalization and justification process a later or secondary feature of our morality.

In the *Herald* story, for example, all parties acknowledge that the ship capsized and people died as a result. The differing narratives emerge at the level of explanation and justifying or defending certain actions. Similarly, postmodern philosophers acknowledge that certain acts are wrong and condemnable: murder, slavery, rape, and so forth. They do not necessarily argue about those issues in specific terms, but examine the wider context in which they occur, closely examine the language and concepts we employ in describing them, and highlight the practical implications they have for social policy.

One of the exciting prospects that the postmodernist view invites is a greater role for the imagination and creativity in framing ethical narratives. It gives us permission to inventively explore the multiple options, as well as to frame issues in ways that demand rethinking them, taking into account their context and the forces that create their narrative arcs.

The power of the narrative is all-important for the postmodernists, and we should take seriously the claim that literature, poetry, art, psychology, economics, anthropology, and other disciplines may be just as effective as moral theory in promoting empathy—in short, whatever works. This is a powerful message, and we should not downplay the importance of presenting the story as part of any ethical project.

Whether we buy into the postmodernists' larger project, it is nevertheless well worth examining just how much of our life trajectory may be channeled in ways we don't often realize—for example, the assumption that a college education creates better citizens or our holidays are opportunities for greater consumption. The postmodernist movement encourages us to view ethics not only as a set of individual choices, but also as a function of institutions and systems that already provide the background framework and color pallette for those choices.

12

Non-Western Ethics

Thus far we have approached ethics from a Western point of view. Before we start to look at specific thinkers and theories in non-Western ethics, it is important to step back and consider how they are likely to strike someone whose frame of reference has been shaped by living in the West. Non-Western ethical theories may emerge from a completely different understanding of the world, and so concepts that may seem obvious and self-evident to Westerners may not be universally accepted. For instance, Western traditions place an emphasis on individual human rights and personal decision-making, but from the perspective of more collectivist societies this stress on the individual may conflict with the value of making choices to realize the goals of the group.

When working with non-Western material it is always useful to be open and sympathetic when we confront ideas that may initially seem odd or incongruous. Ethical views generally emerge from fundamental beliefs about human nature—for example, what it is to be a person and how we relate to the world. The same is true of the ethical ideas of non-Western cultures as laid out on the following pages, and it is therefore important to recognize that although there may be much moral agreement over such basic issues as caring for the young and elderly, not lying, or not causing unnecessary harm, how these issues are framed and put into practice will be significantly influenced by particular philosophical assumptions, as well as other cultural and historic factors.

CASE—SPITTING ON THE BUDDHA

There is a story that the Buddha (fifth century BCE) was sitting with his disciples one day when someone spat on him. The Buddha did not react with anger or conciliation, but looked at the man and said "What's next?" Some of the disciples protested that they should punish the man, but the Buddha told them their reaction was inappropriate and offensive. The man was a stranger, and did not really know him, the Buddha continued, and must therefore be spitting at the image from his mind, not at the real person. Besides, he said, spitting is an act of intense emotion, and there must be more to be said, hence his question to the man. The response shook the spitter so much that he left, and returned after a sleepless night, throwing himself prostrate at the Buddha's feet. The Buddha told his disciples that here again the man was communicating a message too strong for words, and again asked "What's next?" The man then asked for forgiveness, but the Buddha explained that he was no longer the same man who spat the day before, and there was nothing to forgive.

Ethics from different cultures may strike us in the same way as the Buddha's response struck his Buddha's disciples. Perhaps we fail to understand because we begin with different assumptions and conceptual frameworks, so that our natural reactions and intuitions are no longer a reliable guide to understanding.

Several words of caution are therefore in order. These non-Western theories may not be formulated in the way a Western audience expects: In the West, a canon of classic literature has evolved over time, and philosophical criticism and commentary occurs around the accepted essential works in the canon. Thus certain texts and ideas are held to be so important that anyone in the society ought to be acquainted with them. For instance, whether or not we believe in it, people in the West grow up with a common idea of hell, a place where evildoers are punished in the afterlife. Many cultures do not share this concept and would be puzzled by the notion. Similarly, we accept many ideas as part of our cultural literacy such as individual rights or romantic love which might mystify people from other parts of the world.

Moreover, problems in translation often arise; that is, concepts from one culture may not neatly map on to another. This happens in the Western tradition, too, of course. We use language all the time without thinking much about the embedded assumptions we rely on as native speakers. Extending the thought, then, it will inevitably be very difficult to translate certain terms unless we understand them in their temporal and cultural context, and we should bear this in mind when examining non-Western approaches to ethics.

Consider the Latin word *caritas*, which is central to some ethical and religious teachings. The original Latin referred to the quality that makes something valuable—for example, high price or preciousness. This took on the meaning of something that was beloved (and hence the words *care* and *caress*). When it came into English, it was translated as love, but also as charity. Hence even in our own language concepts evolve over time and there are confusions when we try to pin down some ideas—love and charity being good examples.

A ready cross-cultural case in point is the Chinese notion of "face." In English the phrase "saving face," is used to indicate saving someone from public embarrassment. Face is an important concept in China, as it represents the way others perceive you. In Western terms, if we disappoint someone, we are likely to say sorry and consider the issue closed. However, because of its collectivist orientation, Chinese culture emphasizes the importance of one's reputation before the group, and so being able to present yourself well in society matters much more. This in turn shapes behavior toward ensuring that individuals are rarely put on the spot or confronted publicly.

Finally, there is always a risk of oversimplifying and conflating ethics in other cultures. Just as Western ethics has diverse schools of thought and many variations within them, other approaches have been challenged and refined in many ways. We should be careful then, in presenting a broad overview of them, to recognize that a great deal of discourse exists within these various perspectives, and a detailed understanding of the theory will necessitate even further research and inquiry than our introduction here admits. These difficulties should not, however, prevent us from examining some of their major ideas. Broadening our studies to incorporate non-Western views can serve to expand our own approach and methodology. Furthermore, one cannot engage in the meaningful global dialogue that discovers shared principles without having at least some understanding of the historical location and philosophical assumptions that underlie vastly different cultural practices, customs, and traditions.

In this chapter we will look at four selected representative ethical movements. They place the locus of moral concern in the social order, self-consciousness, nature and community, respectively. However, it is important to bear in mind that both in Western and non-Western philosophy there are rich traditions with many thinkers and varied interpretations, and hence we should consider any selection as a brief introduction rather than fully comprehensive.

Some of the traditions we will examine are sometimes thought of as religious. However, while they may include notions of the divine (in the sense of finding the miraculous around us) or have ritualistic aspects, these philosophical approaches do not rely on revelation from a divine authority. That is not to say that someone following them may not have theistic beliefs, but we will specifically focus on the contribution of these various frameworks to ethics, not religion.

CONFUCIANISM

Confucianism involves a commitment to a natural order that applies to the harmony of both the self and the self-in-relationships. Proponents emphasize the importance of maintaining a balance between the individual and others as well as reconciling the various roles we play in life. Confucianism wants us to look inward and become self-aware so that we can good-heartedly develop well-ordered relationships with others and society at large.

Confucius is the name given in English to K'ung Fu-tzu—literally, K'ung "the Master"—who lived in China from 551 through 479 BCE. The philosophy attributed to him comes from writings of his students, especially Mencius, who often added commentary to his teacher's thought. There are nine Confucian classic texts, generally known as the "Four Books" and the "Five Classics." The best-known work in the West, the one most concerned with ethics, is known as the *Analects*, a collection of sayings and anecdotes about Confucius gathered into twenty chapter-length sections or "books." The *Analects* were probably written about fifty years after Confucius's death. The contents are not very systematic, but nevertheless some general themes become apparent. The philosophy is focused around personal character exhibited in our relationships rather than a set of abstract principles.

Confucius believes in a well-ordered universe as a basic value. From his perspective, there is order and harmony in the universe and it is our job to discern how to be in accord with it. He uses the term *Heaven* to represent this order, which does not rely on any particular individual and continues through time and across different societies. Insofar as we promote this order, we participate in this transcendent reality of Heaven.

For Confucius, personhood is defined in terms of relationships with others. That is, we exist by virtue of our connections to other people and the world around us, beginning with parent/child. It is human nature to live in societies, and hence our lives are a web of relationships that demand certain behaviors. If we understand our proper place and duties to others, then we will achieve happiness. One of the central ethical projects, therefore, is to discover our station in life, and the appropriate duties and expectations associated with it. Thus cultivating love in oneself and others (*Jen*) using a set of conventions that mirror the order of the universe (*Li*) will, he maintains, lead to the best life possible.

Consequently his philosophy emphasizes individual growth in order to become a "person of excellence"—sometimes translated as the **superior man**—who is aware of the various demands imposed by society. The hallmarks of this superiority are selflessness, understanding in one's private life, and courteousness in the public arena.

The person of excellence will embody what are termed the "Five Constant Relationships." These are parent/child, husband/wife, elder/younger sibling, elder/younger friend, and ruler/

subject. There are of course many other relationships that affect us, but they are taken to be analogs of the five basic ones.

Within the five basic relationships, the parent/child is the most fundamental and as a result, Confucianism emphasizes the value of the family. This is primarily because a well-ordered family is a model for the child in its later dealings in the world. As one of the famous sayings from another of the books puts it:

> The ancients who wished to illustrate illustrious virtue throughout the kingdom, first ordered well their own states. Wishing to order well their states, they first regulated their families. Wishing to regulate their families, they first cultivated their persons. Wishing to cultivate their persons, they first rectified their hearts. Wishing to rectify their hearts, they first sought to be sincere in their thoughts. Wishing to be sincere in their thoughts, they first extended to the utmost their knowledge. Such extension of knowledge lay in the investigation of things. Things being investigated, knowledge became complete. Their knowledge being complete, their thoughts were sincere. Their thoughts being sincere, their hearts were then rectified. Their hearts being rectified, their persons were cultivated. Their persons being cultivated, their families were regulated. Their families being regulated, their states were rightly governed. Their states being rightly governed, the whole kingdom was made tranquil and happy.[1]

Notably he says there are duties on both sides of each relationship. Consider his view on marriage: A wife should not have slavish obedience to a husband, but both have a role to fulfill. If things do not go smoothly, true obedience would require her to object to unfair demands. Similarly, a teacher deserves respect, but in turn has duties to the students to bring out the best in them and to help them in every way possible. He or she ought to acknowledge the qualities such as hard work, tenacity, or inquisitiveness that students bring to the classroom. In any relationship, if either side lets the other down, according to Confucianism, then there is disharmony in the proper order of things, which should prompt change.

Often the idea of inevitable inequalities seems somehow wrong to Westerners, even though it might reflect the reality of most of our everyday encounters. We should carefully distinguish social equality from moral equality, though. At one level, Confucius is making a sociological observation, and it might turn out that appreciating the various levels of power and position may be a very useful talent. In fact, many of our relationships do involve the judicious use of influence by one person over another, ideally for mutual benefit. The language that Confucius uses implies that the superior in the relationship has authority and the right to dictate, and is due obedience and respect. Nonetheless, we shouldn't be blinded by the terminology. Confucius posits a society where everything is well ordered, and hence those in positions of authority have earned them through merit, and if they are incompetent, they ought to be replaced. Thus, in general, people in superior ranks have done something to deserve their place in society, and they are due the respect and deference of their rank. Confucius argues that some individuals will be morally superior, and we ought to listen to their advice.

For example, Confucius considers the ruler and his relationship to the heavens. Ideally, it would reflect the idea that there is a right order in the universe, and be echoed by a calm and prosperous society. On the other hand, if there were civil unrest or injustice brought about by the prince's poor management, it would be appropriate for things to change, even through outright

---

[1]Confucius, *The Great Learning*, Chapter 1. http://classics.mit.edu/Confucius/learning.html

rebellion. Thus Confucius believes an unwise ruler may upset the natural order, and it would be fitting in that case for him to be overthrown by his subjects.

The Confucian view seems at first glance to go against autonomy in the classic liberal tradition of the West, which holds individual choice as paramount even if it may lead to poor judgments or mistakes. We should be careful to note, though, that Confucius does not actually demand restriction of individual liberties—he just believes that it is in everyone's interest that we follow certain rules and conventions, although ultimately it is up to the individual to subsequently conform or defy convention as he or she chooses. Accordingly, Confucius presents us with an ethical framework and strongly suggests courses of action, but nevertheless he does not absolve people from making moral decisions. Thus autonomy is still valued, but is always thought of in the context of a wider set of relationships and overall societal good.

Jen

Jen—sometimes translated as Ren—comes from a character that embodies both "man" and "two." It is the overriding virtue in Confucian ethics; achieving it allows one to become a person of excellence. The basic idea of Jen is that an individual should cultivate love to bring out the best in both self and others. Translations vary in their attempts to convey this concept. Some commentators refer to it as complete moral excellence. Others simply use "goodness," "charity," "kindness," or "benevolence."

Jen involves doing one's best, and then extending that feeling to others. Recall that for Confucius the human world is one of relationships. Jen arises from the foundational parent/child relationship, and the natural devotion and care that children feel toward their parents (*Hsiao*). Sometimes the concept is translated as "submission" but once again, it is important to not get caught up by the hierarchical terminology. "Submission" to Western ears has overtones of blind obedience. Perhaps a better understanding would be "due respect" or "deference." That is to say, we enter the world already in relations with others, and this submission is not so much submission to another individual, but submission of both individuals to the norms of that relationship.

As the preceding passage highlights, Confucius believes that it is important to know ourselves first because the core of our excellence in all of our relationships is self-knowledge and purity of our heart. Sometimes, to express this, Confucius uses the term **sincerity**. The underlying notion is that we have to engage in honest introspection rather than present an image to the world based on our own illusions or according to someone else's expectations. Only after we have achieved harmony within ourselves can we enter into full fellowship with others. In Confucianism, love and doing good are intimately tied up with knowing how best to serve others.

The converse of Jen echoes the Christian "Golden Rule," but instead of "do unto others as you would have them do unto you," Confucius puts it in the negative. That is, he suggests you refrain from doing unto others what you would not have them do to you.

> [A student asked] "Is there one word which may serve as a rule of practice for all one's life?" The Master said, "Is not *reciprocity* such a word? What you do not want done to yourself, do not do to others." (*Book 15*, #28)

Again, although translations differ, the central idea is that the individual first reaches a place of personal peace and acceptance, and then extends this attitude to others. For Confucius, morality always begins with the self, but necessarily has to be manifested in social relationships. So while there is some emphasis on the individual, the central focus is on establishing right relationship with others. This notion of relationship is not an abstract external ideal, but an immediate quality, one that we already have if only we realized it. He says in *Book 7*, #30, "Is Jen a remote thing? I wish to have Jen, and lo! Jen is at hand"

In another passage in *Book 5*, Confucius is in the company of his students when he asks them what they want most. One responds that he would like to have material goods such as carriages and clothes that he could give to his friends. Another wants the modesty to prevent him from announcing his good deeds. Then they ask the Master what he wants, and Confucius replies "To give rest to the aged, to show sincerity to friends, and treat the young with tenderness."

One interpretation of the passage is that the first student is looking for beneficial outcomes, and the second to do good for its own sake (and here we can see correlates to utilitarianism and deontology). Confucius, though, responds in terms of promoting virtuous dispositions to all people. He extends the notion of familial relations to an idea of the common good for all mankind, in that we are all connected and therefore have interlocking duties. The person of excellence, then, will have an ethical attitude that promotes universal beneficence.

Li

Confucius considers Jen to be a natural human instinct. Because people live in societies with a variety of relationships, he thinks that the best way to express Jen is through a set of conventions that mirror the harmony of the external world. This leads to a set of rituals that govern human interaction. These conventions or rituals of behavior are known as **Li**, sometimes translated as "propriety." Accordingly, at the beginning of *Book 12* we find Confucius saying:

> To subdue oneself and return to Li, this is Jen … Look not at what is contrary to propriety; speak not what is contrary to propriety; and make no movement that is contrary to propriety.[2]

Strictly following convention allows everyone to know his or her place and act appropriately. This creates social harmony and stability. Civil society is, in effect, a commons shared by all, governed by strict rules that prevent individual abuse and consequent mutual harm. This view is reflected in a section from *The Book of Rites* called "The Commonwealth State":

> When the perfect order prevails, the world is like a home shared by all. Virtuous and worthy men are elected to public office … All men love and respect their own parents and children, as well as the parents and children of others. There is caring for the old; there are jobs for the adults; there is nourishment and education for the children. There is a means of support for the widows and the widowers; for all who find themselves alone in the world; and for the disabled … Intrigues and conniving for ill gain are unknown. Villains such as thieves and robbers do not exist. The door to every home need never be locked and bolted by day or night. These are the characteristics of an ideal world, the commonwealth state.[3]

Moreover, Li puts us in the right attitude toward others and spiritual beings. However, we should not think of it as purely ceremonial compliance. It is better regarded as a moderating influence that guides and governs our emotions, avoids extremes, and puts the mind and body in harmony.

---

[2]Confucius, *Analects*, trans. James Legge, 1861.

[3]Confucius, "The Record of Rites," Chapter IX, *The Commonwealth State,* http://www.confucius.org/lunyu/edcommon.htm

Fate

Along with Jen and Li, Confucianism is anchored in the concept of fate. However, this notion is not fatalistic in the sense that everything we do is fixed, because in fact, Confucius repeatedly emphasized the importance of personal choice. Rather, the supposition rests on a picture of the world as ordered according to a certain harmony that we can choose to promote or not. Confucius was not very concerned with outcomes as a moral gauge. He felt the focus should be on individual choice at a particular time. He thought that strategic thinking for personal gain—often translated as *profit*—was an immoral distraction. Thus he was not fatalistic in the sense of believing that things were fixed and could not be changed, with the possible implication that it doesn't matter what we do. A better way of thinking about it is that we should cultivate the best character possible and behave in the best way we can in any situation. Then, if things don't always come out the way we imagined, so be it. We can only do what we can at any moment given our limited knowledge. If we cultivate Jen, strive for excellence, and stop worrying about the consequences, he believes we will live with less anxiety and develop a sense of contentment.

Challenges

The teachings of Confucius did not become widespread or influential in his lifetime. However, they were later taken up as state orthodoxy. Indeed for six hundred years—only ending in the twentieth century—memorizing his works was expected of every Chinese student who aimed to join the imperial bureaucracy that was the main means to a secure job and personal advancement. Widespread adherence to his teachings led China to become a society that relied on strict social conventions and everyone knowing his or her station in life.

Historically, despite the fact that Confucius advocated overthrowing autocratic and ineffective rulers, several emperors used his works to justify their despotism. Yet the basic emphasis on conservatism and collective welfare nevertheless created a system that lasted for over 2,000 years, until encounters with the British in the nineteenth century. Another distortion worth noting is that while Confucian teachings do not directly advocate the subordination of women, it had that effect when it was adopted as state doctrine. Male domination was seen as natural and correct, and women were expected to know their place, exhibit self-discipline, manage the household, and selflessly support their husbands. At the same time, society honored the role of mother within the family unit.

The most striking challenge in Confucianism for many Westerners is the subjugation of the self and the primacy of convention. These issues appear to go against qualities that we prize: personal autonomy and innovation. It would seem that under Confucianism, the individual has to acknowledge his or her role in society and reconcile to doing it well. However, this characterization is not exactly correct. Confucius notes that through industrious hard work, one can rise above his station. Moreover, individuality is not squashed, but rather takes expression in *how* a person relates to others, given the social realities already in place.

It is useful to see how Confucius's thought prompts us to examine whether we are as free as we often imagine. For example, we are bound up in relationships of family, friends, work, and community, and each has its various privileges and responsibilities. Consider the family unit: It is at the same time liberating and constraining for the individuals involved. Parents grant the children freedom and sponsor their activities, yet there will also be rules and assigned duties. On a grander scale, even in Western liberal societies, individual freedom does not mean anarchy where everyone makes up his or her own rules. Instead, there is freedom within certain limits—such as not interfering with the rights of others—with significant punishments if someone disobeys the boundary constraints.

A linked question that Confucianism poses is whether we are actually autonomous. His answer will be that, yes, we are masters of our own hearts and can certainly interact with the world to try to change things. On the other hand, humans are social creatures, and the way we structure communities will necessarily involve reciprocal duties and personal compromises. Inevitably, as part of the human condition we are in the middle of a web of relationships of various kinds. Therefore we should do the best we can in each of those relational roles: friend, colleague, sibling, and so forth. Additionally, our actions are really all we can control; outcomes will be what they will be. Thus there is no point in agonizing about things that are ultimately beyond our power.

Confucians have traditionally emphasized rules of etiquette that govern every action, sometimes so elaborate that they include details about how to address one another or the correct kind of dress or behavior in every social situation. This may seem odd to contemporary Westerners. Here again it is probably best not to dwell on the minutiae, but instead to consider that, in sociological terms, various social conventions are a valuable means of preserving the identity of any community, whether a family or society as a whole. If we look around, we can see many rituals in our own society that may initially seem trivial but are quite important. For example, people in a court will rise when a judge arrives. Or for a school graduation event, commencement ceremonies follow a certain set format. Even in everyday encounters, requests include the ritual word *please*. Social greetings include questions about personal welfare ("how are you?") that follow patterns, and people make negative judgments if someone is impolite or doesn't adhere to accepted conventions.

One important function of these rituals is to remind us of the various social relationships we are a part of, and our relative social standing in society. This may not be obvious until we think about traveling to a distant country where there are different customs. Not knowing how to act around others—whether it is appropriate to look at people in the eyes, or shake hands, for example—is likely to make us feel awkward and embarrassed. Thus although we are not always conscious of the dynamics, we are routinely involved in social conventions that let us know how we should treat one another.

Summary

Confucianism, in contrast to many Western theories, has direct practical insights that tell us how to live a good life. It does not dwell on abstractions as is the case with many Western philosophical positions. Instead, it offers concrete recommendations about everyday behavior and emphasizes the development of personal character by encouraging reflection and disciplined control of our thoughts and desires.

However, it is undeniable that classical Confucianism does not deal well with how a person or society should adapt to changing circumstances, and how conventions ought to evolve. For instance, traditional Western theories are perhaps better at accommodating changing views about the role and rights of women. More recent commentators on Confucianism have addressed these worries, and many feel that the text can be interpreted more flexibly today than it has been in the past.

Confucianism is often difficult for Western readers to accept or fully appreciate. Nevertheless, it suggests that through self-discipline a person can achieve peace and harmony, both internally and in relationships with others, an ambition that can have great appeal as a guiding principle in life.

TETSURO WATSUJI

Watsuji (1889–1960), a recent Japanese thinker is also a useful representative of an ethical approach based in social order. He was well versed in European philosophy, and was instrumental in introducing Japanese ethical concepts to the West. As a young professor he studied and translated Nietzsche and Kierkegaard, but ultimately disagreed with their shared belief that ethics springs from the isolated self.

Ethics is intimately connected with theories about human nature, and Watsuji's views about personhood are foundational to his thought. Watsuji's major work was *Rinrigaku*. In Japanese, *Rinri* can be translated as ethics, and it consists of two characters, *Rin*, which refers to linked relationships, and *Ri*, which signifies order. Linking the two, then, offers a set of ordered connections that indicate how we should behave as people bound together in a community.

Watsuji shies away from using a word for the individual, and prefers to use the term *Ningen*. Ningen itself is composed of two ideograms: one for *nin*, "person," and the other *gen,* meaning "between." A helpful way to think about it is to consider the similar English word *man*. We use the term to refer to particular males, but also much more broadly and inclusively when we talk about, say, "to serve man," meaning mankind. Because the word encompasses both meanings, when we use it, we are reminded that we are all linked by our humanity. For Watsuji, to be a *Ningen* is to be a member of a community.

In contrast, a typical Western view of community is to think of it as discrete individuals treating one another with impartiality; in John Stuart Mill's phrase, "each counts for one and no-one for more than one." However, for the Japanese, community is more than a collection of individuals and more like an organism that has different cells that are all linked and part of the overall entity.

Moreover, Watsuji believes this integration into the wider community means that the idea of personal consciousness dominant in Western philosophy is flawed from the very start. The French rationalist philosopher Rene Descartes (1596–1650), considered the father of modern philosophy, for example, in his famous statement "I think therefore I am" declared that the only thing he could ever really know was that he exists. Watsuji noted that in making his claim Descartes is already using language, and so even the most fundamental idea about personal identity occurs in a shared means of communication that connects the person to others in the culture.

The Individual and the Community

Watsuji held that humans are individuals who naturally live in the context of various communities. The way we assert our individuality is by reacting against the community in some way. He calls this a "negation." For example, we grow up generally doing what we are told and following expectations. At some point, many individuals buck authority somewhat, and in so doing Watsuji sees us denying conformity.

However, as we mature ethically, according to Watsuji, we come to see that there are things that matter more than we do—causes or values that are greater than ourselves. This awareness then pulls us back into the community, so that we suppress our own personal desires for the common good. He terms this a second negation: We begin by positively following societal expectations, go against them, and then suppress our own desires, bringing us full circle back within the community norms.

We can think about separating the individual from society by making an analogy to a painting. Typically a painting has a foreground and background, and the whole work is surrounded by a frame. When we look at it, we can choose to focus on the foreground, but when we do, we are still aware of the background. Even though we can separate the two as a mental exercise, both make up the whole composition. The frame is also important, as it puts boundaries on the picture and defines its space on the wall. Similarly, Watsuji believes that society can be viewed as being made up of both individuals and the community at large, but they are not independent elements. While we can do the mental exercise of separating them, we should acknowledge that both are part of an overall unity. Although we can concentrate on one and not the other, we are the ones who distinguish parts of a complete whole and it is impossible to think of one without the other. Furthermore, as with the picture frame, people in communities are bounded by rules and norms that give them identity and shape.

Trust

Watsuji believes that the bedrock of community is the quality of trust. Here again he finds constructive contradictions: We could not know trust without betrayal. He is well aware that, for instance, pickpockets prey on the gullible. Nevertheless, he says that they could operate only if the norm was one of trust among people, and that is what makes crime shocking. He finds hope in these contrasting negations, since when we say that someone is an enemy, the very language used opens up the possibility of friendship. That is, if someone is my enemy, he is not my friend, but describing him as a nonfriend shows that there is already conceptual space for the relationship to change from one to the other.

Trust, as he presents it, is not a contract and does not rely on evidence. Rather, it is more a precondition intrinsic to human interaction. It involves being true to one's humanity. In business dealings, for example, a person should be trustworthy, that is, operate on the basis that he or she is already trusted by all the various stakeholders in the enterprise; it is not a quality to be selectively used, like a tool, when it is strategically useful. Following this business example, Watsuji's philosophy goes some way to illustrating how Japanese companies aim for long-term customer relationships, as opposed to a quick sale. It also explains some Japanese attitudes of common commitment to an enterprise where for instance, a company will be reluctant to lay off workers during hard times.

Watsuji criticized Americans for having what he termed **reiki shakai**, a profit-centered society based on self-interest and material comfort, often forsaking the love of art for easy stimulation. He traced these traits back to thinkers such as Hobbes, and described Westerners as behaving instrumentally to fulfill their individual self-interest. He thought their morality was overly legalistic, and based on manufactured rights instead of well-established relationships.

The notion of individual rights as understood in the West does in fact run counter to Watsuji's philosophy, which is founded on the primacy of the community and communal good. In practice, Watsuji would prefer that disputes are put to the arbitration of an elder, who will make a judgment based on what is the overall best interest rather than submitting them to a legalistic process to evaluate whether a particular person has certain entitlements.

Challenges

Watsuji's philosophy provides an interesting counterpoint to Western individualism, and gives food for thought about what our true ambitions should be. True, we have fostered material comfort, but maybe at a price. It turns out that by various happiness indexes, people in Western societies are working more, but enjoying life less. Additionally, the stress on individual accomplishment and acquisition may actually mask what is in their best mutual interest; for example, a very successful arbitrage banker may make a great deal of money, while the overall society suffers as a result of his or her own conduct.

Perhaps the biggest challenge for Watsuji's approach is that he considered communities to be benign. He envisioned a set of nested communities—the family, the town, the district, and so on—with the ultimate community of communities being the state. In his writings he considered that the emperor embodied all that was good, and that such a ruler was automatically owed unflagging allegiance. History shows some of the problems this brings. If the ruler is weak, then power can easily fall into the hands of the unscrupulous. Or the ruler might be strong, but not benign. In either case, in the absence of some overarching principles to distinguish better from worse actions at the highest level, a country is at the whim of its ruler.

Watsuji was criticized after the Second World War for his unwavering and uncritical devotion to the Imperial rule, and his writings have often been dismissed because of that aspect of his personal history. Although Watsuji may have been misguided in his uncritical allegiance to those in power, we cannot dismiss his ethics on those grounds alone. The idea that there may be times when we should put our lives on the line for a cause greater than ourselves also resonates in our society; for instance, many Westerners have gone to war and put their lives at risk for the sake of duty, honor, justice, and country.

TAOISM

Sometime around the sixth century BCE, around the same time that Confucius lived, a text that has traditionally been attributed to Lao Tzu ("the Old Master") emerged in China, although it is probably the work of several authors. Its title is the *Tao Te Ching* ("The Treatise on The Way and Its Power"), and its opening lines are these:

> The Tao that can be trodden is not the enduring and unchanging Tao. The name that can be named is not the enduring and unchanging name.
>
> (Conceived of as) having no name, it is the Originator of heaven and earth; (conceived of as) having a name, it is the Mother of all things.

The *Tao Te Ching* has become one of the most cherished of all Chinese philosophical texts. The main idea at work in the text, and in the philosophical position of Taoism, is that nature is the source and gauge of all things. Humans are part of the natural world, and their desires are therefore also natural, so thwarting them through rules of conduct is likely to end in resistance and strife. Thus the Taoist seeks to find the "**Way**," or path of nature, as a guide to personal action. The Way is sometimes described as the "Easy Way," since it means not fighting nature, but flowing with it.

Taoism was refined some three hundred years after Lao Tzu by Chuang Tzu (probably with contributions from a number of anonymous authors). Chuang Tzu's work is most associated with the ethical aspects of The Way. He defines happiness, for instance, as the ability to empathize with the infinite, shedding the petty distinctions and limits imposed by our ordinary categorizations. The approach taken in the *Tao Te Ching* is unlike that of any Western philosophical text, and for this reason its ideas might strike some Western readers as hopelessly unfathomable. Furthermore, the work's declared suspicion of rational analysis not only contrasts it to Western views but also makes any attempt to describe it as necessarily piecemeal and less than fully adequate.

The principal virtues that allow us to follow The Way are simplicity, patience, and compassion. It requires that we deny anthropomorphism, which considers humanity to be the pinnacle of creation. To the Taoist, all creation is part of a harmonious whole. Given our limited senses, we are constrained to thinking of it in certain ways that are likely incorrect, as we may lack the perspective of the infinite. In a famous passage, Chuang Tzu writes about dreaming that he was a butterfly. He says he does not know whether he was a man dreaming about a butterfly, or a butterfly dreaming he is a man, to illustrate the point that it is always appropriate to adopt and use multiple perspectives, and the view of the whole is inescapably elusive.

Adherents regard the Tao as the source of all, and it is so fundamental that Tao itself has no particular characteristics. In Western terms we might usefully think of the Tao as "logical space"—the zone of all possibilities. The Tao has sometimes been compared to the inside of a bowl or an uncarved block of wood. Although the bowl has shape, it creates space that can be used, and in fact its emptiness allows it infinite potential. Similarly the block presents itself as potential for creating something with form and shape. Because there is Tao, things and relationships can subsequently emerge, taking the form of particular objects or relationships that can then be named. Tao itself, though, is prior to naming, and as such resists being put into words, leading to the apparent paradox that only with Tao can there be names, but Tao itself cannot be named. Hence the Tao is usually only alluded to through metaphors and stories.

Tao might also be thought of as that which gives form and order to the universe. It is not a mystical being, but is imminent in the world and manifested in its cycles and harmony. When we observe the natural world, we find that there are always complementary principles: light and dark, active and passive, male and female, and so forth. These pairs represent the dual forces of *yin* and *yang*. There do not always need to be equal amounts of yin and yang in every circumstance, since what matters most is that they are in the right proportion for the situation. In different cases it may turn out to be appropriate for there to be more of one than another, as long as they are in harmony with Tao. For example, there are seasonal changes in the length of the day, or cycles of growth and decay.

Taoist ethics has twin pillars: a basic liberating trust in humanity and a profound optimism. For instance, Taoist writings make the case that if we trust people, they will not repay with betrayal but work cooperatively. Consequentially a Taoist is likely to say the best government intervenes minimally in people's lives, and the best ruler is one who empowers rather than restricts his or her subjects. For instance, current research in workplace settings has determined that employees who work in teams and are not micro-managed seem to be both productive and happier than their counterparts who are consistently monitored.

In the case of conflict, Taoism advocates something it terms **wu-wei**. This can be translated as *minimal effort*. It would be wrong to take this to mean inertia. Rather it suggests that soft and prolonged energy can break down the hardest resistance, like running water can have an effect on the hardest of rocks. Likewise, we could resolve our differences through violence, but this is typically unnatural and wasted energy. If we could channel the same energies to peaceful resolution, seeking the harmony embodied in the Tao, we would be more likely to find a way to a more lasting solution and greater well-being for all.

Taoist Language

Discussions about language and its various uses are central to Taoism. It suggests that many distinctions are imposed by the human mind that first distinguishes characteristics, and then classifies them—day, for instance, is also not-night. Moreover, human language—*names* in Taoist terminology—is inherently relativistic. A mountain, for example, also carries with it the concept of lowland, since we recognize only one in relation to the other. Furthermore, these distinctions do not derive from nature itself, but instead are products of our psychology, and hence are just one way of describing the world.

Additionally, not only do humans create contrasts, but we also differ in our judgments about them. Some may think of, say, a spicy dish as delicious, while others consider it repulsive. Similarly, a person may appear to be in distress when doing hard manual labor, but from a different perspective he may be learning a beneficial lesson about fortitude. In short, a Taoist would say that as we are all different, we can only make judgments based on the context and situation as we see it at a certain time and place. Universal agreement will therefore be impossible according to the Taoist since judgments are likely to vary with each person's individual perception.

Western ethics has various responses to such a relativist challenge. These are usually based on an assumption that there are at least some moral absolutes, and these are just as much facts as scientific claims. For example, the claim that unnecessary suffering is morally bad and should be avoided might be treated in the West as a fact similar to the empirical finding that hot air rises. But the argument that there are absolutes will have no purchase with the Taoist who believes that everything is changeable, including any purported factual claim. Within its own worldview, Taoism is entirely consistent. For example, Chuang Tzu discusses right and wrong with his students, asking who will decide the outcome of an argument. He poses a case where a man on one side of the dispute gets more people to agree with him, but Chuang Tzu points out that this does not make him right. He feels no one is authorized to make an absolute judgment, noting that if something were completely right, then it would be obvious to all and there could be no argument. He concludes "Forget distinctions. Leap into the boundless and make it your home!"[4]

"Leaping into the boundless" can be interpreted as going beyond conventional categories. If we were able to take the viewpoint of an independent, eternal being, then we might be able to see everything in its proper perspective. However, as mortal beings we are tied to the sensory input and mental categories provided by language, and so the boundless becomes an aspiration to get beyond our human limitations.

Critically, the relativist position of the Taoist need not mean that there are no standards or particular behaviors that cannot be condemned. It is true that there are murderers and other criminals, of course. For the Taoist, these individuals are anomalies. They stray from the normal and natural—in effect, they go against the flow of the universe. They are a minority, acting against the backdrop of regular behavior. So if we seek to determine The Way, we will find it much more in the easy and simple cooperative life than in a path of aggression and competition.

Moreover, if we let people take responsibility for their own behavior and let them follow The Way, Taoism asserts they will live up to that trust. On the other hand, Taoism contends that if we continually regulate behavior (e.g., in the many formal rituals in Confucianism) people will inevitably fail to adhere completely, and this unnecessarily creates outcasts from the community. The Taoist would likely point out that most of us have not really fully embraced unregulated trust, and suggest we would have more harmonious and balanced lives if we truly did so. Therefore, Taoism also gives us a vision of respectful dialogue and mutual tolerance, and encourages us to move in that direction.

Challenges

Several ethical implications of Taoism go against traditional Western thinking. First, it seems to assert that there is a plan at work in nature which we can discern. Second, the good is defined by

---

[4]Chuang Tse, *Book 2*, "Discussion on Making All Things Equal."

following that discoverable natural path. Third, there will always be multiple perspectives about any situation, so there will never be an absolutely correct one.

In essence, the Taoist is likely to respond that we have to give up the language of right and wrong; ethics is not to be built on rational moral discourse. Many Westerners may well be confused by Taoism's apparent reluctance to condemn behavior, or pass judgment on opposing points of view. Taoism seems to offer little prescriptive advice. It also appears to have no definitive decision procedure, and avoids rules, codes, or guidelines. Someone who faces a moral dilemma may seem to be forced to rely on opaque stories or vague precepts, with no benchmarks for acceptable behavior.

These sorts of criticism are unlikely to persuade the Taoist. Recall that Taoism is not an algorithm for conduct which relies on outcomes or a rational process. It is more an integrated outlook on life, and its adherents would say that it is entirely practical. Just as the Western Pragmatic approach is based on what works best, all things considered, Taoism asserts that whatever is in harmony with The Way will work best, and it is ultimately futile to try to alter it. For example, consider the use of dams on many rivers in the USA. Although they have been effective in making waterways more accessible to boats, the alterations have often also had negative collateral effects, such as destroying wetland areas that control flooding naturally. Taoists would say the same about human action. Although we can certainly impose rules, and force people to do things against their will, ultimately these systems will unravel unless they are consistent with the natural order.

It might be tempting to think that Taoism, with all its relativism and acceptance of yin and yang, leads to complacency or indifference toward the world, but there is nothing inherent in the teachings to suggest this. On the contrary, discerning the Tao may entail hard work and sensitivity. As anyone who has tried to mediate a discussion over a heated topic will attest, finding the joint merit in differing perspectives requires a significant investment of time, energy, patience, active listening, and empathy.

BUDDHISM

Like the other non-Western approaches we have looked at in this section, Buddhism is more a philosophy than a religion. It does not look to a transcendent God with the authority to provide answers, and it is primarily concerned with individuals reconciling themselves to the world and finding practical solutions. Buddhism suggests that metaphysical speculation about questions such as the infinity of time and space should remain secondary to immediate issues of dealing with suffering in the world.

Buddhism at its core is about overcoming ignorance and reconciling oneself with reality. Ironically, although its starting place is personal awareness rather than community, the aim is to overcome the ego and dampen individual ambition in favor of promoting the welfare of others.

The founder of Buddhism, Gautama Siddhārtha, was born in the sixth century BCE near the Himalayas in northern India. Siddhārtha was born a prince and had a sheltered and privileged upbringing. When he was a young man and left his royal compound for the first time, he was shocked to encounter sickness, old age, and death. In reaction to what he saw, he left his family to seek an answer to the problem of suffering in the world. First he took up religion in the form of traditional Hindu teachings. Not finding what he was looking for, he became an ascetic, someone who gives up the materialism and its pleasures and cares. However, after several years he realized that he was indulging in practices that were opposite but just as extreme as his earlier life of luxury, and that the answer probably lay in a middle way between indulgence and renunciation. According to legend, Siddhārtha sat for many days in deep concentration under a fig tree (sometimes called the Bodhi tree) and suddenly understood the causes of and means to overcome suffering. Afterward, he was known as the Buddha, the "Enlightened One," and spent the next forty-five years traveling and teaching. His followers collected his lectures and sayings. The central tenets of these are contained in *Tipitaka*, or *The Three Baskets*.

A famous Buddhist teaching tells of a story of a man shot with a poisoned arrow who is in great pain. The doctor's primary concern, it is pointed out, should be to remove the arrow and tend to the patient; if he were to wait until he had discovered the nature and origin of the arrow, the age of the patient, or who his parents were, then the man would likely die first. Thus Buddhism deals less with metaphysical speculation than it does with alleviating everyday distress. At its most basic, Buddhism suggests that the truth is within us, to be found through profound self-reflection. Its adherents aim for a state of Nirvāna, or release. This comes when someone realizes the impermanence of things, and is able to combine discipline and knowledge to overcome the cycle of suffering.

Suffering and Change

The paramount fact of life that a Buddhist accepts is that life involves suffering. We are surrounded by unmet desires, anxieties, sickness, and ultimately death. We also of course experience joy and love, but the Buddha believed that these pleasures are transitory. What appears to be joyful does not last, whereas suffering is the constant background condition to human existence.

Another central idea in Buddhism, which is inherited from Hindu thought, is that there is no substance. Many Western thinkers subscribe to the notion that some things are permanent through time and space. They say objects that we perceive—for example, the flowers, chairs, and other people that we encounter—have substance and persist inwardly despite the apparent outward changes of decay, destruction or death. The prime example is the self, since we generally believe we are the same person as we were yesterday. In stark contrast, Buddhists do not believe in a persisting self. Furthermore, according to Buddhism, we are constantly tripped up by the language we use and falsely led into believing that things are substantial and constant. They acknowledge that we may refer to "things" and what we think of as our "selves" by one name at different times; a flower is a flower when fully bloomed and also when it starts to fade, and we refer to "James" when he is a child and even after he dies. But they observe that in fact everything is in the process of decay or rebuilding, even if only very slowly. When we look inward, the Buddha would say we do not discover a soul or a self, only a set of sensory experiences. The most we can ever do is become more aware of our thoughts and sensations, but in doing this, we are never discerning something that is permanent.

An analogy is useful here. Consider muscle fibers. Separate overlapping strands of tissue interweave to form a muscle, but no one strand is continuous from one end to the other. They are linked, to be sure, but it would be a mistake to talk about the essence of the muscle itself. In a similar way, a person experiences a series of selves, each causally connected to those that come before and after.

On this framework, it would still be proper to hold someone responsible for things he or she did earlier; the series is not a set of discrete and individual selves, because of the constant interconnectedness. Thus for a Buddhist, it would be an inaccurate description to say that the world is changing, since the phrase implies that there is a permanent object, the world, that is experiencing some alteration. Rather, we should acknowledge that impermanence is an inherent quality of the world, and say that the world *is* change.

Change is central to Buddhism, then, but change does not come about without cause. Everything that exists will come into being and eventually cease to be. An unavoidable part of the cycle is that everything is itself caused and will also bring about change. This sense of connection is the concept of **karma**, where all thoughts or deeds are prompted by others, and will have causal effects as well. Sometimes karma is characterized in the West as a kind of cosmic poetic justice, where evil deeds will be punished and good ones rewarded. However, it is more accurately explained as a sense that the present world has been brought about by prior events, and the future will depend on what we do now.

Buddhist teaching says that the principle problem for us is overcoming our ignorance of the causes of suffering. Some degree of suffering is due to holding on to material goods, and thus detaching ourselves from the things we prize so highly will be a useful step. If we see possessions in the proper perspective as transient, as means rather than ends, then we can let go of them more easily. Importantly, this does not mean returning to the ascetic state of renouncing the world, but instead purging ourselves of desires that makes us cling to people and material goods tenaciously, when it turns out we can never hold onto them forever. Given that reality, the Buddhist maintains that a full life focuses on bringing about the well-being of others through awareness of the impermanent nature of things and behaving well in the face of that reality. This middle course is known as the Eightfold Noble Path, a set of principles for living. To overcome suffering, one must have:

1. Right ideas
2. Right aspiration
3. Right speech
4. Right behavior
5. Right livelihood
6. Right effort
7. Right mindfulness
8. Right concentration

RIGHT IDEAS The basic Buddhist teachings are outlined in the Four Noble Truths, which are the central ideas of Buddhist philosophy:

1. There is suffering.

2. Suffering is not arbitrary, but has causes, typically cravings caused by desire. We get locked into a cycle of wanting to possess things, yet the transient nature of the universe means that we can never really keep them: any ownership is inevitably going to be temporary, and we will find that gaining them never fully satisfies our wants. This typically means we then crave more. Yet paradoxically, a Buddhist would say that the more we cling to things the more we become separated from others and the realities of life. Conversely, sympathetic engagement with others will reduce suffering.

3. Suffering can only be mitigated by recognizing and addressing its causes. For example, if we judge our happiness in terms of material acquisitions, then we will probably never have enough; we set ourselves up for anxiety and disappointment. On the other hand, if we recognize that suffering is caused by unrealistic cravings, and subsequently let go of those desires, then we can extinguish false hope and achieve freedom from the grip they have on us.

4. Suffering can be reduced by following the Eightfold Path, which is set out in this and the other seven precepts.

RIGHT ASPIRATION   Right aspiration will give us the moral grounding to establish correct values and goals in life. Keeping this in mind, we should not be distracted by what is happening in the immediate here and now but concentrate on higher goals and larger purposes.

RIGHT SPEECH   Words are often misleading, making us believe in the reality of things that have no substance and are inadequate in conveying inner truths discerned through self-reflection. Thus we should be very careful in choosing the best words to express our thoughts.

RIGHT BEHAVIOR   The basic quality of moral conduct is self-discipline. Correct behavior is constituted in five principles of restraint: Do not kill. Be chaste. Be honest. Do not take stimulants. Practice self-control.

RIGHT LIVELIHOOD   We should take up employment that will enhance life and minimize harms to ourselves and others.

RIGHT EFFORT   Morality is not merely the casual avoidance of bad deeds. Instead it is a conscious and disciplined effort that we must engage throughout our lives.

RIGHT MINDFULNESS   The natural tendency of the mind is to wander and get distracted. Hence it is important that we maintain the discipline to focus on those things that matter and are under our control.

RIGHT CONCENTRATION   Right concentration is a meditative practice that incorporates the seven other steps. By removing ourselves from the distractions of sensory experience, meditation allows people the clearest access to pure thought.

Finally, it is worth mentioning the concept of **reincarnation**. Sometimes the idea is lampooned; perhaps to the point where someone might caricature a Buddhist as saying that if someone acts badly in this life, they might awake to find themselves, say, a spider in the next life. The idea is much more subtle, of course, than any such caricature would have us believe.

Perhaps the most straightforward way to approach it is to note that a Buddhist accepts that actions will have both immediate and lasting effects. This means that harmful acts will propagate harm, often in ways that we cannot yet know. Moreover, as noted earlier, instead of thinking about *the self* as a permanent entity, Buddhism regards it as constantly changing. Those changes come about through a series of causes and effects. Recall, too that we should abandon any thought of ourselves as independent and self-sufficient beings and realize that we are all part of an overall unity.

Bringing these elements together with a view that good promotes good, and conversely that harm brings more harm in the world, the Buddhist maintains we should always act to alleviate suffering wherever and whenever we can with regards to other people, animals, and the environment. Although we may not literally come back as a spider, we should treat that small creature, and all other living things, *as if it were possible that we might*. Essentially, this is a different version of the Golden Rule—do unto others as they would do you. Following this precept means we ought to give more thought to what we do by taking into account the potential consequences for everything our actions are likely to bring about.

An ethical life for the Buddhist will involve accepting personal responsibility, seeking healthy detachment, and finding harmony with others. Personal responsibility means accepting our role in the causal chain. Thus, faced with a choice between an act that promotes good and one that is essentially negative, the Buddhist will be guided by the principle of attempting to improve the overall karma by assessing the situation in its widest perspective.

This does not mean that, say, children should not be disciplined or that all conflicts are to be avoided. Instead a follower will ask what sort of response will serve to reduce suffering the most. This might mean that a parent will take extra time explaining to a child why his or her behavior is inappropriate and what is expected instead of imposing a quick punishment. Alternatively, a person at work might be encouraged to react to angry colleagues with acceptance and respect even if they are not behaving similarly. The point is that we are in control of our personal conduct. We should own our actions. We do not have to slip into routine or accepted behavioral patterns when there are possible alternatives that will not add to the amount of bad karma.

Challenges

How should a Buddhist act? Initially, it might seem that because Buddhists accept that suffering is inevitable, it implies Buddhism is about meekly accepting one's fate and therefore becoming indifferent to the world. If, say, someone contracted a disease or was harmed by others, then it might appear that a Buddhist would not react or seek to alter the situation, just like the Buddha when he was spat upon by a stranger.

Yet we should not oversimplify in this brief sketch of Buddhism. Recall that the Buddha advocated a middle way that avoids extremes of indifference or great attachments. In no sense is Buddhism a retreat from the world. The Buddha in the story was more concerned with how to deal with things in a way that causes all parties to reflect on what would be most likely to cause greater good to come into the world. Violent reactions or conciliation both imply a lack of thoughtfulness. Psychological rather than material welfare is paramount for the Buddhist, and *all* actions are believed to bring about change of one sort or another. The mindful person will engage with any situation to bring about good. Therefore, a life well lived for the Buddhist will ultimately be judged in terms of whether someone lives without anxiety, dealing constructively with others and their surroundings.

Buddhists will seek to avoid attachment. This doesn't mean that someone can't love another person or own things. However, it means that we can't possess them, or imagine that they are everlasting. Buddhism is an outlook where people don't define themselves by their occupational title or belongings. Knowing that things are impermanent leads to an attitude where we can enjoy things in the moment and treasure events more than things. Consider the case of a catastrophic house fire. As we might expect, it will leave the owner distressed. At the same time, though, she may be profoundly grateful that no one was injured or killed; she might say that it was a useful reminder that we should put things in their proper perspective and concentrate on the things that really matter in life. Alternatively, if faced with a chronic or terminal illness, the Buddhist would not abandon all treatment and avoid personal encounters. On the contrary, he might accept that he has the illness, but dwell more on making the most of every moment rather than ruing his fate.

A Buddhist will try to engage with other people with an attitude of generosity, respect, and compassion. The "Right Livelihood" approach means that an adherent will look to the broader picture by suppressing egoistic or vain ambitions, and seek what they describe as a "wholesome view," one which avoids thoughts and actions that may cause harm.

Many people may assume that even if we try to avoid deliberate harm, then many actions will bring about some deleterious effects. For example, the principle of doing no harm (described as **Ahimsa**) seems impractical. It might seem that if we were to apply the principle strictly, say, when we protect crops, then we are likely to kill field mice and other animals at least by restricting their food supply, or more actively by setting traps or poison. But note that the principle of refraining from doing harm is not an absolute command, but an ideal, and we do not have to take it to extremes. Instead *Ahimsa* tells us to seek out whatever solution causes the least harm in that particular situation, all things considered, for instance, in this case probably by first taking better measures to exclude unwanted pests from grain stores before spreading toxins.

The attitude of doing no harm might also appear, on the surface at least, to encourage avoidance of all pain. It would be easy for a student facing a test to declare that he would be better off reconciling himself to failure and abdicating the work. However, we can see there are other paths that would also lessen his anxiety level; the most obvious one is that he should study sufficiently to be confident in his exam performance. Consequently a Buddhist approach of lessening harm does not imply distancing oneself from hard work or engagement in the world. Here again, the general thrust of Buddhist philosophy is to move beyond immediate matters and have us make thoughtful and reflective judgments that incorporate concern for the broad effects of whatever we do. For example, the Buddhist would probably not take issue with a cancer researcher trying to establish what prompts genetic mutations, in the hope of lessening human distress. Alternatively, if research seeks to create markets for goods we don't really need, or just creates mindless amusement, then it would probably be condemned by the Buddhist as an inappropriate use of our energy.

Nothing in the Buddhist admonition to do no harm implies anyone should be indifferent to crime or the suffering it causes to victims or society as a whole. Remember that the "Four Noble Truths" state that our suffering can be mitigated and reduced only by addressing root causes, not immediate symptoms. For instance, Buddhist nonviolence is a lifelong commitment to compassion and empathy with others. However, in the face of a violent act, each Buddhist will try to conform in the best way possible to that core commitment. One might insist on a pacifist stance of non-involvement. Another might determine that force is the most appropriate response to save lives or prevent harm.

Aggressive revenge or timidity would go against the basic demand for empathy, but protecting those we love would be completely consistent with Buddhist philosophy. In some cases, then, a Buddhist view may lead to a consciously passive act, such as nonviolence in order to achieve a larger result. At other times, under certain conditions (perhaps defending someone from an attempted rape) a Buddhist might resort to using force if he or she determines that is the best means of achieving the proper ends. Hence nonviolence thus does not preclude the use of force, but it does require clear thinking instead of mere reaction in the heat of the moment. For example, what we imagine as altruistic or heroic action might turn out, on reflection, to be prompted by a yearning for personal glory or satisfaction, and therefore inappropriate. In Buddhist terms, any specific action will matter less than the purity of heart that it exhibits.

These difficult cases point out a vital lesson of Buddhism: We are all on our individual journey, although ultimately connected. The teachings are not formal dogma, but a lens to enlighten our conscience, and make our own choices. Many practitioners would deny that there is such a thing as Buddhism in the sense of a doctrine with absolute rules of conduct. Instead they see it as a set of tenets for individuals to follow by themselves.

Buddhism strives to help people help themselves through deep reflection. It seems hard to deny that everyone would prefer a life of peace and harmony to one of discord and competition. Yet such a life is not easy to achieve. It begins with humility, and then demands continual commitment to the hard work necessary to creatively deal with the difficulties and suffering we encounter as part of the human condition.

To many Westerners, Buddhism appears to advocate eschewing accepted societal norms of happiness and success. Many Buddhists would agree, but point out that those norms are often artificially constructed. They might say that many of the goals and symbols in our culture are synthetic and fairly meaningless at the end of the day. Society and business often create certain goals that aren't what people really want, or at least, what they would want outside the inspiration of those desires through advertising—a bigger house, a luxurious car, a faster computer. The Buddhist challenge is to reflect in a very profound way on what makes us anxious, to strive to take control of our conscience, and then to act to remove the suffering that we impose on ourselves. Doing so, according to Buddhist claims, will give us greater peace than achieving artificial ambitions set by others. The Buddhist would ask us to take seriously the proposition that true enlightenment and peace cannot be found through wealth, status, or power, but rather it is deep within ourselves.

AFRICANA ETHICS

Africa is a vast continent with diverse cultures and history. Therefore, any description of African ethics will necessarily be a broad generalization that fails to do it full justice. We would have the same problem if we looked at European ethics as some kind of unified body of work. Nevertheless, there are some consistent themes that become apparent, some of which show interesting parallels with the ancient Greeks in particular, and that these themes provoke some challenges for the traditional way we think about philosophy.

As we saw earlier, translation issues arise when we look at non-Western ideas and practices. Sub-Saharan Africa has some 1,500 distinct languages, including Swahili, Zulu, Shona, and Akan. Its colonial history also has resulted in English and French being used as common administrative languages. Furthermore, there are distinct tribal groupings, each with particular cultural traditions. This is not to deny that there may be a commonly accepted sense of virtue that many African communities subscribe to. Typically what they have in common is that the operating morality is very much centered on community welfare. It is also practical and immediate: Decisions are often based on their functional implications rather than reliance on abstract principles for their own sake.

This forward-looking, communal, and practical nature of morality can be seen in a quotation from Archbishop Desmond Tutu, the South African clergyman and activist who was awarded the 1984 Nobel Peace Prize. Tutu led the *Truth and Reconciliation Commission* after the fall of the segregationist Apartheid regime, which had maintained white supremacy in his country for over a century through racist and segregationist policies. When Apartheid was peacefully overturned, many people were looking for punishment or revenge. In his book *No Future Without Forgiveness,* Tutu expressed that to take vengeance in this way would be counter to African principles of morality. He referred to a particular term, **Ubuntu**, which is used in the Nguni group of languages, but also found in other African languages, for example as *Botho* in the Sotho tongue. Ubuntu acknowledges our mutuality and looks to future relationships, and hence seeks clemency rather than revenge. The concept puts social harmony as the paramount goal. By Tutu's analysis, revenge fails to resolve issues, and in many cases sows the seeds of future discontent. In his words Ubuntu says "My humanity is caught up, is inextricably bound up, in yours." He continues

> We belong in a bundle of life. We say, 'A person is a person through other persons.' It is not, 'I think therefore I am.' It says rather: 'I am human because I belong. I participate. I share.' A person with *ubuntu* is open and available to others, affirming of others, does not

feel threatened that others are able and good, for he or she has a proper self-assurance that coming from knowing that he or she belongs in a greater whole and is diminished when others are tortured or oppressed, or treated as if they were less than who they are.[5]

Tutu's discussion points out three characteristic elements in African ethics: a certain metaphysical view of human nature, a community-based morality that supports mutual welfare, and an emphasis on character.

Many African cultures believe in a common ancestry, which logically leads to the belief that all are related. Such concepts of brotherhood or humanity include associated duties of hospitality and care. This is even reflected in some conventional greetings, where an inquiry of how someone's day has been may get the response, "My day has been fine if yours has." With such a fundamental notion of shared welfare, we understand that no one person's fate is completely distinct from others. In contrast, Tutu points out that the individual is automatically part of a community: the *we are* comes before the *I am.*

The concept of a person, then, is linked to a community. It follows that the community can also withdraw its acceptance if someone transgresses acceptable norms. For example, in the language of the Kiluba, in central Africa, they reserve the term *Kintu*, which specifically designates someone who has forfeited his or her dignity, that is, a fallen person, or in another translation, someone who has *lost character.*

A good person is one who acts in accordance with his or her moral sensibilities. The same idea is echoed in many other African languages. For instance in Ghana, *suban* is the word for "character"; it refers to someone who has a moral sense or conscience (*Tiboa*). A person with character is *owa suban pa*, whereas one without is described as *onni suban pa*. By this way of thinking, conscience is a uniquely human trait, and distinguishes mankind from the animals. In short, the notion of personhood, character, and possessing conscience are seen as three aspects of the same thing.

Let's pause to consider how we might view moral issues through an African worldview. If we are all connected and share one another's fate, then it is just misguided to think of an individual's own desires; the concepts won't make sense until seen in terms of an individual-within-community. Moreover, the notion of common good does provide an arbitrating principle, perhaps just as much as personal happiness or working out what any rational person would do if an action were universalized. Still, the African view presents challenges for Western thinking because it relies on wise people within the community to determine the common interests, and a body of knowledge handed down through stories and anecdotes. At this point, let us turn to what it might mean to be wise in the context of this ethical tradition.

The Africana Sage Tradition

One general feature of African ethical teachings to note is that they do not rely on revealed religion or a central great thinker. They also lack the literary tradition we often associate with thinkers such as Aristotle or Confucius, so there is no written body of work that students studied and commented on. Thus the themes that emerge are from an oral tradition where stories, often folk tales, are interpreted by wise people within the community. A **sage** is a wise person. In the Africana tradition, ethical guidance is often provided by someone, usually an elder, who discerns the right action and provides advice to the community. He or she might mediate

---

[5]D. Tutu, 1999. *No Future Without Forgiveness*. New York: Doubleday, at p.33–34.

between conflicting parties, for example, or interpret the wisdom handed down through community lore. Incidentally, the importance of oral tradition and practices has recently been recognized through recommendations by the United Nations Educational, Cultural and Scientific Organization, UNESCO, aimed at preserving heritage that is at risk of extinction. In the words of one of its leaders, Amadou Hampâté Bâ, "In Africa, when an old man dies, it is a library burning."[6]

Folk stories and fables are frequently used by the sage to convey moral teachings. In the European tradition we have Aesop's fables, and likewise in the American tradition there are tales of Bre'er Rabbit. African stories often involve stock characters such as a trickster hare (Br'er Rabbit can be traced directly from those African tales), and a great many feature Anansi, the wily spider who is the spinner of tales. In a typical story, Anansi attends a lengthy funeral rite, where it is the custom not to eat too soon afterward out of respect to the deceased. Before he goes, Anansi gorges himself, and when he declines to eat despite much urging, the other guests are impressed by his restraint. After a couple of days, however, he is very hungry and sneaks some hot beans into his hat, all the time saying he is not going to eat. However, the beans eventually leak down and scald his head, and Anansi runs off into a field in embarrassment. Sometimes the story ends with Anansi bald and afraid of meeting his fellow creatures.

The tale appears to have a clear and simple moral lesson: that insincere piety will always be discovered, and falsehood will result in retributive justice. However, much like the way Christian preachers use Biblical parables as springboard teachings that engage particular contexts and experiences, the sage will choose to use a story at the appropriate time to emphasize certain points to various audiences. For example, a sage might stress Anansi's initial motivation to show himself superior, or alternatively that in the story Anansi has several opportunities to confess but each time compounds his lie and the consequences become more severe.

CHALLENGES

The question sometimes arises whether the sage tradition amounts to "real" philosophy, or merely prudential advice. One criticism is that it lacks any written material. Another is that it has no principled basis to move beyond convention. Nevertheless, although little is documented or attributed to specific authors, this does not mean that there is no body of wisdom here. It is worth reflecting that Socrates, who is commonly viewed as the quintessential philosopher, preferred to do his work in public debate and wrote nothing himself. His views were written down only by one of his disciples, Plato. Additionally, some theories of teaching suggest that we learn best when information is presented in the form of stories rather than plain prose, and indeed the postmodernist movement in philosophy suggests that the narrative is a central mechanism that imparts power and authority in current societies. Therefore, it does not seem that African ethics should automatically be precluded from discussion just because its ideas are not written or structured in the same way as other systems of moral philosophy.

The problem of the sage tradition purely maintaining convention poses a more serious difficulty for African ethical thought. The criticism suggests that no matter how bad things are, the lack of principles external to the community means that there is little justification for social change, especially if there is a premium on social harmony. A rights theorist might argue, for example, that human rights talk gives us a foundation for passing judgment on certain practices,

---

[6]Amadou Hampâté Bâ, 1960. Speech to UNESCO, Paris.

no matter whether they are routinely accepted or lead to a well-ordered community. Thus it appears that the tradition often presumes men are superior to women, or that certain punishments are appropriate. Yet as Henry Oruka has noted, there are, in fact, divergent approaches. The **philosophical sage** tradition, as distinguished from the **folk-sage** tradition, maintains that it is the job of the sage to engage in active critique of the status quo. Additionally, it is important to acknowledge that the idea of the common good is not stuck in time but is actually a shifting target. Thus the wise person needs to interpret received wisdom about what constitutes the best interests of the community in light of changing circumstances. Unsurprisingly, this still means that there is a lot riding on the wisdom and integrity of individual sages, especially as societies become more open to outside influences such as television and the internet.

Additionally, much of African heritage has been strongly influenced as a result of colonization, which has served to undermine the sage tradition somewhat. Hence a community may need to face evolving and rival notions of individual welfare and the common good, especially with more developed property regimes and increased transportation and communications. For instance, if a community once relied on hunting and gathering, it may not easily adapt to concepts of individual property rights and competition. On the other hand, an optimistic view might say that greater access to others could possibly result in the notion of a wider sense of shared humanity as a sense of isolated local community diminishes.

A final layer of criticism speaks to the vagueness of concepts such as *ubuntu*, which seems to embody all the virtues in a single term; it can appear to mean whatever the speaker wants it to mean. This is probably less significant than it initially seems to be, though. We can try to distinguish between the motivating concept and its particular manifestations in everyday life. The fundamental elements of *ubuntu* are that there are nonmaterial goods—human well-being is grounded in relationships that exhibit mutual concern and respect—as well as the understanding that we are all connected. Combining these elements means that human welfare is realized or diminished collectively. If we consider those two elements as paramount, then the specific actions matter less than the underlying motivation.

Western ethical theories such as consequentialism and deontology are based on an idea of the rational individual, and therefore have some problems dealing with altruism and impartiality. In other words, they need to explain why we should be concerned with the welfare of others if there is no apparent personal benefit, and why we should not favor ourselves in any moral decision. On the other hand, African ethics emphasizes the fact that we are all intertwined, and something that is good for another is also good for me. This provides a sound basis for the individual to act ethically. So although African ethics does not present us with a unified body of work, it presents us with a sense of collectivism that resolves many persistent problems faced by the Western tradition.

Summary—Non-Western Ethics

In non-Western approaches to ethics, we have seen appeals to models from social structure (Confucianism and Watsuji), self-consciousness (Buddhism), nature (Taoism), and community (Africana). They are all tied to basic beliefs about human nature and what constitutes a life well lived.

Generally, these models do not separate morality from any other aspect of life. They look at what it is to be good, rather than looking at what constitutes good deeds. They are not religions in the sense of being drawn from the authority of a transcendent being. However, some adherents have nevertheless adopted rites around the various views. Significantly, these ethical models have all survived over time and still serve many people around the world, and whether we agree or disagree, it is important that we do not ignore them.

These approaches to ethics challenge the Western view of the primacy of rational and analytic discourse. Western ethics is typically articulated in prose, and then subject to rational analysis. Many non-Western observers might think this entirely wrong-headed.

Consider for a moment the experience of many basic and universal human emotions: We find it hard to convey their meaning and power with simple prose. We must turn to poetry, art, or music to express what we cannot do adequately in rational, linear logical writing. The lesson may well be that we need to find and explore diverse means to convey common human experiences. In a similar vein, many war veterans are unable to express their memories and feelings simply. They may choose to adopt alternate modes, finding that a war poem or piece of art may be much more powerful than prose.

The point of both these examples is to show that there may be limits to what a rational, analytical approach to language can do if trying to express the most complex of thoughts. Similarly, if we shift our focus in ethics from codified forms of behavior to the central facets of our shared experience, then perhaps it would be just as appropriate to express what it means to be a good character in terms of historical myths, moral stories, or other rich forms of communication that reach beyond logical argument.

Take the following verses (#63) from the Tao Te Ching:

> (It is the way of the Tao) to act without (thinking of) acting; to conduct affairs without (feeling the) trouble of them; to taste without discerning any flavour; to consider what is small as great, and a few as many; and to recompense injury with kindness.

> (The master of it) anticipates things that are difficult while they are easy, and does things that would become great while they are small. All difficult things in the world are sure to arise from a previous state in which they were easy, and all great things from one in which they were small. Therefore the sage, while he never does what is great, is able on that account to accomplish the greatest things.

> He who lightly promises is sure to keep but little faith; he who is continually thinking things easy is sure to find them difficult. Therefore the sage sees difficulty even in what seems easy, and so never has any difficulties.

This verse presents us with imagery, not prose. Nevertheless, it conveys a powerful message in a compressed form that is probably more alive and memorable than typical Western philosophical writing.

Whether we agree with non-Western approaches, we must acknowledge their considerable power, complexity, and influence. Their longevity and geographical spread demonstrate a set of approaches to ethics that have delivered a good deal of value for much of humankind.

Finally, to wrap up this chapter, let's pause to reflect on what someone from a non-Western culture might think of a student taking a class in ethics. What does our approach to studying ethics tell us about the way we think about morality in general, and is there anything that other cultures might offer?

Two things stand out. First, since the Enlightenment, Western views have separated ethics into a distinct activity. We often treat ethics as a discrete subdiscipline; we tend to avoid integrating it, for instance, with literature, art, anthropology, or social studies. Second, much of what we do in studying ethics involves the analysis of language to find the meaning and use of moral terms.

Someone from a non-Western culture might well see both of these activities as odd:

They are likely to say that being ethical is an ever-present part of a life well lived. To that person, it makes little sense to distinguish what it means to be good apart from looking at a person's life as a whole, or to believe that one can examine ethics as a separate intellectual activity separated from someone's lived experience.

Moreover, other societies do not stress the primacy of the individual as an autonomous self in the same way as we do. Ethics in the West is often considered a matter of someone making theoretical and independent rational decisions. A contrasting view, as we've seen in several approaches in this chapter, would say that people always exist in a web of interwoven relationships with others, including family, communities, traditions, and nature. Understanding this web encourages us not to compartmentalize our lives into separate spheres or different roles, with one set of rules for our business lives, another for romantic relationships, and yet another for family obligations. They are all wrapped up together, and a good person will exhibit the same values in all their dealings. These relationships extend far beyond us to the full scope of the world we interact with. Thus trying to examine morality apart from these relationships might appear a flawed enterprise at the outset.

The Western focus on moral language might also seem misguided. If, for instance, the Taoist is correct in saying that names and words that create categories act to destroy the very thing we want to examine, it is clear why that person might turn to myths, stories, art, and metaphor instead. Additionally—and in line with an insight from Aristotle—that person might say to you that learning about morality from a book is like trying to learn the piano without practicing, since ethics is primarily about exhibiting good values in practical acts. Accordingly, examining concepts in the abstract misses the essence of morality: Being a good person matters much more than

knowing various definitions of the term. Let's return to the example of love: If you said, "I love you" to someone, who then asked what you meant by the term, it would probably be an inappropriate if not offensive response. The concept may have to be experienced in a raw, unmediated fashion, and attempts to explain the term may ruin the encounter.

In sum, we find a paradox. Western views critique the concepts and arguments about morality and the language we use to describe it. However, other approaches often take this to be a reductive exercise, asserting that the object we are looking for will never be found by dissecting our language or behavior. This leaves us in a difficult position. Can we judge the morality of other societies in terms we are used to if the very essence of their moral structure argues that you cannot dip into another culture and its morality piecemeal and it can only really be critiqued from within the tradition?

It might well be argued that only in avoiding direct scrutiny can we discover what it is to be really ethical by living an ethical life. Moreover, moral stories, art, and service learning projects might be the most appropriate means to developing moral education. Interestingly, we have also relied on examples throughout this chapter to really explain and get at these approaches, echoing the view prevalent in non-Western ethics of marrying theory and practical application.

Perhaps the greatest value in considering non-Western views are the insights that there are alternate perspectives on examining ethics itself. The various approaches developed in non-Western cultural systems may not be right or wrong, but merely different; we should be careful that we try to judge them fairly for what they offer without prejudging them too readily. Further, contrast with other approaches offers the possibility of strengthening our own views by considering likely objections and how they may be overcome.

GLOSSARY

a priori Knowledge that is available prior to experience.

absolutist A person who claims that some acts are always right or wrong and moral judgments about them should not differ depending on individual preference or the context.

act utilitarians Those who judge an act in terms of the consequences of that act alone; that is, they look at the immediate circumstances to determine what particular act will bring about the greatest happiness for the greatest number.

actual obligations A term used by W. D. Ross to describe how people should act when faced with concrete situations. He thinks that duties in the abstract are clear, but become complicated by individual judgments in particular circumstances.

ahimsa The Buddhist principle of avoiding harm. It implies an attitude of non-violence and respect towards all living things.

altruism A belief that people ought to act in an unselfish manner for the good of others without regard for rewards

antirealism A meta-ethical position that holds that there is no objective moral reality.

antirealist Someone who holds an antirealist position.

applied ethics Branch of ethics that applies the principles of ethical theory to particular focused areas and cases.

appreciation of beauty One of the two primary values, according to Moore, that are regarded as good in themselves; people of refined sensibilities discern this quality, which combines the cognition of beautiful qualities with an appropriately positive emotion toward them.

arête A Greek term usually translated as "excellence" or "virtue" referring to fulfillment of human potential.

argument A connected series of claims or statements leading from a premise to a conclusion.

assertion Declaring something without supplying justification.

atomistic Views that consider personal identity as separate from the identity of others or the wider community. It represents the intuition that we are all individuals. In contrast, some philosophers argue that we only become full persons in relationship with others. For example, a baby may come to distinguish himself or herself as separate, but can only do so in the context of a prior relationship of self *with* others such as parents.

autonomous The ability to be self-directed and make independent decisions, from the Greek "self-law."

basic right *See* Human Rights.

benign self-interest The motivation to engage in activities that may benefit others while ultimately looking out for one's own best interest. For example, someone may donate to a blood bank, believing that supporting the institution will be a good thing for him or her in the future.

bounded rationality Proposed by Herbert Simon, the idea that because we have limited knowledge, time, and resources to make decisions, we should make the best available choice given the circumstances rather than always seeking the best possible outcome.

cognitivism A position about ethics that maintains ethical propositions are either true or false and are subject to proof, in much the same way as scientific claims.

categorical imperative Kant's term for an unconditional moral law that applies to all rational beings. It reflects the idea that we should govern our own actions based on principles that could be universally applied, regardless of our own personal interests.

coherentists Ethical coherentists do not deal as much with immutable truths but rather try to understand the justification of moral language in terms of its internal consistency.

collateral damage The damage brought about by the unintended consequences of an act.

communitarian challenge A position taken in debates on human rights that suggests that the welfare of the community might override personal rights. For example, individual privacy rights might be challenged by the security interests of a community, leading to agencies monitoring personal email.

confucianism Practices and teachings of Confucius.

consequentialism A term popularized by Elizabeth Anscombe that asserts the moral value of an act should be judged by its consequences, both intended and unintended. It is often used synonymously with utilitarianism.

consequentialist A person or view that relies on consequentialism.

constancy *See* Integrity.

cultural relativists Those who claim that value systems are not universal but vary from one culture to another. Thus practices such as killing animals for sport or the acceptability of divorce are seen as dependent on the prevailing cultural norms.

deontological Theories or reasoning based on deontology.

deontology A family of ethical theories that suggest we can rationally work out what is morally required without regard to experience or consequences, based on notions of duty or obligation.

descriptive ethics   An approach to ethics that deals with what people do rather than what people *should* do.

difference principle   John Rawls argues that after equality of opportunity is implemented and positions are open to all, inequalities may arise but they will only be acceptable if they are to everyone's advantage.

distributive justice   A theory of justice dealing with the fair allocation of goods and services.

doctrine of double effect   A doctrine that accepts that harm may come from the foreseeable but unintended consequences of a morally justified action, such as civilian casualties in war, or the potential bad side effects of prescribing a drug.

double effect   Multiple results (intentional and unintentional effects) that emerge from an act.

East Asian philosophy   A general term for a family of philosophical approaches from the Sinitic cultures. In broad terms, they examine the relationships found between people and community, or people and nature, in contrast to Western approaches that look for demonstrable truth and objectivity.

egalitarianism   One of the two main theories of distributive justice that affirms human equality especially with respect to social, political, and economic affairs. Sometimes interpreted as maximizing individual opportunities. John Rawls's egalitarianism allows inequalities to arise as long as they are mutually beneficial.

egoism   An ethical doctrine that individual self-interest is the paramount focus of moral concern. Psychological egoism maintains that we are all primarily motivated by seeking our own interests. Ethical egoism makes the normative claim that individuals *should* seek their own self-interest.

emotivism   A meta-ethical view that claims that ethical sentences or moral statements do not function as statements of fact but only express our emotions and preferences.

end-in-itself   A term used by Kant to express intrinsic worth, in contrast to something being valuable because it can bring benefit to someone. Kant believes that we ought to treat humans well because they have value in and of themselves.

energeia   A continuing motivational dynamic identified by Aristotle as necessary when striving for contentment.

epistemology   The study of knowledge, which examines the origin and limits of what we know.

equal opportunity   A "level playing field" where individuals are allowed to demonstrate merit without impediments brought about by being under-privileged, discriminated against, or having fewer resources than others.

equality   Uniformity of treatment that disregards immaterial factors. Thus an employee may be paid the same as others without consideration for gender. It is sometimes used in the sense of making all things equal, perhaps by redistributing wealth. In the United States it is typically thought of as equality of opportunity, which says that no one should be unfairly disadvantaged at the outset and subsequent differences should be based on merit.

equity   A form of fairness that looks to outcomes based on value added to an enterprise. For example, a worker may be rewarded for creating more output than his or her colleagues.

essentialism   A view that people and things have some unchanging characteristics. When used in terms of personal identity, it implies there is a continuing self through time. When used in discussions about sex and gender, it implies that men and women have differing natures.

ethics   The study of the nature and scope of the language of morality, that is, examining human values and standards of behavior.

ethical   Behavior or action judged in terms of moral values such as good and bad, right and wrong, fairness and justice. It can be used broadly to establish general principles, or more narrowly for specific endeavors such as medicine or law.

ethical egoism   A normative claim that says moral agents ought to do whatever is in their self-interest.

ethical egoists   Supporters of ethical egoism who believe people promote their own good and do whatever is in their best interest.

ethical relativism   The view that there is no one universal or absolute set of rules that apply to all individuals regardless of context; that is, each individual has his or her own moral beliefs and judgments, which will usually be based on personal experience or perception of a particular situation.

ethical theory   A theory that deals with the theory and justification of moral principles or values.

ethos   Character or trait; the Greek word for *habit* and the root for the English word *ethics*.

eudaimonia   A state of excellence, variously translated as flourishing, happiness, or personal well-being, considered by Aristotle as the appropriate goal for human existence.

feminism   A spectrum of social theories, political movements, and moral philosophies that are motivated and united by asserting equality for women.

feminist   A person who supports feminism.

folk-sage   *See:* sage.

foundationalist A theorist who believes a moral system has to be grounded in unchanging beliefs that are true for all people at all times.

fundamental right *See* Human Rights.

game theory The use of mathematical models to explore decision making and outcomes. The use of "game" here is non-trivial, as these models can be used to predict strategic behavior in warfare, or economic and political decisions.

gender Behaviors, activities and attributes typically associated with men and women. It can also refer to one's internal sense of being a man or a woman.

gender egalitarian Those who advocate that men and women should be treated equally and reject the notion that one sex is better than the other.

good will As described by Kant, the purest motivation for moral action. He believes an ethical person should act according to his or her duty. While many people have mixed motives, for example, realizing that if they act in a certain way there may be some personal benefit, someone with a good will is naturally motivated to follow the dictates of duty without any other intentions.

hedonism The belief that pleasure is the highest good, and the production of pleasure allows us to determine the right action in any case.

heteronomous Directed by others. Kant believes a truly moral individual should be autonomous, that is, self-directed and not rely on instructions from others. He thinks that although we can listen to advice, it is important that we internalize an action and make it our own, so the individual is the moral agent and consequently responsible for his or her actions.

history of philosophy Works of philosophers across ages and cultures that have been refined through discussion and criticism over many years.

human rights Claims or immunities that people are entitled to. Human, basic or fundamental rights are thought of as belonging to every person by virtue of their humanity. Human rights cannot be revoked, in contrast to privileges, that is, rights endowed by a legal system.

hypothetical A possible situation or outcome.

hypothetical imperatives According to Kant, a line of reasoning that depends on "if…then" calculation. He argues that outcomes are always unpredictable. Therefore he believes that it is more appropriate to reason ahead of time to establish principles that are not dependent on things turning out in the way we hope they will.

imperfect duties A duty that is praiseworthy but not unconditionally demanding. For Kant, a perfect duty is absolute, for example, "do not lie," since going against it would lead to a contradiction. Thus if people lie, truth loses its meaning, or if everyone stole we would have no sense of property. However, there are other duties such as donating to charity that are moral, but not required, because if they were not followed it would not undermine a fundamental moral principle.

imperialism The act of imposing one's standards on others.

integrity An overarching unity in one's moral life; also called constancy.

intellectual virtue *See* Virtue of Thought.

intrinsic In and of itself. Some things are valued because of their instrumental value, for example, a knife is useful for cutting, or a computer for storing data. Others, notably people, animals, or the environment, are considered valuable and their loss would be felt even if they have no apparent instrumental purpose.

intuitionism A view that accepts that moral statements can be determined as true or false, but contends they arise from a human sensibility that enables us to determine right from wrong.

jen Sometimes rendered as Ren, is derived from the Chinese characters for "man" and "two." It refers to the aspiration to bring out the best in self and others.

justice Concepts of moral rightness based on ethical principles.

karma The Buddhist notion that ethical actions have causal effects. Thus our actions may serve to create or diminish the amount of good in the world.

li In Confucianism, li refers to appropriate behavior based on the relationship involved. In English, it could be called propriety or manners.

liberal In social and political philosophy, a person who promotes maximum personal liberty consistent with the maximum liberty of others. It rejects privilege or undue governmental interference.

libertarianism A theory that promotes individual choice as the paramount virtue in organizing society.

logic The systematic study of formal and informal reasoning. It critiques the validity of links between premises and conclusions in arguments.

makoto A Japanese term for truth or sincerity. Sometimes rendered as "good-heartedness" in English. It places the stress in ethics on the nature of the individual rather than rules or rights.

market morality A term that suggests people's values are reflected in their consumer choices. Thus if people say they support recycling but research shows that they are not willing to pay for effective deposit schemes, the inconsistency will be highlighted by where they spend their money.

maxim A moral principle that governs behavior. Kant believed that any maxim could be tested to see if it applied universally without causing a contradiction–for example, if everyone lied, then the concept of truth would become meaningless.

meritocracy A system that rewards merit, such as scoring highly on achievement tests, or gaining profit in business. Sometimes criticized because the definition of merit itself can be vague. For example, scores alone may not reflect the challenges that some students faced in preparing for a test.

metaethics The branch of ethics that looks at the nature of moral language, how it is used, and asks questions about the meaning of moral utterances.

metaphysics The branch of philosophy that deals with the nature of reality and being. It deals with issues that are not addressed by science such as personal identity and the divine.

miranda warning A rule established by U.S. Supreme Court by which law-enforcement officers are obliged to warn a person of his or her rights to remain silent and entitlement to legal counsel.

modernism An intellectual movement that believes human progress will be facilitated by the application of scientific principles.

modernist A believer or supporter of modernism.

moral free space The zone of moral deliberation bounded by certain constraints within which people in a community can develop options for action.

morality Personal and societal values representing principles and behavior that is desirable or objectionable. Often morality is thought of in terms of opposites, such as good/bad, right/wrong, just/unjust, fair/unfair.

morals Particular values relating to personal and societal decisions regarding desirable and objectionable behavior.

natural law A view that sees an order in the universe. The related ethical approach suggests that people ought to act in conformity with that natural order. For example, it may support marriage as an institution based on the observation that pair bonding is a natural feature of human existence.

natural right *See* Human Rights.

naturalism The doctrine that natural or scientific facts are adequate to account for all human experience. For example, naturalists would deny supernatural causes, or might describe experiences such as compassion in terms of a predictable chemical response to certain stimuli.

need A category used in one form of distributive justice as the basis for redistribution of goods or services.

negative right An immunity against interference, such as the right to remain silent, or the right against torture. It is negative since respecting the right means does not require action to be taken.

noncognitivism A meta-ethical view that moral utterances do not make knowledge claims, and consequently cannot be right or wrong. For example, if "Bullfighting is immoral" expresses a personal feeling rather than a fact, it is cannot be verified or refuted in the same way as "Hot iron expands" may be.

normative ethics A theory of ethics that recommends societal norms and personal behavior.

patterning Ordered redistribution of goods and services, justified by some predetermined principles with set outcomes, typically articulated as "from each according to" and "to each according to" such as the communist notion of from each according to ability and to each according to their needs.

perfect duties For Kant, actions that are morally obligatory, since their negation would lead to a contradiction. For instance, if everyone cheated on tests, or if everyone broke promises, the notions of tests or obligations would become meaningless.

personal affection One of the two primary values, according to Moore, that are regarded as good in themselves.

personal autonomy The ability to decide for oneself. Literally, to impose self-law. Thus a patient who is informed of medical choices may decide for himself or herself, but would lose that ability if unconscious or delirious.

philosophical sage *See* sage.

phronesis The capacity of the individual to discern the course of action that is most conducive to the good, after carefully considering the situation in light of personal experience and judgment.

pluralistic deontologist Someone who believes that duty or obligation is the focus of moral choice, but recognizes that there may be multiple or conflicting duties involved. For example, we may have duties to not lie, and do no harm. However, parents routinely say things such as 'a kiss will make the hurt go away' or 'Santa will bring presents' where there are multiple duties involved.

polis A community (Greek city-state) created for the common good of the society.

positive right A claim or entitlement that implies action has to be taken. For example, under arrest, authorities may have to provide a lawyer for a suspect, or institutions may have to make accommodations for people with disabilities.

postmodernism A movement drawing on the insights and methodologies of a range of disciplines, which proposes that truth is constructed by people attempting to make sense of their personal narrative. Typically postmodernists deny absolute or universal principles, and endorse the primacy of personal experience. Postmodern approaches demand a radical reevaluation of categories and structures within society.

postmodernist A follower of postmodernism.

practical virtue *See* Virtue of Character.

pragmatic critiques Analyses that encourage us to give up the search for the exact nature of reality and to concentrate instead on practical ways the words we use and the narratives we create can be employed to enhance human welfare.

preference utilitarianism A moral theory that maintains that a moral action is one which most optimally satisfies the interests or preferences of all those affected.

prescriptivism An ethical approach that suggests moral language not only expresses a personal view, but also serves to encourage others to agree with the speaker. For instance "Age discrimination is bad" not only communicates someone's attitude but also encourages others to think so too.

prima facie obligations Literally "at first face" duties that strike us as obvious and do not need any further justification. W. D. Ross listed seven, including fidelity, reparation, gratitude, non-malfeasance, justice, beneficence, and self-improvement.

primary goods Goods that every rational person would want, as outlined by John Rawls in his book "A Theory of Justice." These include natural goods such as health and intelligence, and social goods such as rights, liberties, powers, opportunities, income, and wealth.

prisoner's dilemma A game-theoretic model that balances individual self-interest against mutual benefit. The dilemma arises in the absence of full cooperation and trust, since there is an incentive for participants to take advantage of others. For example, it is in everyone's interest to minimize pollution at the cost of some personal inconvenience. However, if some people are going to disregard mutual interests, then it would be rational for everyone else to look to his or her personal benefit instead.

privilege A special right, advantage, or immunity granted by a legal authority, such as the right to drive or the right to vote. It may be forfeited or revoked under certain conditions.

psychological egoism The assumption that we are all ultimately motivated out of self-interest. Even in cases of apparent altruism, such as putting one's life at risk to save a child from a burning building, the psychological egoist maintains that actions are motivated by personal satisfaction, or the avoidance of future guilt.

pure justice A system that sets up initial fair conditions and then does not interfere with the outcome. For example, a pay scheme rewards those who produce most, or a lottery open to all and won by a very rich person.

reiki shakai A Japanese term for a society based on material possessions and comfort.

rational Based on reasoning and valid argument. Sometimes positively contrasted to intuition as a source of knowledge.

realism An ethical theory that maintains there is an objective truth to moral claims.

rectification The process of redistributing goods and services to correct perceived imbalances in a system. A government may tax individuals and redirect their wealth, for example, or a college could adjust entrance requirements if a student is from an underprivileged background.

reincarnation The Buddhist notion that our actions have personal repercussions. Contemporary interpretations consider rebirth figuratively, often as a person evolving morally, or recapturing some of the moral energy they expend.

relativists Those who claim that humans understand and evaluate beliefs and behaviors only in context, that is, relative to other situations. They deny there are universal or eternal moral truths that can be established without regard to particular circumstances.

reparative justice A theory of justice that focuses more on repairing harms than punishing offenders.

restorative justice A theory of justice that looks to restoring those harmed by injustice or crime. It attempts to find means that allow all parties involved to heal and move on.

results-based theory In ethics, a theory that looks at the aggregate benefits and harms of any proposed action.

retributive justice A theory of justice that is concerned with giving people what they deserve. In the case of wrongdoing, it seeks to punish offenders proportionately to the harms involved.

rights Claims and immunities that people are entitled to. Human rights, sometimes called natural, basic, or fundamental rights, are considered universal by virtue of being human, for example, the right to free speech or freedom of religion. In contrast, some argue that rights are a function of particular legal codes.

rule utilitarian Someone who follows a version of utilitarianism that looks beyond the immediate case and considers which rule or principle would result in the greatest happiness in the long term.

sage A wise person in a community who people often turn to for advice. A folk sage is a keeper and interpreter of traditional communal wisdom. The philosophical sage actively critiques behavior and society.

satisficing A combined word using "satisfy" and "suffice." It is a process where decision makers lack the ability and resources to arrive at the very best possible solution, and opt to find an outcome that is good enough for the task at hand.

sex Biological features that distinguish males from females.

sincerity A term used by Confucius to describe authentic self-awareness that subsequently allows honest interaction with others.

sociobiology The branch of science that deals with the study of evolutionary aspects of social behavior in humans.

sour grapes An expression that demonstrates that we are likely to adjust our preferences and ambitions based on our perceived chances of achieving them.

teleological Ethical theories incorporating notions of overall purpose or destiny.

teleology The belief in purpose, goals, or ends in the universe.

telos A purpose, goal or end. Aristotle maintains that humans strive for well-being or flourishing, which he calls eudaimonia.

theism A belief in the existence of at least one God. Many theists maintain that God has an active role in human existence and our ethical duty is to align ourselves with divine commands.

theistic Views that refer to God or deities to explain features of the world and human existence.

tit-for-tat A strategy in the game theory that has proven to be the most effective in a prisoner's dilemma. An agent will initially cooperate, then respond in kind to an opponent's every move.

ubuntu The term in some African languages that reminds us that we share and partake in the lives of others and a wider community. It implies social harmony and reconciliation.

universalization The process of applying a line of reasoning to all moral agents.

utilitarianism An ethical theory that holds that the rightness of an action is determined by the result that produces the greatest happiness for the greatest number of people.

value-based theory An approach that include judgments about the relative merit of particular goals and behaviors.

veil of ignorance A thought experiment popularized by John Rawls that asks people to create general principles for society. Subjects are aware of the basic facts about the world, but ignorant of their particular situation, and hence their vested interest in any specific outcome. Rawls believes that under these conditions people will create policies that give fair opportunities for everyone.

virtue Moral and intellectual qualities that represent the mean between too much and too little. For example, someone may be too courageous or too timid, or too generous or not generous enough. Aristotle believes it is vital to judge the right application of each virtue for the specific circumstances.

virtue of character Also called practical virtue. Aristotle believes that there is an experiential component to moral development, which comes about through training and experience.

virtue theorist Those who emphasize character and virtues demonstrated by a person over time in determining his or her ethical behavior.

virtue of thought Sometimes translated as intellectual virtue. For Aristotle, the theoretical knowledge that is a basis for morality. Like learning to play a musical instrument, he believed that theory alone was insufficient and had to be supplemented by practice.

way In Taoism, the natural order that individuals should follow. Discerning and living in harmony with the way should be a guide for our everyday lives.

wu-wei A term used in Taoism sometimes translated as minimal effort. It suggests that if we live in harmony with the natural order, then things will take their course, and we should not struggle to impose artificial order or false permanence.

INDEX

intrinsic value (good will), 77
intuitionism, 18
    Moore, G. E. and, 18
    moral statements and, 18

J

Jaggar, Alison, 126
Jen, concept of, 150–151
    basic idea of, 150
    "Golden Rule" and, 150
    parent/child relationship and, 150
A Jury of Her Peers (Glaspell), 121, 126
justice, 102, 111–118
    challenges, 116–118
    concept, 103
    distributive, 112
    pure, 113
    reparative, 111
    restorative, 111–112
    retributive, 111–112
    rights and, 102–119

K

Kant, Immanuel, 35, 76–84, 86–87, 95,
        131, 133
    categorical imperative, 78–80
    duties, conflict of, 81
    end-in-itself philosophy of, 77
    good will, 77–78
    on human nature, 78
    human psychology and, 87
    on human rationality, 82
    hypothetical imperatives, 80
    impartiality and, 87
    moral decision procedure of, 79
    on morality, 77, 83
    outcome-dependent reasoning and, 80
    perfect and imperfect duties, 81–82
    personal autonomy and, 87
Karma, concept of, 161, 163.
        See also Buddhism
Kierkegaard, Søren, 154
Kiluba, 166
King, Martin Luther, 94–95, 99
Kintu (person who has lost character), 166
Kipling, Rudyard, 98
knowledge, 137–138
    Foucault, Michel view of, 137–138
    power and, 137–138
Koehn, Daryl, 109
Kohlberg, Lawrence, 122–123
K'ung Fu-tzu. *See* Confucius

L

"language games," 134
language(s)
    Akan, 165
    English, 165
    ethical, 134, 135
    Foucault, Michel view of, 138
    French, 165
    games, 134
    Kiluba, 166

modernism and, 134
Nguni group of, 165
postmodernism and, 134–135
power of, 138
Shona, 165
societal institutions and, 135
Sotho, 165
Swahili, 165
Taoist, 157–158
Wittgenstein, Ludwig on using, 134–135
Zulu, 165
Lantos, Tom, 29
Lao Tzu, 156
law
    ethics and, 10–11
    moral, 79, 80
    morality *vs.*, 11
    natural, 14, 28–29
    religious, 12
    self-imposed, 80
Le Guin, Ursula, 67
The Leviathan (Hobbes), 24
Levinas, Emmanuel, 140–142
    concept of Other, 140–142
    human nature, views on, 140–142
    interpersonal relations, importance
        of, 142
    knowledge and, 140
    le visage, 141
    on morality, 140, 143
    on traditional ethics, 140
le visage, 141
Li, concept of, 151
    civil society and, 151
    spirituality and, 151
libertarianism, 113–114
    individuals' choice and, 113
    market morality, 114
    meritocracy, advocation of, 116
    Nozick, Robert, 113–114
    pure justice, 113
The Life You Can Save (Singer), 66
The Limits of Trooghaft (Stewart), 107
literature
    Asian, 48
    classical, 48
    Foucault, Michel and, 137
Locke, John, 92, 113
logic, 5, 134. *See also* reasoning
    modernism and, 134
    postmodernism and, 134
logical positivism, 134
    ethical language and, 134–135
The Lord of the Flies (Golding), 22

M

Machievelli, Niccolo, 23–24
    domination, advocation of, 23–24
    egoism and, 23–24
    on self, 23
    self-interest and, 23–24
MacIntyre, Alasdair, 95–97
    external rewards and, 97

internal rewards and, 97
justice, approach towards, 118
morality and, 96–97
practices, 97
science and ethics, analogy between,
    96, 97
views on virtue-based theory, 96–97
Madness and Civilization (Foucault), 137
Magna Carta, 102
makoto, 109
market morality, 114
Marx, Karl, 137
maxim, defined, 78
medical ethics, 7. *See also* ethics
Mencius, 148
meritocracy, 116
metaethics, 16–19. *See also* ethics
    antirealism, 18–19
    cognitivism, 17–18
    conceptual analysis, 16
    key elements of, 16
    noncognitivism, 18
    realism, 18–19
    reasoning and, 16
metaphysics, 6
Mill, John Stuart, 61–62, 96, 113, 131,
        133, 154
    women's suffrage and, 61
Miranda warning, 104–105
    negative right, 105
    positive right, 105
    types of rights, 104–105
modernism
    defined, 131
    ethical theory and, 21
    language and, 134
    logic and, 134
    postmodernism views *vs.*, 131
    science and, 133–134
Moore, G. E., 18, 64, 133
    education, ethical sensibilities and, 133
    on intuitionism, 18
    on naturalism, 18
moral consistency, 6
moral decisions, 6, 8
    delegation of, 8
    ethics and, 8
    individual preferences and, 19
    moral imagination and, 41
moral development in children
    conventional role-conformity, 123
    pre-moral level, 123
    self-accepted moral principles, 123
moral equality, 149. *See also* equality
moral free space, 41
moral imgaination, 40–41
    moral decisions and, 41
    social psychology and, 41
moral imperialism, 39–40.
        See also imperialism
    colonizing powers and, 40
    human rights, example of and, 40
moral infractions, 7